AND SHE WAS NEVER THE SAME AGAIN

A MULTIGENERATIONAL MEMOIR

NATASHA PRYDE TRUJILLO, PH.D.

And She Was Never the Same Again: A Multigenerational Memoir

Published by Violet Echoes Press
Denver, CO

ISBN: 979-8-9895443-0-1

AUTOBIOGRAPHY / Psychologists

Cover design by William Dalton Frizzell, copyright owned by Natasha Pryde Trujillo, Ph.D.

CONTENTS

FOREWORD

THE ALCHEMY OF GRIEF: AN ACADEMIC'S INVITATION TO EXPLORE

I need to begin by noting how honored I am that Dr. Trujillo asked me to write this foreword. She and I have known each other since 2015, when she was admitted to the doctoral program in counseling psychology at Purdue University. However, after reading *And She Was Never the Same Again,* I realize how little I have "known" her or the depth of her experiences and layers of her personhood. Dr. Trujillo was a true master of control—driven to meet each deadline, accomplish each milestone, and move through the program at a speed that I had never before witnessed. The extent to which I can now make sense of her approach is profound.

For her three years in the doctoral program, Dr. Trujillo met weekly with a group of like-minded scientist-practitioners, members of my research team. We read and discussed thanatological (i.e., the study of death and dying) theory and research—and worked to expand our application of these concepts to a broader range of non-death loss life experiences. Examples of life events of focus for the team during this time included the transition to college, life-altering injuries, romantic breakups, and parental absence. We acknowledged and honored the layers of loss and the glimmers of gratitude that were possible in all of these challenging life experiences.

When I look back at letters of recommendation I wrote for Dr. Trujillo, I consistently emphasized her work ethic; her time management skills (as a double-edged sword!); her choice of projects that were clinically, empirically, and personally relevant; and her commitment to acting on her convictions. She used all of these elements of her character to bring this book to fruition.

However, more than anything else, she brought her desire to better understand herself and her family—and to make a difference in the lives of you (her readers) through vulnerable sharing and authentic reflection. Perhaps the greatest contribution of this book is Dr. Trujillo's willingness to bring all of who she is to light. She has taken the audacious step of opening herself to the world—an almost complete 180 to her prior way of being and moving in the world. To say that I am proud of her as a person and a psychologist is an understatement.

What you will find in this book is Dr. Trujillo's practical and moving illustrations of the theories, concepts, and empirical findings that were discussed by our research team. She has made these concepts her own and integrated them into making sense of herself, her family, and their collective narrative.

To begin, our team developed the Gain/Loss Framework of Impact,[1] with the main assumption being that most significant life events, regardless of desirability or undesirability, are likely to involve perceptions of both gains and losses. With a primarily desirable life event (e.g., a new job), the perceived gains (e.g., higher salary, new learning) are likely to be initially most clear, whereas the losses (e.g., questions of competence, missing of familiar colleagues) are likely to unfold over time. In contrast, with an undesirable life event (e.g., the death of someone close), the losses (e.g., the support they offered, their physical presence) initially eclipse the gains that may appear over time (e.g., lessons they taught, greater understanding of the true friendships in your life). The challenge for us all and for society in general is to hold the complexity of life experiences; life is not dichotomous and linear but rather dynamic and circular. With loss comes grief, and with gains comes gratitude. These are not mutually exclusive but rather intertwined and, in some ways, complementary.

Next, the concept of grief is often only associated with death-related losses. Dr. Trujillo has poignantly demonstrated that grief is also experienced after a whole range of non-death loss events. Grief is the passive, involuntary, and multidimensional reaction to a whole range of losses. We do not choose how we grieve; it is a natural reaction to loss and emerges from the uniqueness of our personhood and our general mode of responding to stressful life events.[2] Grief does not move in stages but rather is specific to every single person and to each of the losses they experience. Although grief is often associated with crying, it is not equal to sadness. Grief is emotional, cognitive, physical, social, and spiritual. It can be so overwhelming *because* it affects all domains of human functioning. Grief does not end—it is an unfolding that shifts and changes over time. It is a reflection of love and attachment, an ongoing honoring of an important connection.

In contrast, mourning is how we seek to cope with loss and grief. It is active, voluntary, and intentional. Like grief, it is specific to each person. Although mourning is generally associated with external, public, and community-focused events (e.g., funerals, memorials, graveside services), the most powerful acts of mourning are often internal, personal, and private. Mourning includes any actions we take that connect us back to the loss/death in a meaningful way. These can range from mentally reviewing memories to organizing photos and other memorabilia, picking up a new hobby, and annually gathering with friends for a picnic. The forms of effective mourning are as numerous as our creativity will allow. I have no doubt that writing this book has been an act of mourning for Dr. Trujillo.

My hope is that you (her readers) take courage from Dr. Trujillo's willingness to move toward the losses in her life—to raise up and "stay with" the material that society often indicates we should bury. Rather than developing, planning, and implementing this book in isolation, Dr. Trujillo initiated conversations with her family members and friends about topics that had long been taboo. In order to study her own life and the lives of her family members, she gathered crucial qualitative data from many others. A key mantra of our research team was "to make the untalkable talkable"—and Dr. Trujillo took that lesson to heart. She did not engage in these interviews to determine blame or to force resolution. She engaged in them to reestablish connections, respect differences, and renew narratives. I hope the risks she took to ask the questions and truly listen to the answers may inspire you to do the same in your own lives.

Dr. Trujillo has taken the theories, concepts, and research related to the field of loss and grief—and she has lived them, reflected on them, and integrated them into her personal and professional lives. They have made a difference for her—a revelation that moves me deeply—and I am as certain as she is that they will make a difference for you too.

The narrative of this book does not end in a neat and tidy way. How could it? There is no end to the losses and gains in the world. They will continue on—as will the associated grief and gratitude. There is also no such thing as an individual experience; we are all connected to those who came before us and to those who will follow. We live in story—and the story continues on.

Heather Servaty-Seib, PhD, HSPP
Professor of Counseling Psychology, Purdue University

PREFACE

MY WHY

From the moment I committed myself to this project, I knew what the very last sentence of the book would be. The rest took more time to bring to life. When working with clients as a counseling and sport psychologist, I often encourage them to find their "why" for any given pursuit. My "why" for writing this book is because of how it ends. *Her.* Just to try and survive required intense effort to fight against self-destruction brought on by profound losses. It began with the loss of *her* and culminated with the loss of myself, what could have been, and my naive certainty of what should be. Tragedy rode in on the coattails of rebuilding my life after losing my beloved Grandma Pryde, whom you will soon get to know. I needed a way to keep myself busy from debilitating pain but to somehow balance distraction with the need to be with my feelings, the only true way to move through grief. So, I began to write. I wanted to better understand myself and why those I love the most are the way they are.

The content of this book can be heavy and evoke intense emotion at times, so I want to caution you to be sure to take care of yourself through the process, as there may be parts that are triggering and difficult to sit with. My intention is to spotlight the multifaceted losses most of us try to hide from or don't see, *and* to encourage people to acknowledge the gains inherent in the most despairing events we miraculously survive. I hope you experience both an attraction and a repellent reaction to each person in the book. I attempted to showcase the many sides to people, some that are easy to love and digest and others that are hurtful, confusing, and unbelievable at times. It is clear that some characters (such as my Grandma Pryde) are more challenging to reflect negatively on, while others may be a bit easier to paint in a villainous role. I will own that I have biases that influence the way these stories are composed, yet I have tried my best to paint a comprehensive picture of the duality that exists within all of us. I firmly believe that when you love someone, you have to accept that perfection does not exist, and for all the ways we can honor and respect someone, flaws will forever be present as well.

I hope to normalize that multiple losses (death and non-death) across a lifespan are a standard part of being human and that the sharing of vulnerable, lived experiences can empower and strengthen our capacity to find connection and meaning. I wanted to tackle issues of grief and loss in a more comprehensive way so that people can call grief out when they see it and not be afraid to name it. To say the hard things they think and be with the hard feelings they feel. I wanted others to find self-compassion and other-compassion in the messy process. I wanted to honor those who mean the most to me. Most importantly, I wanted readers to see themselves in these stories and become more accepting of the fact that grief never truly goes away but we can learn to handle "hard" better by accepting the suffering inherent in life and the growth that is never too far behind it. I urge you to consider how you might respond or react from the viewpoint of each character you come across. What are your own values, your own needs, and your own experiences that may lead you to make the same or different decisions? Whom in your life can you be more curious about after the telling of these tales? What do you need to say that hasn't been said, and how do you reconcile that in cases where you may no longer have the opportunity to do so?

PROLOGUE

THE HOW AND WHAT'S IN IT FOR YOU

Bringing this book to life was an exhausting endeavor. I spent solitary, reflective time generating a list of the varied losses I have endured and the broader losses that my family has suffered, whether I was a part of them or not. It feels strange and disrespectfully hierarchical to pick and choose the "most impactful" experiences, as I risk sending the message that hardships not highlighted aren't as valid or are perhaps insignificant. That people I lost but haven't written about didn't mean as much, or that losses not featured means there were no long-term effects. That is not the case. Rather, I selected stories that I felt fit the themes and intentions that sustained the motivation to compose the book you now hold in your hands. From there, I narrowed down which losses (at this point in my life) seem to be the most poignant regarding the way I look at the world. I asked myself which losses affect me the most and why. Which ones influence my thoughts, beliefs, behaviors, desires, and biases? Which ones affect my emotional functioning and the way I experience and interact with others? Which ones help bring light to grief's existence of losses inherent *within* life, not just *of* life? Which ones have profoundly moved me, and which ones did I think just might move you, too?

This collection of narratives speaks to profound experiences that have contributed to my life in meaningful ways. While some areas focus specifically on my own lived experience, I am simply a unifying thread in the retellings of others. Even so, the events and the characters within them have significantly helped shape who I've been, am, and will become. This book is about my family, biological and chosen. It features some people I know well, some from a distance, and some I've never met, yet all of them have a role to play in my emerging understanding of myself, other people, and the world. These stories are multigenerational and span the course of several lifetimes. The chapters are arranged in chronological order in my life, organized by the time in which the relevant story began to intersect with my own development.

Once I had an outline of what each of the twelve chapters would be (my favorite number), I began interviewing the main characters of each story as determined by who was still alive, who was present and highly involved in the narrative, and who would be reliable and engaged in the process. It was paramount that everyone included was also willing to tell their story. I spoke to both family members and non-family members, depending on the topic and their involvement in the tale. The last two chapters were the most difficult for me to manage my own emotional experiences around, thus I wrote them much more quickly, a telling testament to my own struggles in being *with* the prominent grief inherent in those pages (and one of the biggest takeaways for you, the reader).

I spent the first week of each month conducting interviews that I recorded on my phone. The interviews were loosely structured and open-ended. Much of what I asked and gathered depended on the flow of the conversation. I tried to do as many as I could in person to capture the body language and other observatory markers that would help me emotionally connect on a deeper level while I was bringing the stories to life, but some were also over the phone. It's worth expressing how profound the palpable connection of each conversation was. I felt a deeper understanding and appreciation between myself and the interviewee with each story relived. Grief took both physical, emotional, and spiritual forms that you could sense beyond what meets the eye. It was common to hear apologies for overdue tears that hadn't been given permission to flow. For buried tension to find its way to the surface and cause physical discomfort not yet felt due to consistent attempts to avoid it. I am exceptionally grateful for each person's tolerance of my incessant (and likely irritating) prying into the depths of their suffering and can only hope that it also brought about a sense of relief, catharsis, and perhaps deeper sense-making or healing on some level.

After I collected all the interviews, I also gathered as much objective data as I could. Hospital records, police reports, newspaper clippings, and anything that could help elaborate on the anecdotal evidence. Please note there may be errors in the medical descriptions included. I did not have a physician review for accuracy, I only relied on the written and verbal sources available to me. Then, I replayed the recordings and let my fingers go to town. For some chapters, I wrote my own experiences and ideas first and then jumped into the recordings, but for most, I started with others' recollections and waited to add my commentary until the end. The structure of each chapter is slightly different, in that some chapters cover one singular event, whereas others focus on an expansion of a series of events and interactions over time. Both contexts are important, as each give you a clear window into how grief and loss can sneak into your soul. I also felt it was important to share stories that focus on acute moments of distress and ones where there's a slower build-up. As you will hopefully see, both are impactful in shaping our development over time.

Next, I edited it twice. Once reading internally and once out loud to myself. Then, I gathered my parents, Uncle Tom, and Aunt Tammy (all of whom you will get to know), and I read each chapter out loud. Most of the time, Tom and Tammy would come to my house and be with me in person while my parents listened over the phone since we live in different cities. Other times, we were all together, and sometimes, it was all via conference call. There is no doubt that I was more comfortable *not* being in the same physical space as my parents for many of the chapter reveals due to the raw vulnerability and confrontation of challenging memories and facts of our dynamics.

A few of the chapters I read or sent to others if they were featured but not interviewed, as I wanted to be sure that I captured their memories honestly and that I was being as respectful as possible. A further note on respect: being raised in a large Spanish family, it is customary to always greet your elders with appropriate prefixes. Even cousins of older generations, distant relatives, or close family friends are often referred to as "Aunt" or "Uncle." For the purpose of pacing and flow, I provide the correct relationship of each character as they pertain to me at the beginning of each chapter but then refer to them only by their first name OR by how their relationship is defined with the other character(s) in a given scene. I mean no disrespect and believe it keeps you, as the reader, less confused and more engaged in the narrative itself. Selfishly, I also need to name this to avoid lectures from my family about any lack of respect in my writing. Along those same lines, getting each person's consent was key to having their information included. I gave everyone the opportunity to change their name if they wanted, but no one did. For those people I was unable to track down or who had minor roles in the stories, names were changed. For the deceased, I spoke with my family at length and chose to keep their real names intact. A few characters don't have names at all but are only referred to by the role they played in a story (e.g., a coach, a doctor).

One of the most difficult decisions I've had to make throughout the process is to determine how to respectfully synthesize information to help readers better understand how life events contribute to who we become over time, an aspiration behind this project. I risk criticism of "psycho-analyzing" my family, scrutiny about disclosing personal details in a way I'd never do in a therapeutic setting with a client, and backlash about making determinations that may be inaccurate or arguable about my loved ones. The weight of even writing those words is quite heavy, to be honest. I am a psychologist by trade, someone who examines behavior and conceptualizes how and why people struggle. I look for interconnections and pose tentative theories, aiming to make sense and more fully integrate life events into a narrative that can help us continue to move forward and, hopefully, do a little better than we did before. I can't completely separate my training from myself as an author, particularly when writing about the things so near and dear to my heart that have led me down my career path.

You will read my own reflections about how and why some of my loved ones show up the way they do. For those still living who were part of the interview process, I shared each detail of my writing and my process and checked the accuracy of my assertions to the best of my abilities. Some they agreed with, and some they didn't, thus many difficult conversations were had, and I made changes as I felt reasonable and appropriate. I dug deep to check my own assumptions and ensure integrity as best I could, even if that meant respectfully disagreeing. I worry that perhaps I will regret the vulnerability brought to light in this book or that maybe my conclusions now may shift over time. But in some ways, I hope that I do. The discomfort with being this forthcoming, my willingness to change my mind about my experiences and those of my loved ones, and my pledge that I very well may have missed something or gotten it wrong all show me that I'm still open to learning and don't have all of this figured out yet. This is a vow I take seriously both as a person and a psychologist: to never stop learning. It's a process I hope you, as a reader, can also take away and find compassion for yourself through trying. I believe the gains of moving forward with this work outweigh the losses that may hold me back or cut me down. Thus, I persisted, and I hope you will too.

I want to acknowledge the intersections of privilege and oppression you will come across in this book. I urge you to keep in mind that, as humans, we hold many different social identities: race, ethnicity, class, religion, nationality, citizenship, education, sexuality, gender identity, native language, and more. The ways in which these identities work together or against one another are beyond the scope of this book, but I recognize that I have privilege in many of the ways I walk through the world that have influenced how these stories played out. I had access to education. I am a bi-ethnic, cisgender woman who passes for White in most cases. I have financial stability and access to resources that have made several of the complications I've faced much easier. Each of the people represented also has a unique makeup of identities that have both helped and been disadvantageous to them throughout their lives. I encourage you to consider these intersections and to reflect on your own, as they truly cannot be separated from who we are and how situations in our lives are impacted by traits we cannot change.

Ultimately, this is a book about you. It is about your family and your friends, everyone you've ever met and all the strangers you have yet to meet. It takes you on a journey of gains and losses that stretch generations, cultures, identities, and decades of time. Losses that are individual and collective, death and non-death. It awakens you to the inevitable and makes you look at the things most people want to avoid seeing. It explores near-death experiences, medical trauma, the stigmatized death of a partner, intergenerational trauma, perfectionism, death's destruction of a family's composition, individual trauma, what it means to be an athlete, chronic illness paired with the denial of death, first loves, identity transitions throughout life, and the gaping holes that become permanent fixtures within us when those we love the most die. Each chapter is told through in-depth narratives crafted by weaving together perspectives from the key players and concludes with a synthesis of how grief was manifested and maintained over time within and outside the self. It educates you on various aspects of grief and encourages you to take away questions for yourself and your loved ones. You will notice numbered endnotes that you can reference for more in-depth knowledge about the topic of interest. I was deliberate to not include footnotes, as part of the power of this book is to force you to sit with all the feelings without distractions or avoidance. I want you to learn but to learn through feeling *and* intellect; this won't be your usual academic text.

I also want to issue a warning: it is not a "how-to" book. There is not just one way to grieve, and to suggest there are universal, concrete steps that must be taken discredits the human experience of suffering and the uniqueness we each embody on our respective paths through pain. I challenge you to focus on both the gains and losses of these life events. Contemplate how the characters in the stories have gotten torn down but also how they have been rebuilt—how they have created something beautiful from the rubble. Undoubtedly, you may spot growth that I haven't illustrated, and you may even disagree with some that I have. That's okay. The point is that we don't return to our former selves when loss strikes. That's also okay. You will feel, you will learn, you will grow, and hopefully, you will never be the same again.

1

THE NEAR-END OF THE BEGINNING

On September 8, 1990, at 3:53 a.m., my then-twenty-year-old mother became everything she ever wanted to be. Even at that tender age, she felt in her bones that motherhood was her destiny. As newlyweds, she and my dad (exactly one year older) welcomed me into the world with fierce, unconditional love and a chaotic, overbearing village behind them. Although married and working full time, they were just kids themselves and had no idea what terror was coming just two weeks after one of the happiest moments of their young lives.

In the days following my birth, my mom felt understandably fatigued but without major alarms. There were no red flags warning that her body was slowly turning against her. She was tired, pale, and struggling for stamina, but as her motherly instincts kicked in, her focus was on building a bond with me, the tiny bundle who relied on her for survival. Her attention was homed in on each noise and movement I made, too busy with the newness of motherhood to question how her body was healing from giving birth (without drugs, I might add: total badass). She easily dismissed her waning pallor and energy as benign, reminding herself she had just delivered an infant and her condition was to be expected. She believed everything was normal because she wasn't bleeding and her physician voiced no concerns. Many assume the white coat surrounding doctors' human bodies protects them from mistakes, as if the achromatic pureness erodes the aptitude they all possess for error. She simply did not know; no one did.

My dad and the rest of the family noticed her skin tone slowly becoming more transparent and the additional effort she put toward moving about. They, too, chalked it up to typical post-partum symptoms anyone would experience after being a human incubator for nine months. They never questioned whether her appearance could be a forewarning of a life-changing crisis. Their incognizance made the sudden nature of her near-death experience all the more gut-wrenching. Heart-stopping, even, especially for her.

The evening of September 24, 1990, did not start out unusually. In fact, there is no memory of mundane nor illustrious events that would, in hindsight, indicate how our lives would change forever. We spent the day with family: my mom's brother and sister (Tom and Tammy) visiting from Palm Desert, California, and Denver, Colorado, respectively. A picture of the family was captured that day, with no trace in their smiles of the foreboding pain and suffering to which they would soon bear witness. Everything was fine. Everyone was fine. My parents went to bed close to midnight, having just said goodbye to Tom and Tammy, who would spend the next two hours driving back to Denver from Laramie, Wyoming, our hometown. My mom checked on me, and I was quiet, comfortably swaddled next to my parents' bed in a bassinet for the time being, totally oblivious to the imminent stress and injury lingering in the shadows of our first family home. As she lay in bed waiting for sleep, she felt herself bleeding. She thought about the peculiarity of what she was feeling. She knew it was too soon to have a period and hadn't experienced any bleeding since my birth, thus confusion clouded her mind.

She got up to investigate further and heard me start to fuss. Given no blood-curdling screams, she appropriately assessed that there was no urgent need for intervention and walked the few steps from their 1980s king-size waterbed to the bathroom. She entered the bathroom from the hallway and quickly sat on the toilet. She saw blood filling the toilet as if a valve in her had been turned on but then broken off. She began to feel shock. Her body was dispelling blood at an uncontrollable rate. She anxiously flushed the toilet three times in a matter of minutes, scared the blood could overflow onto the gray tile that lined the bathroom floor. She questioned what was going on and became embarrassed by the amount of blood she was losing. She tried to remain quiet as her fear grew louder, not wanting to wake up my dad and have to explain her body turning against her. She was determined to stop the bleeding herself, so she sat a minute longer until she felt confident she was okay to move. She took a deep breath and prayed she could return to bed without incident. As she talked herself through the courage needed to get up, she heard me whimpering. Focused on consoling whatever affliction I had, she entered the hallway and began to walk into the bedroom. She looked over at my father, sleeping soundly (or so she thought), and experienced a lightheadedness that frightened her. She thought she might pass out and yelled at my dad as her bewilderment and dizziness both grew at rapid speeds. He got up, discombobulated but activated by her scream, and ran over to her as he oriented himself back to consciousness. He grabbed her around the waist and led her through the bedroom and onto the waterbed. She calmly said that she wasn't feeling well, but they both knew it was much more serious as he saw the growing stains of blood on her clothes and puddles on the floor that they were unable to contain merely seconds after leaving the bathroom.

As she lay in bed and became increasingly honest with herself about the severity of the situation, she tried not to pass out while instructing my dad to call her mom (Grandma Pryde), a registered nurse, who was working a night shift at the local hospital on the pediatrics unit. Pryde directed him to call 911 and informed him that my mom was likely hemorrhaging. She said her plan was to go down to the emergency room to prep them for my mom's arrival. Once they hung up, my dad, confused and becoming more terrified by the second, left my mom in bed and went to my bassinet to briefly try to console my restlessness. He did not stay with me long and stepped away to grab a couple of towels to lay around the ever-growing pool of blood. The blood was too plentiful and too red for his mind not to question whether she would live. He shivered, then batted away the notion as quickly as he could. He knew he couldn't handle whatever was to come on his own.

As he left my mom, now cushioned with towels in bed, he ran to the phone and dialed his old home phone number. It was late at night, but he knew he needed to wake his mother (Grandma Becca) and get her to the house stat. His brother (Uncle Tim), a carefree seventeen-year-old at the time, was still awake, watching TV and winding down from a shift at the local Kentucky Fried Chicken. When Tim heard my dad's voice, he immediately knew something was different and felt a chilling sensation travel from the base of his head all the way down his back. My dad was not the kind to behave erratically or display fear or unsteadiness (his embodiment of machismo[1] ever-present, ugh). He told Tim that something was wrong with my mom and he needed them to get there right away because he thought she might be dead. Now afraid, Tim rushed to their mom's bedside and shook her awake. After a few moments on the phone, all Becca knew was that my mom was bleeding, my dad thought she was going to die, and she was needed. Without allowing Tim any notice to even put shoes on, she yelled that they had to leave right away and sprinted out to his 1987 red Nissan pickup truck. He drove the approximate two miles from their house to ours in record time.

As this phone call was occurring, my mom was fighting for her life ardently but unknowingly. With tenacity and a steadfast commitment to me, her self-talk became both aggressive and survivalist. She thought she may be feeling better and told herself she could not just lie there. She felt more blood escaping her and was fervent on making it to the bathroom again, mortified at the mess she was making. My dad ended his phone call just in time to help her get up, using his surprisingly reliable strength for the slim young man he was to steady her. The whole way to the bathroom, she continued to lose blood in a solid flow they could not decelerate. They made it only as far as the entry to the hallway, a few steps at most. She stopped abruptly and tried to turn herself to the right to enter the bathroom but was unable to move any longer. With incredible force, a blood clot the size of a cantaloupe erupted from between her legs. With it came her underwear, ripped completely off her body. The clot broke like a water balloon when it made contact with the floor. As the dark red, gelatin-like substance succumbed to gravity, the blood splashed onto the floor, walls, ceiling, and both of them. Operating on pure horror and adrenaline, my dad screamed as he tried to get her a few steps closer to the toilet, but her body became limp and unresponsive. He had no choice but to lay her on the bathroom floor as gently as he could.

While my mom danced to an unpolished beat with consciousness, my dad initiated the call with 911, sprinting up the stairs at lightning speed to ensure the door was unlocked and wide open. As he did so, he exhaled a pronounced sigh of relief as he saw Becca and Tim arrive. He first noticed Tim as he burst inside, running with focused hurry down the stairs with only socks on. Tim was immediately drawn to the crying emitting from my bassinet. Perhaps I could sense the fear in my protectors, or maybe I realized on some level the trauma of the evening would shift my life forever. Before he tended to me, he watched Becca, who had immediately run toward my mother's lifeless body. Becca heard my dad's amplified voice on the phone and saw him fidgeting above my mom but not actually doing anything. "She's going to die; she's dying as we speak!" he pleaded with the dispatcher, each phrase an octave higher, trying to explain the blood loss, as if his escalating pitch would propel the ambulance faster. Tim only briefly got a glimpse of the blood-filled bathroom before Becca directed him to soothe me. Tim noted his mom's incredible ease. Her calm takeover of the situation helped him hold back an overbearing feeling of nausea and do as he was told, trying to make sense of the confusion and fear in my dad's eyes at the same time. His mind was warped as he attempted to process my dad yelling that his wife was going to die, begging a stranger to help save our family.

In moments of alertness, my mom's brain was swirly, at best, and she was mostly unable to make sense of what was happening, only knowing with certainty that she was full of pure terror. She came to at one point with her head in Becca's lap, and she reasoned that Becca and Tim must have arrived while she was passed out. Becca sat on her own lower legs and feet, trying to prop my mom's head up while gently tapping both sides of her face with cold water. Steady and calm, she repeated, "Come on Lynn ... Lynn ... please wake up, Lynn, come on, jita!" only pausing to overhear how the 911 call was going. If there was any comedic relief in this entire experience, it was Becca trying to help my dad communicate with the dispatcher what was happening. He was frantically screaming, "She's hammering, she's hammering so much!" When he paused for a breath, she gently relayed, "Jito, she's *hemorrhaging.*" English is absolutely my dad's first language, but there have been several times throughout my life where that has not been an apparent fact, a quirk that makes me both laugh and love him more at the same time. At the advice of the dispatcher, my dad instructed Becca to pack more towels around my mom as tightly as possible and to try to keep her awake until the ambulance arrived. Intermittently, he would yell my mom's name in her direction to try to keep her conscious and to give Becca's voice a break from doing the same thing.

My mom noticed an unflinching, matter-of-fact voice in her head, telling her she needed to get back to me. *You need to take care of Natasha. You have to survive this.* She had moments when she questioned if she were still alive and tried to cling to anything in the environment that would ground her to reality. At one point, her attention was diverted into the hallway, and she noticed my dad pacing. She could make sense of his panic given the frantic nature of his walk and tone and was somehow able to grasp that 911 was instructing him to bag the clot in order to determine how much blood volume she lost. She cringed as she thought about the clot as her cause of death. He began repeatedly yelling, "I need a bag for the blood, I need a damn bag!" Astonishingly (but so typical of my mom), she mustered what energy she could and directed him, "The bags are in the closet in the nursery upstairs." She felt increased fear seeing my dad so beside himself. She had never seen him this way; his typical calm and steady demeanor had completely disappeared. As the terror overtook him, she succumbed to more blackness as her body shut down from the deluging blood loss.

Meanwhile, Tim picked me up, carried me into the living room while I wailed, and gently rocked me. After a few minutes, he heard the ambulance's sirens and set me back down in my bassinet, having achieved no relief for my discomfort. He rushed up the stairs and caught the ambulance driving by our house. In spite of the fact that we lived on a dirt road and he had nothing protecting his feet but socks, he sprinted after the ambulance, yelling, "Stop! Turn around! Come back, please hurry!" Eventually, they noticed they were off the mark and pulled a U-turn. He ran into the middle of the street, furiously waving his arms to direct them. When they pulled up, he could hear my screams from outside and was envious he couldn't do the same. As the three male paramedics burst through the door and headed downstairs, he came back to my side and picked me up, trying unsuccessfully once more to console me, just rocking, back and forth. As he held me, he watched both of my parents leave the house as if it were a 3D movie. One lifeless and one riddled with agony about what it would mean to become, yet again, a family of just two.[2]

When Dusty (one of the paramedics) got the notification that he was being summoned to my parents' house, he was surprised, concerned, and apprehensive. As he heard a brief summary, he homed in on the immense pressure he now faced. This was personal to him, given that he knew my mom and the rest of my family. He had respect and admiration for them. He also knew that a hemorrhage of this capacity was a critical situation, and there would be no room for error. He was early in his career as an EMT, having just joined the fire department not even a year before. He went to high school with my mom's older siblings and lived down the street from them growing up. His confidence as a newer professional wasn't where it should have been to call himself seasoned, but he knew the job he had in front of him needed to be done well. When he arrived at the scene, he descended to the basement and assessed her status for himself, recognizing the most pertinent steps included slowing down her bleeding, getting an IV started, and delivering her to the ER as quickly as possible.

Jerked awake yet again, my mom woke up with Dusty standing over her. Dusty was someone she considered a friend (not to mention someone she found hopelessly attractive, a fact she never excludes when bringing him up and one that gives us all a good laugh). Although relieved to see him, she was also ashamed that he was seeing her in such a vulnerable and sickly state. As she tried to orient herself, she noticed three paramedics now surrounding her. They swiftly lifted her body and set her on a stretcher on the floor in the hallway. They moved about with great exigency, traipsing all over the basement to secure her in place and carry her to the ambulance. At one point, the paramedics asked my dad to get out of their way so they could work more effectively. He was watching every one of their moves. He watched them open and utilize all sorts of medical equipment he had no language to identify. He saw needles, blood pressure cuffs, bags of fluid, and other items that served only to intensify his fear. As they carried her up the stairs and secured her in the ambulance, they shouted brief commands to him, "Sir, her vitals are not good, we will do all that we can to save her. You need to follow us to the hospital. Now." They slammed the door and blasted the sirens, peeling out of the driveway without waiting for a response. Now alone with an unhappy baby, Becca and Tim couldn't help but stare from the brand-new life in front of them to the bloody footprints that left dark red reminders of the upheaval. Their eyes traced the pathway from my parents' bedroom to the bathroom, through the hallway, up the stairs and entryway, and into the driveway, where the ambulance had sat running just moments before.

Once en route to the hospital, Dusty stayed by my mom's side and set to work starting an IV. Of all the EMT job responsibilities, he was most confident in his IV skills. He knew he needed to work on getting some volume into her and had to walk a delicate line of trying to catch up with fluids she had lost, while not flooding her system. His self-talk erupted. *Okay, Dusty, if the IV flows too quickly, you'll risk making her blood pressure too high, causing her to bleed out faster. You can't go there.* He chose to use a sixteen-gauge needle because he assumed a blood transfusion would be imperative based on his assessment of her blood loss. The sixteen-gauge needle would ensure that the red blood cells would not be damaged and would allow for whole blood transfer once she entered the operating room. *Come on, Dusty, you need precision and ease in your stick. You got this.* With his direct pep talk, he smoothly slid off the plastic cathlon and used the steel needle to pierce the skin and go directly into the vein, then he secured it to her arm. As he pressed the needle into her vein, she noticed blood shoot straight up and land on the ceiling. Faintly, she whispered, "I'm so sorry" before again giving way to blackness. He tried to keep her conscious and calm as she waxed and waned between life and death.

As he worked to restore her vitals and remind her she was being tended to by someone who truly cared for her, his colleague engaged in a fundal massage to help stimulate contraction of her uterus to slow down and prevent further blood loss. Given that her bleeding was internal, they knew it was impossible to attempt a direct pressure route to stop it. Dusty placed an oxygen mask on her with the hopes of overloading the oxygen-carrying hemoglobin with extra oxygen. He knew that the fluid from the IV was helpful, but it did not carry oxygen into her body, given that it contained no red blood cells, thus no hemoglobin. In other words, the fluid was useful, but her body's oxygen-carrying capacity had deteriorated. Not necessarily worthless, but like watering down the Kool-Aid, if you will. As they worked, they also tried to estimate the amount of blood lost. Blood volume of any person can be estimated based on an individual's weight (body weight in kg x 70ml = total ml of blood). During pregnancy, a woman's blood volume increases to accommodate the growing fetus. They knew my mom had given birth about two weeks prior, thus they were hoping that her body hadn't completely returned to normal yet and she was still storing some additional blood volume, a potential key to survival.

Meanwhile, Becca and Tim began to problem-solve how to clean the blood-soaked chaos left behind and allay my discomfort. After seeing what he saw, Tim believed that my mom was going to die. Wrapping his head around that, he became frightened about what would happen to me. He did not think my dad was capable of taking care of me on his own and was worried about how we would live. He told himself he wasn't even sure that my dad knew how to change a diaper or prepare a bottle on his own. Becca sat staring at the remnants left behind and equated the visual with a murder scene. She followed the bloody footprints with her eyes: up and down, up and down, and prepared herself to spend the next several hours cleaning relentlessly. Partially to help rid the home of the physical reminders of a life likely lost, and partially trying to cope with her own fear and certainty that her daughter-in-law was going to die.[3] She sent Tim back to their house to get some supplies to begin the deep cleaning that would continue for weeks.

She was finally able to calm me down (an incredible gift she seems to have with all children). She silently cried and prayed the entire time Tim was gone. When he returned, she regained her composure and got to work right away. She told herself she was unfazed by the blood when she set the goal of erasing all traces of it from the home. She had to go over the same spots multiple times and was diligent in looking into all the cracks and crannies to get it all. On her hands and knees, it took all night and then some. With each fierce thrust of her arms on the heavy stains, her brain worked in overdrive to come to terms with the fact that she was likely going to have to help my father raise his daughter in a much more involved capacity than she initially anticipated.

It is unclear why my dad wasn't allowed in the ambulance, but he was instructed to follow them. He quickly started his 1977, dark green Chevy Sierra and tailed the ambulance to the hospital. Going down Grand Avenue, the longest street in the entire town, the scenery on both sides was a complete blur. It was well past midnight because all of the streetlights were blinking yellow. He saw his odometer exceed one hundred miles per hour on a street where the speed limit was thirty. When he arrived at the hospital, he was not allowed inside the operating room and instead had to remain in the waiting room, alone. There was a brief moment of relief for him in seeing Pryde standing in the emergency room entrance. He trusted that she would know what to do and longed for her presence as she disappeared behind the scenes. He paced in a cold, lifeless waiting room with no distractions but his own catastrophic thoughts. Disbelief stunted his ability to express emotion at all, so although no tears made their way down his face, the threat of inevitable loss began chasing him. He thought his wife was going to die and was terrified at what it would take to raise me on his own. *How the fuck am I going to raise a daughter without Lynn, and who will be there to help me?* He was convinced by the sheer amount of blood that there was no way my mom would survive. He acknowledged his fear but felt paralyzed and could do nothing with it. His thoughts were a broken record on repeat with no solutions in sight.

According to the history and physical report from the hospital, when the paramedics arrived at our house, my mom's blood pressure was 90/0. In the less than ten-minute drive from our house to the hospital, they had restored her blood pressure to 106/60 and her pulse to 82. At the hospital, she continued to drop in and out of our world and the other. When coherent, the first thing she noticed was that her mom was there, somehow standing patiently at the garage door where the ambulance parked. She was immediately wheeled into the operating room, where Dr. Kay entered the picture. Dr. Kay was periodically my mom's physician throughout her pregnancy and was a friend of Pryde's. Dr. Kay taught Pryde how to crochet baby hats while her hands still worked (osteoarthritis is a bitch), and the hats became a staple in the community for newborns. What remained from the clot my mom expelled was also transported into the operating room. It sat in the bag near her, on display for the surgery team to assess. Dr. Kay murmured something inaudible under her breath, likely expressing a sense of hopelessness that my mother could survive such overwhelming physical trauma. They prepped her for surgery and performed a dilation and curettage that she unfortunately felt. The discomfort was a combination of intense pressure and pain. The force was such that she envisioned them scraping her insides, making her completely hollow instead of actually repairing damage. A D&C, as it is called in shorthand, is a procedure done to remove tissue from inside a woman's uterus. They hoped that this procedure would stop the heavy bleeding and clean the uterine lining that they learned was still littered with placenta from my delivery. A careless human error made by the delivering physician.

Dr. Kay quickly made her way out to speak with my dad. "Troy, the surgery was successful, but she will likely need a blood transfusion to fully recover." She also explained what had gone wrong, but all he was able to make sense of was that Lynn was stable. To him, that meant maybe he wouldn't have to raise me all alone, that maybe he had a second chance to have his wife back and live out the future they had planned together. So she was stable, but very, very ill. They admitted her overnight for observation. It was estimated that she lost approximately 1500cc of blood. To put that in context, it is about 3.17 pints of blood. An average adult has between eight to twelve pints of blood. My mom is a petite, small woman, about five foot two. She lost somewhere between 26 and 40 percent of all of the blood in her body. As a result, the next order of business was determining whether to do a blood transfusion to replenish her lost blood supply.

I was born in 1990, so context on a societal level is needed to better understand the potential ramifications of this recommendation. The AIDS epidemic was in full swing by this point, and blood transfusions were an incredibly risky and, in some cases, a prohibited medical solution. Dr. Kay told my mom that they needed her consent before being able to move forward with a blood transfusion. At the time, for individuals who had planned surgeries, a protocol was in place where they could donate their own blood ahead of time to be kept for them should the need for a transfusion arise during their procedures. Since this event was catastrophic and not scheduled, this was not an option. However, due to the intense uncertainty caused by AIDS, my mom refused to consent to a blood transfusion. She informed the medical team that if that was necessary, she would ONLY accept blood from her sister, and she was even hesitant in her comfort with that option.

To back up just a bit, at some point during the chaos and with the alert of a likely blood transfusion, Pryde managed to call Tom and Tammy. "Lynn has hemorrhaged and is really sick. You need to get back to Laramie now. Tam, we may need your blood for a transfusion. Please hurry." They hadn't quite returned to Denver when they received the call, so it was easy enough for them to turn right around on the interstate. The ride back to Laramie felt like it took years. The car was filled with trepidation and unease. It was hard to breathe as they both choked on the words they wouldn't allow themselves to say. A sense of powerlessness took over as they both knew they could do nothing but focus on safely arriving. They knew it was not helpful to pester their mom with calls for updates. They knew trying to make sense of it in the moment was pointless, given the abundance of questions that consume the waiting game. They silently considered, for the first time, what it might be like to bury a sibling, and they shuddered at the anticipatory grief and imagined new normals of a life without their baby sister. As the city lights became faint dots in the sky and the Wyoming wind grew stronger with each mile, neither could bring themselves to acknowledge the fear sucking the air out of the car. They could not speak the uncertainty running through their minds into an audible existence. It was not the time to make sense of what was occurring, but their brains were all-consumed anyhow, isolated in the depths of expectant dread.

When my mom woke up the next morning, she attempted to reach the bathroom on her own and passed out on the way, too weak to support herself. Once again, they advised her to give consent for a blood transfusion, but my mom declined, determined to heal on her own. Despite multiple fainting episodes, by the second day, miraculously, it was discovered that a blood transfusion was no longer necessary. By the end of that day, she was released, having regained enough strength to function independently. She felt enormous relief (as did everyone else) and was insistent on returning home as quickly as possible because, after all, she had me to take care of.

In the days and weeks following the near-tragedy, there was relief that my mom was alive, sure. However, a large and stubborn shadow was cast over my family. Uncertainty, unpredictability, confusion, and fear bled through the fabric of my family's now-shattered sense of permanence and safety. Everyone worried more. Everyone tried to look for signs of trouble and spot them before another disaster unfolded without warning. These newfound processes were mostly unsaid, internal, and alone. As the flames of shock died down and turned to ashes, complex grief emerged as the individual nuances of each person's experience silently competed with one another. They all wondered how to take care of others and also how to handle themselves. Questions about whether to honor their own needs versus ignoring them to focus on me plagued them. It seems as though focusing on the latter is what won out. There wasn't much individual compassion to be had, as everyone seemed to internalize a need for grit. They observed one another and watched the reactions of each other, unsure of what was allowed or what was the "right" way to handle things, fighting inner turmoil about what to address and what to unmind.

It was no secret that my mom had anxiety before. This experience unknowingly solidified a lifelong battle with uncertainty for her. She held anxiety about the future, a pursuit to know what cannot be known and to anticipate and protect her family at all costs. This discomfort catapulted her worry to exponential heights and has characterized components of her parenting and our relationship throughout my life.

She developed fears over her own mortality and for the safety of her family, but more than anything else, her need to protect me flew off the charts. She was protective even before this, but her brush with death drew her closer to a desire to control things and protect *my* life at all costs. I hadn't been the one who got sick, *I had actually been the cause of her illness*, yet she healed with a vengeance to protect me, as a grave threat to me would be the loss of my young mother. In the aftermath, she told Tammy she felt she had died but needed to come back because it just wasn't her time. This realization ignited death anxiety that, in many ways, prevented her from ever living fully again.[4] Reckless young-adult behavior that characterized her early teen years was no more. Along with a sense of maturity and great responsibility came the loss of her ability to be carefree, to live in the moment without worry of future suffering and safety. A way of life was washed away with the incessant scrubbing of the blood she left in the basement. Perhaps even more detrimental, her already iffy self-image became riddled with more insecurities. Deepened embarrassment and shame about a medical trauma she had no control over intensified her already rocky connection with herself.

My dad's former perception of the world slipped away following this experience. He was more attentive to me, more on edge in general, and became constantly worried about the future survival of our family. He became obsessed with considering how to plan for the future and ensure I would be okay at all costs. He was fixated on problem-solving and replaying *what could have been* over and over. All of this obsessing was done internally, of course, never providing an explanation for his anger or seeking support to manage the fear he worked so hard to keep hidden and at bay.[5] Shutting off any emotion is how he functioned throughout the majority of my childhood and well into my adulthood. In fact, it is only within the last few years (since I moved across the country to Indiana for graduate school) that we have seen any cracks in the surface of his soul through moments of vulnerability. As he reflected on his memories for the first time during the interviews with me for this book, it was notable how he had to pause, often mid-sentence, and stare into the distance. I saw his eyes narrow and his body tense in an attempt to ward off the budding emotion. Fighting back tears, he said, "You just never come back from that." He is exactly correct. He never did return to his former self and likely didn't acknowledge it until that very moment.

The rest of my family was not immune to lasting changes from what they witnessed. This experience forever changed the fallacy of safety and shed light on the inevitable multitude of losses[6] that accompany traumatic events. Uncle Tim, to this day, is always prepared with shoes on. He keeps them on in his house, only taking them off when it is time to crawl into bed, and doesn't leave them too far out of reach. Grandma Becca clings more to her faith, which she describes as spiritual growth that allows her to be more realistic.[7] She talks about the uncertainty of life and is always careful not to make plans too permanent, since "you just never know," as she so often says. She remains strong and steady, and I am never too certain exactly how things hit her. She is the rock, the person with whom others fall apart the moment her arms encircle them during hard times.

Despite the ongoing fear that was born from a near-fatal experience mostly internalized on all fronts, the event itself and my mom's ongoing health were not talked about much once the crisis had subsided. It brought reality to the surface of what *could* happen, a good thing to acknowledge in moderation, and then life moved forward. No lawsuit was filed, even though malpractice was the direct cause of the tumultuous start of our family. Space was not made to process the impact, likely because no one knew how. What do you say? Are there even words to truly capture the emotion in such a trauma? Although my mom's hemorrhage was and continues to be something they think about from time to time, rarely does it find its way into the spoken narrative of our lives in a meaningful way.[8] Interestingly enough, it is fascinating to consider the details each person remembers the most, all of which I learned during the interviews. The most traumatic parts get center stage. The blood, the lifelessness of her body, the devastation they believed I'd experience growing up without a mother. But more than that, you could see the personalities of each person emerge as they focused on the components that most add up in the narratives of how they view themselves. For my mom, it was the fierceness of motherly instincts and the equally untamed anxiety. For my dad, it was how quickly his truck went down Grand Avenue and his focus on being a provider. For Uncle Tim, it was the realization of how people change when things change. And for Grandma Becca, it was the neatnik homemaker inherent in her excessive scrubbing.[9]

Less than two weeks later my mom returned to work, and just like that, she had to figure out how to manage a full-time job alongside the role of wife and mother. And she was never the same again.

2

BEASTLY BEAUTY

The next nearly two years passed mostly without incident. No major crises or experiences raising philosophical questions. My family had simply "moved on,"[1] as they say we do in life. The fear and incessant worry had been woven into the double helix of their DNA, but their skin protected them from ever having to see or speak of the changes to their neural and emotional structures—the changes to our family structure. Everyone acted as if they were totally over the hemorrhage—as if it had never happened at all. I had been born healthy, and other than a few sniffles now and again, my medical history was unscathed, not unlike most other two-year-olds. By February 1993, my mom was six months pregnant and eagerly anticipating what life would be like when we became a family of four. Her pregnancy had been uneventful. As we now know all too well, we can never get too comfortable in life, as happiness, permanency, and safety are forever fleeting; the opposites never out of sight, often disguised or hidden in the shadows of the what-ifs.

February 23, 1993, was a typical wintery Wyoming day. Inches of white powder fell steadily, made more ferocious by the gales Wyoming is known for. I was recovering from a non-threatening ear infection. I was stuffy and coughing, had a raspy voice, and had turned pale in the face.

As the day went on, my mom decided it was best to take me to the doctor. She was concerned that I just didn't look right and noticed increasing difficulty in my ability to breathe without conscious effort. She took me to my pediatrician, a good friend of Grandma Pryde's. Being kin to Pryde often made others in the medical community give special attention to our family. Unfair? Perhaps, but it was a result of how beloved she was to all who knew her. My doctor chalked up my symptoms to a viral respiratory infection and instructed my mom to monitor me and give me Dimetapp as needed. She was informed she could call back should any of my symptoms worsen, but with the help of OTC medicine, that scenario was not anticipated. Notably, there was no sign of immediate distress, no perceived urgency to treat me, and no forewarning of what would soon become our reality.

We went home, and my mom did as she was advised. As the hours came and went, I became increasingly more lethargic. As a verbally advanced child, my vocabulary was bigger than that of other children my age, and I had no qualms about showing that off. However, I seemed to regress with alarming speed as my symptoms worsened. I had no interest in speaking, and my usually busy body ceased to engage in the customary exploration by a curious toddler. By 10 p.m. that night, my pallor had become ghost-like with a subtle yet striking blue tint to my lips. I had a high fever (about 103 degrees), and my chest had morphed into a concave formation. With every breath I took, an immense dip in my bone structure highlighted the growing effort it took to get any air in. The sound that my small, nearly twenty-five-pound body made as it gasped for air seemed to physically hurt both of my parents to witness. As my dad lay on the couch, my mom shared her growing anxiety that something was seriously wrong and she felt I needed to be taken back in. My dad was dismissive at first, assuming I would be fine and just needed a good night's rest. My mom waited a while longer and eventually could not stand it anymore. She made the solo decision to take me to the ER, and my dad agreed reluctantly after noticing the stark changes in my body temperature shifting at breakneck pace. My dad wanted to get to sleep for the long workday he had ahead of him, so my mom drove the ten minutes across town with me on her own. Before leaving, she called her mom, who impetuously announced she would meet us at the ER to provide support.

By the time we arrived, I had stopped nearly all engagement with the outside world. My mom carried me into the ER with my arms and legs wrapped around her body. I was motionless and nearly unresponsive, unrecognizable from the feisty personality I had come to develop. As my fever worsened, I became exponentially warmer, making it uncomfortable for her to hold me so close as she was already sweating as a result of circumstance. As the ER staff began their work-up, they allowed me to stay seated with my mom, where I remained until we were forced apart by the protocols they had to enact to save my life approximately twelve hours later. Hospital records show that my pulse was 190 beats per minute, my respiration was between 70–80, and my pulse oximetry was in the low 60s. I did not once move voluntarily. I whimpered in pain, my mumbles mostly incomprehensible. As they took my blood and began an IV, they moved me around as they needed to, being careful to preserve the physical connection both my mom and I desperately needed.

Before the dawn broke, they decided to admit me to the pediatrics floor due to my escalating fever and my deteriorating lung function that were irresponsive to the ER's attempts to restore them. The diagnoses listed on the ER paperwork included bilateral pneumonia, dehydration, bilateral otitis media, hypoxemia, and a rule-out for respiratory syncytial virus. In the early 1990s, respiratory syncytial virus (RSV) was a serious concern, and they completed two washes to test for it before admitting me. The tests were abrasive and uncomfortable, particularly for a small child, yet all it evoked in me was a small whine and the flittering of my eyes, another sign to my mom that she was not overreacting. Both swabs came back negative, which led them to admit me for further testing. At this point, I was a mystery to all, but the urgency and concern were becoming more certain. My mom called my dad to update him; he would stop by shortly before heading off to work.

Once admitted, they transferred me to a hospital bed, allowing my mom to join me. She sat upright with her legs outstretched. I remained cuddled as closely as I could to her chest, still immobile, my face visible just enough to ensure the oxygen tube they had taped to my cheeks was securely in place. They gave me nebulizer treatments with supplemental oxygen to assist my shallow breathing. My oxygen saturation level (the percentage of oxygen in a person's blood) continued to drop despite the introduction of such strong drugs to counteract it. Nothing they were trying was improving my condition. My body temperature continued to get warmer; my mom felt my skin nearly burning her own. She was eager for my dad to be by our side. Across town, he had gotten himself ready for work earlier than usual and picked up his father (Grandpa Teddy) as he always did. He stopped by the hospital with plenty of time to get an update before work. Although he knew I had become sicker throughout the night, nothing could prepare him for what he walked into. He could not pretend or speak away the seriousness of my illness once he saw my motionless body clinging to my mom. I was hooked up to wires and completely uninterested in his arrival. I moaned in distress but was unable to say anything as he came over to greet me. He was immediately taken aback by how hot my skin had become.

My parents, Grandma Pryde, and Grandpa Teddy sat together in the cold, sterile hospital room, watching staff check vitals, write things down, share troublesome looks, and vanish after offering forced smiles of hope. As dawn broke, two male pediatricians walked into my hospital room together. Tension grew to enormous heights. Grandma Pryde was the first to recognize how uncommon it was for two doctors to walk in together to tag team whatever monster was fighting me with inexorable force. Her reaction, even though silent and subtle, caused the others to be alarmed, and it was intensified by the apprehension evident in both doctors. They moved slowly, using coerced strength to make eye contact and deliver news no parent ever wants to hear. They sat down on either side of the bed my mom and I laid in, undoubtedly trying to level the power imbalance and improve their bedside manner. Both doctors knew our family and had great respect for Grandma Pryde, thus delivering this news was a personal blow to them as well.

Dr. Pav took the lead. "Despite our best efforts, Tasha is continuing a rapid descent and we do not know the cause. We have to insist that the next move be to initiate a flight for life, given that all attempts at resolving her distress have failed."

Dr. Klep continued, "If you choose not to pursue the flight for life, we do not believe Tasha will live through the day, and we are concerned that even the flight for life may not be able to reverse whatever is attacking her."

Dr. Pav took a deep breath and took over once more to show the seriousness of their recommendation. "We have already made calls to arrange for the aircraft to transport her to the nearest Children's Hospital in Denver. We suspect that she only has hours, at the most, for any chance of survival because of how quickly her vitals are crashing. We spoke with the head of the pediatric pulmonary department at the receiving hospital who will prep their surgery unit for an immediate tracheotomy procedure once she arrives."

They didn't let the silence linger before they threw an additional sensical yet nauseating blow, swapping eye contact as best they could between my mom and grandma. "Lynn, due to your pregnancy, you aren't allowed to travel with Tasha on the helicopter."

My mom didn't hesitate, adamant that I would NOT be flying alone without familial support. "Then my mom will go with her."

I would imagine, in some ways, that not only did the doctors know that would make my parents feel better, but it also made them feel better, knowing there could not be a more empathic and capable medical professional on board who just so happened to love me more than life itself. Without further hesitation, it was decided. No other questions were asked, and both doctors quickly excused themselves to continue making the necessary arrangements. My dad and Grandpa Teddy could not bear to look at my mom, already sobbing quietly, inconsolable. Instead, they looked directly at each other, and both burst into silent tears, looking away quickly in attempts to compose their collapsing upper bodies. My dad had to take a couple of extra seconds to gain his footing because his legs had given out; he grabbed the wall to steady himself. Grandpa Teddy rushed to his side, quickly hugging him and then backing up to give him room to breathe. Unsure how to hold the mounting emotion, my dad stepped out of the room to make phone calls to my extended family. First, he called his mom.

Grandma Becca was instantaneously concerned when she registered it was my dad on the other line. He never called during the workday, and she could sense something was awry before he spoke. She heard deep, forcefully controlled breaths and could tell he was fighting to keep himself composed. With the first couple of words he uttered, she had flashbacks to a similar call she had gotten just two years before and knew irreparable loss was imminent once again. She tried to make sense of what he was yelling with guided urgency. She made out that I was sick, the doctors said I was going to die, they were flying me to Denver, and she needed to get up there now. They hung up without finishing the conversation. Grandma Becca immediately phoned her mom, my great-grandma Claire (our tough-as-nails matriarch). Before she hung up, she heard Grandma Claire start to pray the rosary in Spanish and held back conflicting feelings of faith and nausea as she ran to the car.

My dad then called my godmother, Aunt Corina. Repeating himself but still struggling to believe the reality of his words, he demanded, "You need to get to the hospital now. They're flying Tash to Denver and think she's going to die. Come now, get here now!" He couldn't remember if he had told her that yet or not. He felt a brief stint of relief in that he knew both Becca and Corina would make phone calls to the rest of the family to spread the news, and the village would soon be on its way.

Grandpa Teddy stiffened up just long enough to follow my dad into the hallway, not making eye contact or saying anything to my mom or grandma. As he opened the door to leave, he looked over at my still, depleted body. I was his first grandchild and the first girl in his family. His head buzzed with rage and puzzlement as he tried to wrap his head around the doctor's words that I was likely going to die. He couldn't sustain his gaze on me for long. He stepped into the hallway and ensured my dad was several steps ahead of him. No longer able to contain the overpowering anguish, his body jolted and he began to cry, trying with all of his might to bury the feelings. He paced up and down the hospital floor, only paying attention to the symmetrical lines dividing the tiles. He couldn't touch his own emotions or fathom what was happening internally for my parents, so instead, he tried to problem-solve.[2] What would be the most helpful thing? As my dad came back into view after making his calls, Grandpa Teddy took out $300 from his wallet. "I'll have Tim get the truck ready for you." With that, he gave my dad a facile hug, tried to swallow every ounce of emotion that had bubbled up, and walked away to make the call.

Meanwhile, as the men exited the hospital room, my mom sat stricken with paralyzing terror. She could only feel my rapid heart rate, desperately needing to reposition herself but holding back any inclination to move at all so as not to disturb or worsen my failing body. She realized she had not eaten or drank anything since before taking me to the ER, and she had not even gone to the bathroom (quite a feat for being six months pregnant; again, a serious badass). She realized that I, too, had not done any of those things, which catapulted her fear that my body was shutting down permanently. She shrieked internally, a firm sense of nausea taking over, but she knew she could not go there. There were too many thoughts running through her head to make sense of any one of them. She brought herself back to the room, imitating her mom, who remained a pillar of strength by her side, only leaving to speak to hospital staff as necessary.

During one of her brief escapes, Grandma Pryde had to again be the bearer of bad news and make a phone call to Aunt Tammy. Tammy's stomach dropped as she could tell by her mom's tone that yet another potential tragedy was on the horizon. Steady as could be, Pryde began, "Tammy, Tasha is having a really hard time breathing, and I am going to be airlifted with her to Denver; you need to meet us at Children's Hospital." Gobsmacked, Tammy alerted her boss of the situation and began the commute to the hospital where she would spend what felt like an exorbitant amount of time waiting for us all to arrive. Grandma Pryde also called Grandpa Bill (her husband). After giving the objective details, she showed a rare moment of uncertainty. "I'm worried and scared, Bill. Her prognosis is not good." He wanted to ask if she was okay, but thought better of it, knowing the answer and that prolonging the conversation would not do either of them any good. Instead, he assured her that he would be right up.

As minutes that felt like eons went by, my mom could hear more commotion coming from the hallway and realized my dad's family was arriving in flocks. News spreads incredibly fast in my family, especially given that Grandma Becca is one of eleven children, seven of them women. It only takes one call and then the game of telephone begins. I would bet good money that nearly half the town knew what was happening to me before the chopper was prepared for takeoff. As my loved ones made their way to give me what they thought was their final goodbyes, they gathered in the hallway. Perhaps unsure of what to say, or trying their best to prepare to witness a child in such distress, it's not surprising that no one came into the hospital room except for the staff, my dad, and both of my grandmas. Everyone had come just close enough to smell preemptive grief[3] in the air, to taste the bitter pain withering everyone's tongues, and to see the impending wreckage that would bury the entire family.

Once the ambulance was ready to drive Grandma Pryde and me to the local airport, the hospital staff wheeled the bed into the hallway. They left me there to allow for a morbid parade of sorts. Family members were ushered to either side of the hospital bed. Notably, it was only female relatives that surrounded my bed. The men who had come stood a short distance away, likely trying hard to avoid any outward sign of emotion and uncertain of how to contain the pain spreading like wildfire.[4]

The women were all huddled close together, holding hands to steady each other's grief-stricken fragility. The sight of tubes, budding bruises, wires, and the evident incapacitation of my breathing literally took their breath away. Each of my great-aunts and my great-grandma took turns as if they had rehearsed this scene a hundred times before. Their strong Catholic faith took main stage as they tended to me. Both me and the bed were covered with rosaries and scapulars as they cried and prayed over me simultaneously. Grandma Claire was sure to put a scapular around my neck, which she blessed with a Spanish prayer, and it stayed on me through the entirety of my hospitalization. "Our Father who art in heaven ... Ay mi jita linda ... no puedes morir ..." It was hard to trace the words to the speaker. Their words shifted between Spanish and English, sometimes directed to me, sometimes to each other, and sometimes to a being that had no physical presence. They were trying to tap into angels in a heaven they believed so strongly in, to either protect me in the flesh or carry my spirit safely to what they believed lay beyond. Although I continued to lie motionless, I emitted small whimpers, perhaps in an attempt to cry alongside them, yet I seemed rather unfazed by their anguish. Their faces and bodies shifted in sorrow, grief making its way into clear view through the streams of tears and the unsteadiness of their hands and gazes. They were saying goodbye to me while also trying to put themselves in my parents' shoes and batting away the unspeakable emptiness they foresaw.

The hospital staff eventually had to step in and remind my family of the imperative nature of the situation and the need to move me. As we arrived at the ambulance, the staff moved me from my mom's stomach for the first time since we had entered the ER. I didn't put up much of a fight. However, the separation was devastating for her. She let go reluctantly, unstoppable tears welling in her eyes. She pushed away thoughts that this could be the last time she would ever hold me.

She made eye contact with Grandma Pryde, who jumped into the ambulance, getting as close to me as possible. "I'm right here, Sugar Plum. You aren't alone, and we are going to ride together. Okay?"

She tried with all her might to communicate hope and resilience to my mom and to remind her that they had been through a near-death experience before and escaped it. "I love you, Lynn. It's going to be okay. She's strong, and so are you." The doors shut as the lights and sirens came on and we sped off toward the waiting helicopter.

Once at the airport, I was moved to a smaller, rock-hard stretcher. I was covered with patches, tubes, and wires to monitor every possible sign of life. The aircraft was small, and they were concerned about any potential unintended aggressiveness I might enact during the ride. As a result, they had to take big white straps and fasten them over my body. They put one across my bottom half, about mid-thighs, and another across my chest, with my arms stuck underneath. They fastened them tightly, which I distinctly remember because it scared me. Two pilots were in the cockpit—a man and a woman. Grandma Pryde was seated at my feet to the right, trying to soothe me and hold me as tightly as she could. I was crying forcefully at this point, yet too sick to explain why. I remember the woman pilot asking me, "Do you want some juice, Sweetie?"

"Please let me up." I winced through needed breaks for more air. I was angry that they weren't listening to the few words I was able to muster, and I was appalled that words were being wasted on asking me if

I wanted juice. Luckily, the most prominent sensation was Grandma Pryde orienting every ounce of love in her body toward me to make me feel safe.[5]

Meanwhile, the second my parents saw the ambulance drive away, they rushed to our house to pack a few things and head over to my dad's parents' house, where they would pick up the truck and Grandma Becca to accompany them on the drive. My dad drove, fully aware that my mom needed him now more than ever to be strong and get them there quickly, without commotion. He saw her slowly breaking and knew there was nothing he could say, so instead, he drove. There was no communication. Everyone was consumed by their own thoughts: thoughts so treacherous they were using all the mental energy they could to redirect them. It was blizzarding. My dad white-knuckled the entire drive, knowing with certainty it was the worst snowstorm he had ever driven in. He talked to himself the whole way, repeating, *Pole to pole, just find the next pole,* in an effort to distract from his own pain while also recognizing the immense risk to their lives, given the weather. Visibility was next to nothing, which extended the usual two-hour drive to a little over five hours total. Extra hours to silently stew in the unthinkable. To cry in isolation, each person trying to regulate their tension enough to stay intact for one another. They heard each other's cries but did not address them. What can you say? Nothing was going to ease the pain, and attempts to do so would likely create anger the car had no room to hold.

When my parents and Grandma Becca arrived at the hospital, the first thing my mom did was make a call to Aunt Tammy to see if she had been united with Grandma Pryde or knew where I was. Then, they asked staff for directions to the correct floor. Although they knew what they wanted to ask, it was noticeable in their voices just how difficult it was to ask what direction dying toddlers were in and the easiest way to get there. They had not heard anything about my condition during their drive. As they scoured the massive facility, they experienced destabilizing moments of wondering if I was even still alive. After multiple interactions with less-than-helpful employees, they were directed to the children's ICU and cancer waiting area. There, they met Aunt Tammy and Grandma Pryde, who were waiting impatiently for an update. At the very least, my parents and Grandma Becca were able to exhale as Grandma Pryde confirmed that I was, indeed, still alive and fighting. I had even slightly improved while in flight, rendering the scheduled tracheotomy procedure unnecessary for the time being. Grandma Pryde praised the flight crew and shed some light on our journey while they waited. Eventually, a nurse led them all into a small, isolated room in the cancer hall, where I would remain for the next four days. Even though I tested negative for RSV two times, I had to be kept in strict isolation since they were unable to definitively label my respiratory distress. The discharge paperwork from my brief admittance had shifted slightly from the ER's notes and now listed otitis media, bronchitis, severe pneumonia with marked respiratory distress, severe hypoxia and acidosis due to respiratory distress, dehydration, and near-apneic episodes as the primary concerns for my new medical team to conquer. They feared something worse was still at play, so the profusion of testing began.

The next several days crawled by, as if the tenseness and anxiety overwhelmed even time itself. It was a series of haphazard routines, almost never executed by the same staff twice. The variety of doctors, nurses, and lab techs who would come in to check vitals, administer medications, or run tests made it hard to establish rapport or trust in the team for my family. The staff had a brash bedside manner and made little effort to empathize with my family or provide a sense of safety or comfort to me. Because I was in isolation, most of the staff never came completely into the room, trying to decrease exposure risk, which could have contributed to their own fear and quick, stoic interactions as they set supplies down on the counter nearest the door. For those who had to take a more hands-on approach, they moved my body about as they needed to, without warning or explanation. As the poking and prodding continued, I would often murmur, "No more, please no more treatments." I had been conditioned to realize that each time the door opened, there would be my pain mixed with the fear and helplessness in the faces of my family.[6]

To me, there was almost a sense of invisibility in that the staff carried on as if I weren't a real person. As if the suffering worn by my family in the room was a set of inanimate drawings on the walls. An interactive museum dedicated to the families of those with sick children. Looking back at it, I now try to give the staff the benefit of the doubt. Perhaps it was because of the nature of their work. They were working in a children's cancer unit, where they knew most would lose their battles. Maybe they needed to desensitize and separate themselves from the misery to get their job done efficiently.[7] Maybe they had learned to master staying focused on the task so as not to carry home the stench of dying young lives that never got to live. Now, I can see and have empathy for these healthcare workers, acknowledging the secondary trauma and immense exposure to grief and loss they bore witness to. However, that does not excuse the impact this experience had on my family.[8] At one point, a nurse entered and observed my mom leaving the bathroom connected to my hospital room. She reprimanded my mom, stating she wasn't allowed to use the bathroom because she wasn't a patient. Really?

The only exception to the demeanors of the staff was Tony, a tall and muscular man who consistently served as my respiratory therapist. My family loved Tony, and they still talk about his compassion and support to this day. Tony took the time to announce himself in a soft voice. He came all the way into the room, not once treating me like I had been doused with some toxic chemical agent. He prepared my nebulizer treatments and explained what he knew about my illness. He reported that I was being given incredibly high doses of antibiotics and steroids, and they needed to be diligent about around-the-clock nebulizer treatments to combat the unknown attackers in my lungs. As I cried and asked Tony to stop the treatments, he artfully practiced a way for me to demonstrate autonomy. "Tasha, can I move your hand over here to this side?" and "Tasha, can I touch your chest and help you breathe this in a little better?" He gave me the capacity to feel like I was giving him permission to move me about as he needed to, something that settled me and allowed me to feel more of the independence I was used to demonstrating at home.

Initially, it was explained that part of the process would be to meticulously monitor every ounce of fluid that came into and exited my body. The fluid would then be tested for further conditions they were trying to rule out. Due to my weakened state, there was no chance I could get up to go to the bathroom, so I wore diapers, which would be weighed as they were changed. This became a stressful process that left my family feeling neglected, dirty, and worried about the staff's ability to treat me. Each time my diapers were changed, they would be weighed but not disposed of. As the days went on, piles of diapers were left to rot on the counters, where staff continued to use dwindling extra space for other equipment and preparation tasks. My family asked what could be done, which was often met with "I don't know" or "That's not my job." To make matters worse, within the first full day of being there, nothing had been given to me to eat or drink. Although I was not complaining of hunger and still barely conscious most of the time, my family knew the importance of fuel to help me battle the illness that was clearly winning. Attempts to meet my nutritional needs fell flat, with staff members passing the buck to other staff members. My family was not allowed to bring anything in, given the need to analyze all of my input and output, thus, they were stuck. They, too, hadn't eaten (or slept), so I would imagine fine-tuned emotion-regulation skills[9] were in short supply, which only exacerbated intolerance of the less-than-optimal care and courtesy from healthcare workers.

My family refers to this particular memory as the "Terms of Endearment" moment (from the 1983 movie with Debra Winger and Shirley MacLaine). Once it had been nearly forty-eight hours without any food in my system, my mom took the lead in communicating with the hospital staff. After her first time asking, a nurse reported, "She has to remain on a liquid diet due to our uncertainty about her condition and fear that anything new introduced to her system could lead to a swift decline." Okay, fine. She let that sit for a while.

She asked different staff a second, third, and fourth time. Finally, a staff member changed the tone and said, "I can bring in some Jell-O or ice cream." They waited awhile longer, but nothing was brought in.

By now, my mom was unable to contain herself any longer. She marched out to the nurses' station and noticed a small refrigerator with Jell-O inside. There were three nurses at the station. My mom said, "Can one of you hand me some Jell-O?" Shockingly, not only did no one respond to her, but they also barely acknowledged her presence. With a primitive leap, she banged the counter hard and loud with closed fists, abruptly catching their attention, and demanded, "My daughter needs some fucking Jell-O!" Without any verbal communication, one of the nurses promptly got up and grabbed two Jell-O's from the refrigerator and a spoon. She cautiously handed them over, crouching and inching closer, as if my mom were about to pounce on her. Perhaps my mom would have if this woman had not finally heard her. I'm glad we never had to find out. I happily ate both Jell-O's as she fed them to me. It was clear her motherly instincts were right; I just needed some damn Jell-O.

The test results continued to come back negative or inconclusive. I was tested for cystic fibrosis, different types of cancer, and other autoimmune diseases, with no clues to pinpoint what was happening, meaning no insight into the best way to treat me. The most common communication was ongoing uncertainty, which left everyone feeling depleted. The days were spent with my family huddled in the room, slowly watching me decline then rally, too exhausted to address their worst fears openly. Instead, they talked about rather boring, pointless things to fill the space. My mom was the only exception to this. She verbalized fear that I wasn't going to make it. Everyone felt pangs of disbelief and nausea but had no idea how to respond. They tried to invalidate her warranted emotion and say things would be okay and quickly distract her to a less-somber topic. Grandma Pryde took the reins in these instances, doing her best to curb my mom's anxiety and exemplify hope and remind them of my strength.

They put movies on the TV in the room, even though I showed no interest. They played in the background, with my family knowing how much I loved them when I was well, and hoping a scene would eventually catch my attention and help bring me back to life. At night, a cot was brought in for my mom to sleep on, with my dad taking a chair. Given the circumstances, they both knew without saying that no one would be comfortable or able to sleep anyway. Throughout my stay, my mom only left the hospital one time to take a shower after a united front insisted she must tend to herself and her unborn baby. My dad would leave my room usually one to two times a day to take a brief walk and to shower. He could hear the squeaky wheels of little red wagons in the hallway and came to understand that the other dying children, if well enough, were given the opportunity to take rides around the ward to change their scenery, if only for a few minutes.

When visiting hours were over, my grandmas and Aunt Tammy traveled a few miles away from the hospital to stay in Aunt Tammy's tiny one-bedroom apartment. My Grandma Pryde slept in Aunt Tammy's room, my Grandma Becca on the couch, and Aunt Tammy on the floor. On the way home, they would grab something to eat, which they really never consumed. At the apartment, they took showers and then tried to sleep. They were stricken with an impounding fear that verbalizing any of their fears might actually will them to come true. Thus, conversation was limited to trying to identify positives, clarifying medical hodge-podge by Grandma Pryde, or filling the silence with current events. Unspoken but forever solidified between the three of them, they all felt a strong sense of camaraderie and tried as best they could to reassure each other and recharge themselves to be strong for my parents.

Two pivotal moments turned my prognosis around, and given the lack of scientific and medical explanations to this day of what happened to me, perhaps these can only be described as the moments in which love and connection conquered illness and saved my life—results no medical tests will show. First, my dad visited the gift shop. Feeling powerless and completely out of control, he was focused on finding me the perfect stuffed animal to make my hospital bed cozier. He was drawn to a small dog. It was a sandy light brown and seemed to be lying on its stomach with his front and back legs stretched out. He had big, floppy ears and black, piercing eyes made of plastic. On the side of his back left leg, there was a tag with the name DOOZER etched on it. My dad bought him and laid him next to me. I perked up a little bit, given that the sterile nature of the hospital room wasn't particularly comforting, and everyone was relieved that something had seemed to bring me a sense of alertness, if only momentarily.

The second piece is always told with laughter and lightheartedness. The same day, they decided to play *Beauty and the Beast* on the VCR. They had cycled through a few of the Disney classics they had access to, but *Beauty and the Beast* was my favorite. I was obsessed; I could recite the entire movie from memory on cue. I had a strong affiliation with

Belle due to her love of books and the ladder bookcase she swung on. (This fact has never changed, and I have a ladder bookcase in my house, which I hope will continue to get bigger as my book collection grows.) At the beginning of the movie is a short, relatively meaningless scene that you have to have a sharp eye to catch: a small deer running through the brush. Given that I had watched the movie likely hundreds of times, I had inspected every inch of every frame. Out of nowhere, when the deer came on, I made eye contact with the TV and called out, "Big Josh!" My dad is an avid hunter and has always had mounts in our home. As a child, he had a huge deer in our house that I aptly named "Big Josh." Through overaccommodation,[10] I had determined that all deer had that name. As I called out his name, it was as if the magic from my imagination had spilled out into the room. I perked up, only briefly, but it was as if everyone in that moment knew I would be okay.

Some may call it a miracle, some may call it science, some may call it something in between, but I'm arguing that it was a combination of things that we can and can't wrap our heads around due to the uncertainty that remains in the in-between of life and death. Why are some young lives like mine spared, while other children aren't given the same chance? What does one do to deserve to continue to live (yet suffer) or die (and feel no pain, supposedly anyway)? Are there winners and losers? However you want to look at it, I finally began to improve. Just as they couldn't identify what had been wrong, they couldn't fully identify what was going well either. But my vitals were regulating, I was responding to the medication, and eventually, they relayed confidence that I could be discharged.

In the last few hours prior to discharge, the elevated joy couldn't be measured. The only true diagnosis from that time that would follow me through life is severe asthma. My parents and grandmas all went through training to get a full understanding of how our lives would change to accommodate a strict medication and treatment regimen that would last indefinitely. With relief also came a forgotten awareness of the exhaustion and constant turmoil everyone's nervous systems had been undergoing for several days prior. Similar to how grief can manifest, relief can also be a strange sensation, and it was experienced differently by each of them. For example, my mom was sitting on the windowsill, watching my family pack up their things as we waited for the final approval to leave, once again as an intact family, and strangely began laughing. Bellowing, uncontrollable laughter. It came out of nowhere, not triggered by anything that was said. The rest of my family was equally confused and disturbed, looking around at one another, trying to make sense of the young mom acting as though she'd been at Disneyland for the last several days, riding the roller coasters and meeting the princesses. It seemed she had hit her breaking point and was experiencing a bit of delirium. She described it as an almost out-of-body experience that was completely out of her control, triggered by happiness because she was taking her baby girl home, alive.

Once I was given the green light to go home, Aunt Tammy stayed behind while the rest of us piled into the truck. I did not have a car seat; thus, I rode on the laps of both my grandmas the whole way home, being gently passed between them as their legs went numb and they needed breaks. Once home, the oxygen company set up machines and walked my parents through the basics. Aunt Corina was at our house, along with her husband and both of my grandpas. She had cleaned, filled my room with goodies from the flower shop she worked at, and prepared a feast for the family to enjoy together. As low as it had gotten for my family to come to terms with the reality that I could die, they were on an equal high as they were able to say out loud that I had lived.

As my parents worked to restore their own homeostasis, my mom was given enough space to acknowledge that the unborn baby inside of her had not moved since the day I got sick. Terrified of what that might mean, she was forced to name this fear. It was too much to acknowledge or verbalize during the hospital stay, and she did her best to put it out of her mind so as not to overwhelm her heart with considering the loss of two children at the same time. On the second night home, she worked up the courage to tell my dad she was afraid because the baby still was not moving, and she had started to spot. My dad, no longer shaking off medical issues of even the smallest nature, encouraged her to call Grandma Pryde. Thanks to Grandma Pryde, they arranged an emergency appointment where my mom would get the one and only sonogram performed throughout the pregnancy. After some searching, the doctor identified a heartbeat, captured a brief arm movement, and reported that all seemed well with baby #2. Waves of relief overtook my mom. It was yet another narrow escape of death.

It wasn't until three months later that we would find out my mom had actually been pregnant with twins and had miscarried one of them at an unknown point during the pregnancy (although I have a pretty good guess of when it occurred). The evidence was apparent after delivery, when two placentas but only one baby arrived. More loss. This complication may have impacted the trauma of my brother's (Dalton) introduction to the world. He was delivered breech, vaginally (again, without drugs, so if you haven't caught on to it yet, my mom is likely the strongest woman on the planet), and with the cord wrapped around his neck. It was a brutal delivery. The following morning, my parents effortlessly agreed that my mom would tie her tubes, severing any potential for the traumatic losses and near-losses they had suffered in pursuit of creating their family. Even given their youth, the doctors didn't question their decision for a minute. Who could blame them?

My mom's initial anxiety and trauma from her own medical history only grew following this experience. She struggled to let me out of her sight. She spent most nights in the ensuing months getting up to put a mirror under my nose to ensure I was breathing. She checked my vitals constantly, poked me to be sure I would move, and had multiple baby monitors put in my room to listen for any signs of danger. She felt immense guilt, despite knowing she didn't do anything wrong. This is a testament to how we logically know something but feel the opposite anyway—a staple of grief.[11] She was concerned about how her stress would impact her second baby and questioned her skills as a mother. Motherhood was all she ever wanted, but she doubted her abilities to keep her children alive, thus increasing her own insecurities and desire to protect us. She wasn't able to acknowledge or accept that some things in life were simply out of her control, and the uncertainty gnawed away at her.[12]

My dad further retreated into the quiet, outwardly well-composed young man he had always been. He paid closer attention but didn't broadcast most of his observations. Once he visibly saw improvements in me, his brain shifted to an entirely new set of stressors, worrying about what this incident was going to cost our family financially. At that point, they did not have the financial cushion they eventually built for themselves, and he believed his role was to be a solid provider. He already had an incredible work ethic, but this strengthened his relentless desire to volunteer for extra hours and road calls that he struggles to this day to turn down. He remarked during his interview for this story that work was his way of trying to control the only thing he believed he could—the financial stability to manage the pattern of medical ruins. He alluded to a sense of guilt in not taking my mom seriously that first night when she voiced concern for my welfare. Had she listened to him, I likely would have died at home that night. How do you ever make up for that? That realization was too much for him to bear, thus work became his outlet; he wouldn't let me down in that sense.

This event also seems to coincide with the time frame in which my parents stopped communicating effectively. Neither knew how to help the other while also managing their own distress. How much can a young couple go through? In some ways, they simply gave up trying to understand one another, as they couldn't figure out how to understand themselves. The village of family members seemed to respond by consistent visits to check on me, touch me, and watch out for me more closely. Gratitude for my health was often shared, but the thread of trauma wasn't often woven into the storyline of our communication. They didn't necessarily treat me differently; it was more of an understated worry on their faces that they worked hard to disguise. If anything, the only spoken changes were reminders to my cousins to be careful around me or for me to be more careful with myself. I was indirectly labeled sickly; someone to be monitored in a different way than others, and wow did I hate that.

Similar to chapter one, of all the intense and traumatic moments you just vicariously witnessed, it seems the most vivid and emotional memories for my family are the audible wheezing, the tubes taped to my face, and the visible struggles as I fought for air. They remembered my depleted whines, my politeness in asking people to "Please stop hurting me." They recalled seeing the contrast of the pitch black in my long, thick hair next to the variegating whiteness of my tiny oval face and huge blue eyes. At the same time, I find it interesting that in the retellings of this particular trauma, there was also a shared sense of fuzziness in their memories. We all moved forward, and some even forgot entirely, a surprising consideration of what the mind can do to help protect us from things we'd rather forget. They described being suspended in time, uncertain of what was real, stuck in disbelief and tunnel vision, just trying to hold themselves steady through such turbulent fear and overpowering sorrow. Mental blockages became stronger over time to help rid the helplessness and desperation of what is always lurking around the corner: loss, destruction, and death. They spoke to a meaning-making process[13] of how lived experiences allow us to see the inanimate, ordinary things as intricately emotional reminders once we have a little perspective. A cement pad where we know a helicopter may land, an oxygen tank with a hose wrapped around its neck in the corner of a room, a small red wagon with four wheels and a long handle waiting to be ridden. These are just things we see until suddenly someone we love has to land on that cement pad, be tethered to that oxygen tank, and take rides in a wagon in a terminal cancer ward. There were also similarities in remembrance of relief. Perhaps one can't experience grief without relief. Do sorrow and gratitude really go hand in hand?[14] If I had died, would my family's unwavering dedication to their faith have shifted in some way?

The impact on me has morphed over the years. Interestingly, there is full consensus that I did not seem to change at all following the experience. I didn't ask about what happened, I didn't complain about my new schedule and routine of doctors' offices and treatments around the clock. This shocks me, given that I was an inquisitive and curious child. I asked questions about everything and was keenly aware of the world around me. I wonder if I sensed that no one knew how to talk about it. That perhaps they were still so consumed by their own fears the other shoe would drop that I concluded I had to sort out my questions on my own and protect them. I simply returned to my pre-traumatic nosey, bossy self and moved right along with them into the future.

I often wonder why I remember only two quick snapshots out of the whole ordeal: the women hovering over me in the hallway, and being strapped down to the stretcher before takeoff. I know they are my pure and honest recollections because as I got older, I was the first one to reminisce about them and have them verified by others who were present. I have come to the malleable conclusion that they were, perhaps, the most traumatic of the events I experienced, and that is why I remember them. Strange that I leaned into the pain rather than striving to avoid it. But, maybe even more than that, they are two moments in which I was faced with the inevitable truth of what it means to be alive. I learned that nothing is permanent and that grief and loss are both multifaceted and nearly everywhere when you really look around. I believe that this experience fundamentally shifted my understanding of myself, others, and the world and jumpstarted my fascination with death, dying, and the process of grieving. Yes, I was only two years old, but I have vivid memories of seeing the incredibly strong and resilient women in my life crushed at the prospect of my impending death. The tension could have easily been cut with the dullest of knives. Their typical, no-nonsense bossiness had melted away, leaving stains of fear and sadness covering their faces and shirts. I remember the crying and the praying in both languages. I remember being smothered by their hands and moist faces, and I remember that I actually was scared, but I could not show it. Their misery had expanded to such depths that my own seemed to have no place. To a toddler, what is death, anyway?

Although I have no personal memories of the two bright spots that embody the rounded corner to my survival, their significance in my life also bears a follow-up. For one, *Beauty and the Beast* is still my favorite movie. When the 2017 version of the film with Emma Watson came out, I was living in Indiana, working on my doctoral degree. I flew back to my hometown for opening weekend and took both of my grandmas and my mom to the premiere. All three of them cried the entire time. It was one of the best decisions I have ever made. (If you're wondering, I didn't cry at all, an idea we will visit later, but hey, it isn't a competition.) Second, Doozer remains in my bedroom to this day. I have no shame in admitting that on my worst days and my scariest nights, I hold him the entire time. He is likely only held together by the years of tears he has endured. He has seen me wrestle with my despair and anguish more than anyone else, and I'd bet that he will be with me on my true deathbed someday.

Perhaps the greatest lasting impact on me has been my pursuit to defeat the odds that professionals place upon me. I have always had a seriousness to me, even as a child. I was goal-driven and fierce in my pursuits. I didn't have time to "play" and leisurely explore my world without intent. I grew up quickly, and I do not doubt that even though I was a new inhabitant in this world, my own near-death experience taught me that I needed to be strong and resilient.[15] I could not show weakness nor allow myself to be the cause of such emotional upheaval as what I saw in the false alarm of final goodbyes that was pulled by my brush with death. That has proven to be both a blessing and a curse. I carry the resiliency with pride but also recognize I have pushed boundaries when I shouldn't have. I got comfortable being the identified patient, a complex and multilayered internal tug of war. I have said yes to things when I should have said no. I have held myself to standards that are unfair and expectations that define perfection that put me in my own way sometimes. My desire to be strong comes with the unaffordable cost of running from being vulnerable because of the way I learned to define it. And I was never the same again.

3

THE GROWTH IN ULTIMATE SUFFERING

Uncle Tom decided to move to California in September of 1987. He moved to Denver after graduating from college in 1982 but came to feel like Colorado no longer served him. He was searching for something more. As a gay man, he was still mostly closeted and wore that shame in perfectly ironed creases. He grew up in Wyoming, receiving overt messages about what it meant to be a man. Physical strength, higher education, financial freedom, and of course, marrying a nice girl and passing on the Greek traditions and expectations taught to him by his father. But he knew from a young age that he was different. To him, different wasn't just about having dissimilar interests or a quirky eccentricity here and there; it meant he was at a deficit—defective and damaged in some way. He spent most of his life trying to blend into the crowd as best he could while denying his own authenticity by administering heavy doses of self-loathing. His discomfort prevented him from doing much self-exploration, thus California presented a chance for him to figure out who he was. Moving to Denver was a good first step toward being able to leave his conservative, close-minded community. But, regardless of the more progressive and supportive external fixtures in Denver, he still struggled with overwhelming self-rejection and wished to be someone entirely different. Perhaps leaving was an attempt to run from himself, or a search to find something that would be the key to unlock his internalized homophobia.[1] Or, maybe leaving would wake him up from this "phase" he was in, as he so desperately wanted to believe.

California held the promise of sunshine, a more accepting community, and distance from his home that had perpetuated the oppression that forced him into his disgraced shell for protection. The first few months there were rather uneventful. Although he carried his shame[2] inside of him, his extroverted nature and genuine empathy for others made it easy for him to connect and build relationships quickly. He lived in small, modest quarters as he adjusted to his new job and began to take in the scene, already more accepting of and dedicated to welcoming others like him. In March of 1988, a group of friends invited him to spend a birthday weekend in Palm Springs, and he jumped at the opportunity. The first night there, they indulged in top-notch food and were eager to check out the nightclub scene. They bounced around to a few dynamic spots and landed at a place called CC Construction. It was packed from wall to wall with a dance floor, strobe lights, and the hottest music at the time. Overwhelmed with the sensory stimulation, he found a place where he could blend into the background. He began to look more closely into the faces of the people around him. His eyes were drawn across the dance floor to a young man sitting on a stool, observing the club with the same curiosity as him. They made eye contact and oddly held it for a few moments, exchanging smiles. He had a quick gut reaction; he needed to meet this person. It was as if the universe had spotlighted him just in time and initiated a magnetic force he couldn't resist.

The man had his entourage around him, about six men in total. He was sitting in the middle, as if being preserved so that others could only admire him from afar. Tom spoke up to his friends and pointed out the man, expressing a compelling sense that he simply had to say hello. Although very unlike him to be so brash and confident, he strolled over and gently invaded the circle, finding himself directly in front of the man, who was even more attractive up close. He was tall, tan, and built. He had a gorgeous smile, impeccable hair, and deep hazel eyes. With surprising ease, Tom introduced himself, and they began a casual conversation. That was it. From that moment forward, Tom and Jeffrey began building their life together, officially beginning to date that very weekend. Jeffrey was initially the strong, opinionated, stubborn leader of the pack who oftentimes intimidated those around him with his success and confidence. Tom carefully embraced vulnerability. He was emotional, sensitive, affectionate, and a people-pleaser. What they loved about one another is what they wanted to work on for themselves. There was a striking balance between their traits that was met with significant admiration and appreciation for their differences. Soulmates, meant to be, undoubtedly made for one another. It was a mutual feeling sensed by them both right away, and it didn't waver. However, the happily-ever-after story we hear so frequently in love stories is far from what their eight-year relationship would endure.

Tom lived in Long Beach and worked there during the week but traveled to Palm Springs each weekend to be reunited with Jeffrey. It didn't take long before he was able to land a job in Palm Springs and make the move. From the beginning, the two of them were very open with one another about their sexual histories and status, given that they were living in the mecca of the AIDS epidemic during its highest peak. Tom explained that he was negative, got tested every six months, and would continue to do so. Jeffrey had a different attitude about it. He chose not to get tested regularly and was firm in his belief that he didn't want to know. He explained that if he contracted the virus, he wanted to go on living his life as long and as well as he could. He didn't want to know about how the disease might affect him or acknowledge that it could mean death. Surprisingly, there wasn't much conflict between them about this, as they chose from the beginning to always practice safe sex. They gobbled up education and resources as they were published to ensure they were following the best guidelines available to them. Tom continued to follow his routine, and Jeffrey would go on living his life without attention paid to the fear the epidemic bred. They had a mutual respect for one another's personal choices and agreed they would not sacrifice their own medical values or a sexually satisfying life despite the stigma.

What neither of them knew at the time is that Jeffrey was already HIV-positive when they met. He had no symptoms and no suspected or confirmed evidence to believe he was infected. Living life was more important than searching for potential causes of death, particularly for Jeffrey. The first five years of their relationship were nothing short of bliss. They chose to live in Palm Springs due to the desert being a more open and welcoming community for gay men than most other areas of the country. It was a diverse region that promoted acceptance in a way that allowed them to feel comfortable identifying as a couple in public spaces. Although nothing was completely safe, particularly with the fear of AIDS continuing to rise throughout the country, they didn't feel as on edge for their own safety. They bought property together as a way to solidify their union, given that marriage or other formal acts of commitment were not allowed. They also became dog dads, had thriving careers, and were a main source of entertainment and connection for their friends and family. They were submersed in Palm Springs gay culture and knew many men in the community who had been infected or had lost their lives to AIDS. It was not a topic that could be avoided, but as Tom's biannual test results came back negative, that was enough evidence for Jeffrey to assume the same for himself.

Tom eventually made the decision to travel home and tell his parents in person that he was gay. He was grateful that California had offered him a new start, a place to be authentic and perhaps learn to truly love and accept himself as an equal and deserving human.[3] He had always told himself that if he ever got into a serious relationship, he would come out to our family in an open and honest way. Early on in his relationship with Jeffrey, he knew he had found his match and wanted to follow through on the promise he made to himself. After a flight and a long drive, he arrived home about 2 a.m. His mom was up waiting in her reclining chair, as she often was, likely reading a mystery. He was short and direct in his demeanor after the general greetings.

"Mom, there's something I'd like to tell you, and that something is that I'm gay. I want to tell dad right away too."

"Thank you for telling me, Tom, but I don't think you should tell Dad." She emphasized the point with much conviction. Even though her intentions were likely to protect her oldest child, the impact cultivated further shame, as she sent the message that this part of him was better kept a secret, especially from the man who was supposed to love him most in the world. He sensed support and unconditional love from her but also believed she struggled internally and was disappointed, even though it was never directly named.

"Did you already know?" he asked.

"I did suspect it, Tom, but I thought it was maybe a phase you would grow out of." Yet again, with uneducated but good intentions, the impact was another punch to his gut. With new layers of shame freshly added, he listened to her advice and did not say anything to his dad during the visit.[4]

Returning to California, Tom continued to build his life with Jeffrey, not once considering HIV or AIDS as a character in their love story. At that time, the two biggest physical risk factors for AIDS were unexplained and rapid weight loss and/or skin lesions that could appear on any area of the body. There was discussion that fatigue could play a large role, and oftentimes, those infected would begin to shift aspects of their character to accommodate decreasing stamina. Tom was the first to notice Jeffrey's unexplained weight loss and his shifting aptitude for productivity. Jeffrey was an incredibly driven and ambitious person. He worked hard, owning a successful hair salon in a thriving part of Palm Springs. At first, nothing was said about it, although concerns were internalized, a never-ending game of ping-pong in the back of Tom's mind. Trying to be respectful of Jeffrey's desire to live, Tom consistently bit his tongue and tried to stave off the fear, reminding himself that it could very well be nothing. Fairly quickly after the notable physical changes, Jeffrey began to come home from work early to take a nap in the afternoons, which never previously happened. Putting those things together, Tom knew this was a telltale sign and that Jeffrey was in complete denial. Without addressing HIV or AIDS specifically, he asked Socratic questions,[5] inquiring about potential reasons for fatigue and pointing out the personality changes. Jeffrey was dismissive, noting he didn't feel well but was ultimately fine.

This back-and-forth lasted about six months. Jeffrey's mother and sister noticed the same things, but attempts to share worry were met with rejection of all talking points. Friends would either completely ignore the obvious or would make somewhat disguised remarks of concern without any follow-up. The avoidance made each day longer.

The shadow of death grew bigger, taking over more square footage in their house, with very few spots of sunshine left that could warm the iciness that angels of death carried. The somewhat individualistic cluster of symptoms each AIDS patient suffered was more fuel for Jeffrey to talk away what he was experiencing and shut down worry. It was as though he built a wall, working to manufacture barriers to stay stuck in his own naivete and ignorance. Eventually, due to Tom's increasing rumination and inability to fight his fears, he began to speak more candidly, insisting Jeffrey visit a doctor to assess the situation.

Jeffrey's severe respiratory fits began about this time. He spent hours each day gasping for air, coughing, and writhing in pain, unable to catch his breath. Each episode lasted for about an hour. His energy slowly diminished, and he became less able to follow through on his job duties. Wasting syndrome also set in, a term used to describe unintentional weight loss of more than 10 percent of an individual's body weight. The weight loss was commonly accompanied by fever, general weakness, and diarrhea. It was most noticeable in Jeffrey's face; it became gaunt and lost much of the bronze glow that he was known for. As the signs made it harder to shy away from, Jeffrey clung to both a lack of acceptance and full denial of what was certainly the cause of his pending death.[6] Their lives would go on this way for a couple more months with amplified conflict in an attempt to dissipate their growing suspicion. Neither slept much due to the respiratory fits that consumed their nights and the quiet terror that led them through each day.

Tom became obsessed with determining a way to get Jeffrey to the doctor. He considered all types of scenarios: things he could say, people whose help he could enlist, even what he could threaten. He spoke frequently with Jeffrey's mom and sister and felt brief moments of connection because he was not the only one consumed by feelings of desperation and powerlessness. It was during one of his own check-ups with his beloved doctor, Dr. Sunjon, where he was able to get a solid plan in place and take back some of the power Jeffrey's denial had stripped from them both. Dr. Sunjon gave Tom a clean bill of health and provided a safe space for him to express grave concern about Jeffrey. Dr. Sunjon was empathic yet forceful in stating that it was of dire necessity that Jeffrey be seen, as he suspected that Jeffrey's condition was far more advanced than Tom had thought. On the drive home, out of pure despair, he decided that the only way to get Jeffrey to seek help was to threaten to leave the relationship. Jeffrey was his soulmate, and the thought of leaving him for any reason, including AIDS, was laughable. Nonetheless, he was certain that he had to sell the threat if there was any hope for Jeffrey at all. He called Jeffrey's mother, a close confidant, and told her the plan. He assured her that he would never actually leave Jeffrey, but he felt he had no other choice and that it was possible it was the only scenario in which Jeffrey would be motivated. With her approval, he got home and prepared himself for what he thought would be one of the most difficult, emotionally-charged conversations of his life.

He sat on the sofa across from Jeffrey, who was lounging in a dark green leather chair in the corner of their living room. Jeffrey was having another one of his respiratory fits, moving his body around to reduce the pain and noise. As he watched Jeffrey struggle, Tom sat stiffly, rehearsing over and over in his mind what he was going to say. He knew he needed to be convincing, without a sliver of doubt in his presentation. When the fit was over, Tom launched into his speech.

"Jeffrey, I love you. I love you so much. I can't keep watching you suffer in this way day after day, week after week. Things are not getting better; if anything, your condition is worse."

Jeffrey put his emaciated arm into the air and firmly signaled the STOP sign.

"Tom, I'm going to go to your doctor." That was it. They sat and cried together for hours. No words, just tears that exchanged the security of their partnership and proved to be more unifying than any marriage license could ever achieve. Their natural traits and roles within the relationship began to reverse permanently from this moment forward. Tom had to become the strong, stubborn, no-nonsense protector. Jeffrey had to learn to be vulnerable, accept help, and acknowledge his emotional journey as he faced inevitable death. The next day, Tom got Jeffrey in to see Dr. Sunjon, and the beginning of their end began.

Dr. Sunjon was a gay man specializing in internal medicine at Desert Hospital in Palm Springs. Tom had initially sought him out for primary care because he wanted to ensure that he was working with a doctor who understood what it was like to live in his shoes as a gay man; someone who could comprehend the fear and pressure attached to the identity. He needed a doctor who would show compassion and not treat him like a leper. Someone who would acknowledge the stigma and treat the person. Dr. Sunjon was the perfect balance of goofball and expert. Tom does not know the details of Jeffrey's first visit. He sat in the waiting room to give Jeffrey the opportunity to build rapport with Dr. Sunjon and to allow for autonomy and power over his own healthcare.

During the visit, Jeffrey was diagnosed with pneumonia and admitted to the hospital the same day. In addition, at the insistence of Dr. Sunjon, they set in motion the process of taking formal steps to solidify their existence as a couple. Wills were updated, powers of attorney were created, assets were moved from both their names solely into Tom's so that Jeffrey could get placed under Medicare's insurance to pay for the treatment he desperately needed but wouldn't save his life. Albeit necessary, Tom could see the defeat in Jeffrey, given that every step taken seemed to deconstruct his identity a bit more, stripping him of power, control, and oftentimes dignity. First, it was his ever-prominent physical appeal and stamina, then his career, then his assets. Many times, strangers would look a little longer or a little harder at Jeffrey or physically move farther away, likely fearful of "catching" the death sentence that was AIDS. Jeffrey knew the stares were because of his deterioration; he now looked similar to the other men dying of AIDS; he'd lost his previously strong and attractive presence. He rarely spoke of these changes, but it was apparent that it tore him down. It broke them both down. It was not often addressed because, again, what can be said? The fear was overpowering, their minds forecasting the horror of what was to come.[7] Such grief both in the moment and in anticipation of the inevitable. It was all they could do to just simply hang on.

Jeffrey's family played a critical role in how things unfolded from that point onward. Since they were his blood relatives, they had automatic rights to be with him and have access to his healthcare while he was hospitalized in a way that Tom did not. Marriage for gay people was not legal, so there was nothing in a court of law that would support their commitment. Jeffrey's family was not only accepting but fully embraced Tom as part of their family and saw merit in the life they had built together. They made it clear to hospital staff that Tom was family and was to be allowed in any hospital room, be present in any family meeting, and receive any noteworthy update whether they were there or not. This alone eased immense potential suffering that both Tom and Jeffrey could have felt, because had Jeffrey's family not been willing to do this, Tom would not have been allowed to visit him. My heart breaks for the countless others who did not have this type of unconditional love and validation. How many died alone, separated forcefully, suffering in isolation? The thought is sickening.

As Jeffrey fought to accept his condition and address problems directly, both of them began to consume as much research and education about the epidemic as they could. They read academic and medical journals, read news articles, watched specials, and talked to their friends and the surrounding community to be sure they were absorbing the most up-to-date information. After about six months of this routine, his condition worsened. It was a nauseating seesaw of symptom improvement and hope on one end, then quick crashes and hospital stays on the other. He had medical appointments at least once a week. The main goal was to get his T-cell count back to an adequate level and treat symptoms from other illnesses as they arose. After much thought and deliberation, Dr. Sunjon made the difficult recommendation that Jeffrey transfer to a different doctor and hospital, an infectious disease specialist named Dr. Point at Eisenhower Hospital, who would be able to admit Jeffrey into different drug trials with the potential to decrease distress and prolong the quality of his life. Jeffrey was adamant that he wanted to try absolutely everything available to stay alive, so he agreed, and the bittersweet change was made.

Over the next two and a half years, Jeffrey endured countless controlled trials of drug cocktails. Due to the need for trials to be blind, they never knew if he was actually on a medication or on a placebo, which created a unique set of stressors. They were happy to be part of the trials and felt good about assisting researchers, but they also wanted to stick with a certain regimen anytime they noticed even a small improvement they could hold on to. They were hopeful that in times when he rallied that it was due to a drug that could reverse his trajectory. They assumed placebo when he would regress and require unwanted but vital inpatient treatment. This is about the time that conversations around death and dying became more frequent between them, both logistically and spiritually. During longer hospital stays, Jeffrey began asking questions of the hospital staff about what his family would see and feel as he left this realm. He asked about what he could do to ease the pain and trauma he couldn't take with him when he died. A nurse at Eisenhower named Patty took the lead with most of these conversations. She was a spiritual, new-age nurse. She was of average height, not thin nor heavy, with short, dark hair and tanned skin who spent her afternoons engaged in hours of conversation with Jeffrey while Tom was at work. In the evenings as Jeffrey slept, Patty would update Tom, letting him know what components of death they examined that day.

"Today we talked about the difference between spiritual and physical death."

"Today we discussed whether or not he can control who is in the room with him when he dies."

"Today he wanted to know if it would be painful to die."

"Today he asked how you will go on and be happy again."

Patty said she'd ask him questions he could ponder to help him feel as in control as possible of the way he wanted others to experience his passing.[8] As time within the hospital walls increased, they saw other patients in similar situations, discharging and readmitting, many ultimately losing their lives to the virus at alarming rates. The presence of death was all around them, and there always seemed to be a weary guardedness among the living. They tried their best not to predict who would be next but were unable to stop themselves from looking around and placing their unspoken bets.

Although there was much sorrow and pain during this time, it is not a complete retelling of their story without acknowledging the happiness and fun they had during these years too. They had always been entertainers and continued to do so for their friends and family as often as Jeffrey's body would allow. With time, they were able to anticipate if Jeffrey would have a good day or not, or how many more days he could have at home before another hospital stay. Although they stayed home nearly all the time, they worked hard to provide meaningful experiences and were sure to laugh and find joy in the small things. They had pool parties and backyard barbecues with the latest music and hottest fashion on display. On particularly good days, they were able to leave the house and soak in the California sun. It was a strange balance of anguish and gratitude, given that each new trauma they witnessed reminded them of their luck in having one another on the journey. Although it was ripping them apart, it was also interlocking their hearts with unbreakable chains.

In the few months prior to his death, there was a surplus of experiences of pure agony, both for Jeffrey and Tom. Jeffrey physically suffered so much and often wondered aloud if he could take any more. He would cry out both in physical and emotional despair, inching closer to the acceptance of defeat. Tom watched helplessly, his heart and gut wrenched, trying to offer comfort and expressing that they would do whatever it took to make Jeffrey more comfortable and keep fighting, if that's what he wanted. It became more frequent for Tom to have to clean up messes of all types of bodily fluids that Jeffrey could no longer control. His own shame couldn't be sanitized away, even though Tom did his best to minimize the impact. At times, Jeffrey's pain levels were so high he couldn't be touched, and at other times, all he wanted was to be held as securely as possible, trying to cement the memory of what it felt like to be one with the one you live for. They had hard conversations to get funeral wishes and arrangements understood. Jeffrey chose cremation and a celebration of life but was open to a church service should his mother really want that. They even explored potential outfits that could be worn for the services, all pivotal acts that helped Tom with his own grieving process.

Jeffrey's last trip to the hospital fell over the Fourth of July weekend and strangely coincided with a planned vacation for Dr. Point, an infrequent and unexpected occurrence. Jeffrey was admitted a week before July 4, and Dr. Point initiated the typical protocol to make him comfortable and start the cocktail of drugs to ease his symptoms. Dr. Point informed them of his vacation, and they discussed a few broad plans to follow while he was away. This visit was a bit different in that hospice was brought up for the first time as an alternative setting. A place where he could be more comfortable without the constant buzz present in the hospital. Nothing was officially decided, but it was as if that conversation was the final warning sign that their book was almost complete. Patty indicated that she felt his death was even more likely given that Dr. Point would be leaving. She provided her opinions about how she thought things would unravel. Although many may see this as a bit far-fetched (me being one of them), she spoke with such conviction that it was hard not to accept her opinions as scientific fact. Can we really control elements of our own death like who is present and who isn't? Who gets to see us take our last breath versus who gets to be notified by an outsider? The time, the date? Do we get a say? A planning session with some higher power? Does a higher power even exist?

Dr. Point left for his vacation on July 2, his departure deeming him the conductor who perfectly orchestrated Jeffrey's final symphony. On the same day, just hours after Dr. Point left the hospital, Jeffrey dropped into a nearly comatose state. Within a matter of hours, he lost any sense of orientation to this world. All drugs were stopped, and he was placed on a morphine drip to control his pain. He lay in the bed in a nearly fetal position, curled up in an awkward way that did not resemble any of his typical go-to comfort poses. He looked incredibly uncomfortable, in fact, but there appeared to be a sense of peace around him, in that his face wasn't fraught with pain. Now, Tom knew what was happening and began making phone calls to their friends and family, explaining that this was their last opportunity to say goodbye.

The sole person Tom called from our family was Tammy, who had been anticipating a call for what would likely be a quick and expensive trip to be there when the time came. She saw herself as "on-call" and had tried her best to plan accordingly. The astonishing ease in getting to California was both shocking and unexplainable. It was a holiday weekend and a last-minute flight, but for some strange reason, she found one ticket for only $150 round trip. She had been saving for weeks, anticipating several hundred dollars more, and couldn't believe her luck. Was it luck, or was it something bigger? She contemplates that to this day, and even though we'll never really know, the way things shook out confirmed for her that a higher being does exist. It was important for her to be there for Jeffrey. Throughout his illness, they had become closer than ever and spoke weekly, often about Jeffrey's fear of dying. It seemed as though he was more comfortable discussing elements of leaving this world with her rather than with Tom, perhaps because he knew his death would have the biggest impact on him.

The day of July 3, most everyone important to Jeffrey arrived at the hospital to gather and wait out his remaining life together. Visitors came and went, tears were shed, and words of love and pain were whispered to his unresponsive body. The day was long and tense with the anticipation mounting: a constant wondering of which moment would deliver the final note of tragedy. Tom left the hospital for a few hours to pick up Tammy from the airport. They stopped to grab something to eat on the way back to the hospital, arriving close to midnight. The conversation was somber. Tom did his best to prepare her for a ghastly, thin, raw, and unpolished version of Jeffrey.

As midnight passed and signaled the commencement of Independence Day—July 4, 1996, Jeffrey was surrounded by his mom and dad, sister and brother-in-law, best friend John and his partner Dennis, and Tom and Tammy. About ten minutes after Tammy's arrival, it was clear that Jeffrey's family was exhausted, so they decided to leave for a few hours of sleep before heading back in the morning to continue the vigil. They all kissed Jeffrey and exited the room, walking down the long hallway to the elevators. Tom walked them down to their car to catch a few moments alone to process the day and offer any support he could to their aching hearts. Tammy, John, and Dennis stayed behind in the room with Jeffrey. John was sitting on the windowsill to the left of Jeffrey's bed, and Dennis was on a chair near the window, also to Jeffrey's left. Tammy chose a chair at the foot of the bed, a few feet away from Jeffrey's feet, centered with the bed. They exchanged surface-level pleasantries: how their travel was, features of the facility, and things that stood out to them about the long day.

Out of nowhere, a loud and audible SNAP emerged from Jeffrey's bed, and a strange coolness, much colder than the blasting air conditioner in the room, sent chills through all of them. They all looked at Jeffrey and watched as he shot upright, his legs straightening in front of him, and his back and head perfectly aligned and poised. He opened his eyes and looked directly at Tammy. He smiled at her, not uttering a word, but held a brief gaze. She yelled his name in disbelief, raised her arms, and exclaimed, "Jeffrey, Jeffrey, I'm here, Jeffrey, I love you!" He did not respond. As quickly as he had risen, he laid back down, but this time, directly on his back with his arms outstretched comfortably on either side of him and his legs straight and relaxed. As his body flattened on the bed, all three watched in equal parts fear and awe as they saw his spirit leave his body. It was colorless and swirled up toward the corner of the room, disappearing through the crease where the ceiling and wall met. Its exit left an overwhelming sense of peace, serenity, and warmth none of them had ever felt before. It is described more as a *feeling* of a being than a visual simulation of one. The simultaneous dichotomy of both fear and peace is something I'm told language cannot do justice to. From the windowsill, John screamed and began crying, while Dennis and Tammy were utterly unable to communicate with the outside world. The machines Jeffrey was hooked up to all went off at once, followed quickly by nurses running in to check the objective data and ask for anecdotal retellings of what had happened. His heart had not yet stopped beating, but the time was close. Dennis swiftly left and started running down the hallway on a mission to find Tom.

As Tom walked through the automatic sliding doors back into the hospital, he sensed an eerie calmness that he hadn't felt before. The air was different, the people looked different, it was as if the unthoughtful décor and chairs had been swapped out and were being seen under new lights for the first time. Same external shell but completely reorganized interior. Although he felt a strange sense of peace and tranquility, he couldn't help but wonder if things had actually changed or if he had just never paid attention to his surroundings so closely before. He proceeded to the elevator and waited patiently. As the doors slid open, he heard loud, harsh footsteps echoing nearby. He heard Dennis ushering toward him, screaming his name.

"Tom! Tom! Come quick, we need to get you back to the room!" Tom's heart sank as he feared that he had missed Jeffrey's last breath, and he immediately felt the weight under him succumb to gravity.

"Dennis, what happened? Is he gone!? Tom yelled as he simultaneously began to fight his body and run back toward the room.

Dennis managed to respond, "No, I'll explain, just hurry!"

Tom noticed the time (12:15 a.m.) on his watch and rushed in, yelling, "Is he gone? Is he gone?" struggling to pause to hear an answer. He was confused at how different everything in the room seemed to be. Tammy, John, and Dennis were all pale as ghosts, dumbstruck, and unable to form coherent sentences. It was warmer than he remembered, and the eerie sense of peace from downstairs seemed to have followed him, even though he was in such a rattled state. As he looked at Jeffrey lying in the bed, he noticed he had been readjusted from the awkward, tangled locus he had been in for the last two days to a relaxed and serene position. A position he had seen Jeffrey sleep in peacefully so many times over the previous eight years. He asked for an explanation and listened with fixed fascination as Tammy retold the details of what they believed was his spiritual passing that Jeffrey had been working so hard to prepare them all for. As they each tried to regain a sense of emotional stability and ground themselves back to the present, Tom made calls to Jeffrey's mom and sister, the details of which he can no longer recall. Within twenty minutes, they returned and surrounded his bed. Patty continued to check in with them and offered updates without responses. Tears were the only form of communication, with subtle glances and quick squeezes of one another. They watched the remaining machines Jeffrey was connected to, listening for the sounds of death and focused on the increasingly shallow breaths and the prolonged silence in between them. About two hours later, Jeffrey took his last breath, solidified by the unsavory noise indicating he had flatlined. An annoying, cringe-worthy beep was the lone sound signaling the end. Patty turned off the machines and told them they could stay as long as they needed to. Because of what they had witnessed, Tammy's head was spinning. Given that Patty seemed to have a somewhat unusual attentiveness to Jeffrey, Tammy couldn't stop herself and asked, "Can people choose who they want to be with when they die? Did Jeffrey?"

Patty echoed her undying beliefs as she summarized, "I think people can pick who they *don't* want to be present when they die, but not necessarily who is there. Jeffrey wanted witnesses who were close enough to his most beloved supports who could testify to his soul's passing but didn't want Tom, his parents, or his sister there directly."

Tammy then pondered aloud, "How was he able to sit up and open his eyes? What was that about?"

Unfortunately, Patty wasn't able to offer much. "I can't say for sure; it was just the last reflex of his body."

One by one, they took turns saying tearful goodbyes and exiting. Tom was the last to leave; adamant that he complete the nightly routine he had become so accustomed to over the last several years. He walked around the room slowly and tidied each area, throwing away trash, reorganizing belongings, and cleaning solid surfaces. He turned the lights down low to prepare Jeffrey for a good night's rest, and kissed him goodbye for the last time. About 2:15 a.m. on Independence Day, he thought to himself, *How ironic this is, that on freedom's birthday, it is Jeffrey who is finally getting freedom from the pain and suffering of a fierce and valiant fight against AIDS.* With that, he walked out of the room and met Tammy, who was waiting for him by the elevators. As they drove back to Tom and Jeffrey's house, the only thing he said on the way home was, "Tammy, what am I going to do with my life now that Jeffrey is dead?" All of his plans, the life he had carved out for himself, his soulmate and the love of his life, were all gone.

I can't do full justice to the abundance of gains and losses inherent in this story. To begin with a win, thankfully, because they did not avoid the concept of death and had planned what would happen after death, most of the arrangements were relatively easy to put into motion. Peace and gratitude surround the courage it took for them to plan Jeffrey's death. They did it together, as best they could. Jeffrey's family and their friends filled their home for the next several days as plans were solidified; even Patty stopped by to offer condolences and share her perspective and memories of her conversations with Jeffrey.

Chillingly, a couple of months after Jeffrey's death, Tom went back to the hospital to find Patty and thank her profusely for her short but monumental role in their lives. Upon arriving at the correct station, he was informed that she no longer worked there. He exhausted his search efforts but was never able to find a trace of her. None of the other nurses knew anything about where she went or what had happened to her. She remains a mystery to this day, although she is often referred to as an angel by those who met her.

On the flip side, a glaring theme present during the interviews with Tom was the isolation he experienced and the various reasons that contributed to that. A prominent cause of sadness is how solitary this experience was for him, especially prior to Jeffrey's official diagnosis. With the exception of Tammy, he did not disclose the stress and dread devouring most of his waking moments. He did not call our family with updates or to process the latest recommendations or budding developments of heartbreaking symptoms he helplessly watched Jeffrey suffer through. He did not reach out to friends for support, sometimes out of avoidance and a desire to try to distract from or forget his own reality, but more often because of his own internalized homophobia, lack of self-acceptance, and fear of how their image would be degraded. Even though he was living in a mostly gay-friendly and empathetic community, he knew that outside of his bubble, there was a world that equally feared and hated him for the simple fact of who he loved. Moreover, he recognized the stigma he had to fight as the partner of a man who had died from AIDS. People automatically assumed he either was infected or would be at some point; thus, they treated him as though he were contagious and had a stamped pending death date. The harmful effects of both implicit and explicit bias and discrimination ensued as a result. When he informed people of his negative status, he got used to the disbelief in their reactions. Even Tammy described living in puzzling fear, just waiting for the positive test to confirm he would suffer the same fate. Even though he tested regularly, he had those fears himself. They tended to oscillate in intensity as he saw the physical and mental despair eroding the love of his life. As he continued to run into homophobia, his response was to retreat further into himself. To shove his needs away, working harder to please others and provide them with unconditional validation and support he didn't believe anyone would show him. He worked hard not to put himself on display or "shove his sexuality in anyone's face," as he described.

He only initiated two calls to his parents during the entire three-and-a-half-year journey about the most profound experience of his life. He acknowledged an internal tug of war in that he wanted them to know what was happening, but shame and a desire to protect Jeffrey's privacy prevented him from expressing details. The first call was after an official diagnosis had been made. He called and matter-of-factly said that Jeffrey had been diagnosed with AIDS. It was at this time that he indirectly came out to his dad. After what felt like an eternity of silence, they asked if he was infected as well; he assured them he was safe and would continue to be safe. They also wanted to know how to help, which was met with relief and reassurance that he was loved. He was grateful to be met with compassion to the best of their abilities. The second call was right after Jeffrey's death. He told them together and heard deep sighs through the phone. They asked if he wanted them to fly out and what else they could do to support him. He thanked them but declined their offer, insisting he had sufficient aid. Part of this response goes back to his own shame and not wanting to "throw his life" in their faces, and it breaks me to my core that even in his deepest moments of grief, he still sought to protect others rather than meet his own well-deserved needs for belonging.[9] My family rarely, if ever, discussed what happened in detail, during or after. Throughout the interviews, no one could recall family conversations about losses that he suffered outside of simply naming that Jeffrey's death occurred. This chapter serves as the most informative guide they have to what he lived through. Heartbreaking and infuriating, if you ask me.

I was not mentioned in this story at all. I don't have a lead role, or even an extra's role, honestly. I grew up with Uncle Tom bringing "roommates" home, visiting once or twice a year. I did not know any openly gay people and don't remember conversations early on with my parents about what sexual orientation was. But as I aged, I started to put things together on my own and concluded that he was quite obviously a gay man. When I was in high school, I noticed how reserved he was and became curious that he never spoke about his life in California, other than big flashy stories here and there. I realized I didn't know him at all, and that made me sad. Why was he hiding? Why did he seem so uncomfortable in his own skin?

Once I got to college, I realized I was actually a promising LGBTQIA+ ally, sprouting from my love for him and lack of understanding of the fears he carried. The impact of watching him suffer with his own authenticity and internalized shame is a contributing factor that heavily influenced my own career aspirations. In October of 2013, I heard about a documentary being released called *Matt Shepard is a Friend of Mine.*[10] Matthew Shepard was a college student at The University of Wyoming in 1998 who was brutally murdered by two local young men because he was gay. The documentary was advertised to allow viewers to get to know Matt as a person, not just as the gay murder victim the world came to know, a narrative I was deeply interested in, in part because I felt like I didn't know much about my uncle either. I asked him to attend with me. I sat next to him and watched tears stream down his face in silence throughout the movie. I resisted my own urges to cry the entire time and fought myself nonstop about whether or not to reach out and touch his hand, my own discomfort with vulnerability on full display. For my own selfish reasons, I did not (wrong move, Tash—wrong move).

The movie was compelling and permeated my soul in a way I don't have words for. As soon as the lights came up and the applause started, I decided I needed to be the person to bring this film back to Wyoming, back to the community where this vicious crime took place. I was lucky enough to meet with the director, Michele Josue, following the film. We became fast friends, and when I returned to school, my sole goal was to figure out a way to get a screening set up at the university. But not just any type of screening. I wanted to gather a group of individuals from the film and present a panel to the public where this murder could be addressed and questions asked of law enforcement in a way that had never been done before.

To make a long story short—as my goal is NOT to make this about me—I got connected with the Shepard Symposium on Social Justice, which was composed of a group of brilliant and outstanding human beings who put together a phenomenal conference to support social justice efforts every year. I became an event coordinator, and with the assistance of dedicated advocates, we made the vision a reality. I gave a speech prior to the film, where I did my best to say that I loved my uncle more than he could ever imagine, and there was not a damn thing wrong with him. I felt it was time we acknowledged that and supported an opportunity for him to be himself in a way Matt Shepard would never have. In conversations with my uncle since this time, we both credit this experience as leading to the strength and closeness of the relationship that we have now. He has not fully transcended into self-acceptance (who has?!), but now he is a much different man. He is more open and willing to share himself in a candid and unapologetic way. Everyone who meets him falls in love, and his vulnerability leaves permanent marks on others that make us all want to be better humans. I am proud that he is able to see himself in a light he couldn't step into before. I look up to him in ways words cannot capture. His devotion to optimism and persistence, despite overwhelming odds, motivates me on my worst days. I am often in shock of the way his life experiences push him onward, not backward, and I cowardly admit that I am not sure I would have the strength to do the same in his shoes.

For instance, he frequently emphasizes that he is living proof of what education and following safe sex practices can prevent. He and Jeffrey were together for eight years, and he never contracted the illness. He was steadfast and firm in communicating this information to my parents as well, delineating sincere advice to educate my brother, Dalton, and I on this illness and on safe sex practices, which my mother did beautifully in time. He also speaks with deep admiration for Jeffrey when he acknowledges that Jeffrey's willingness to participate in the drug trials contributed to the eventual approval and dissemination of the medicines that thousands of people take today. Medication that allows them to live a relatively symptom-free and healthy life post-diagnosis. Uncle Tom's biggest loss and Jeffrey's biggest sacrifice are significant factors in the ability for couples just like them to not be robbed of the opportunity to live a long and prosperous life together. He reflects a sense of pride that he and Jeffrey were a small part of what has made a community they both belonged to more safe, open, and accepted. I've never heard him feel sorry for himself or ask why he had to suffer so immensely in order to now witness such change and nascent opportunity for the younger generations. Sometimes he will comment about the lack of awareness and gratitude that others benefit from without understanding the struggle of those who came before. I can't help but relate that to how often that narrative is highlighted for all types of social justice issues we face. If we don't talk about the history, it disappears, but the effects are still woven into our anatomy. This premise serves as a motivation for me to analyze my family's hardships, both within ourselves and within the larger communities in which we exist.

One of the most mind-boggling facts of this story is how elegantly Uncle Tom balances the gains and losses of it all. Even while he was going through it, he was astoundingly able to identify the beauty in what he was witnessing as the two of them worked together to ease Jeffrey out of this life and into whatever comes next. He highlights the power of what it means to change, grow, thrive, and fall apart together. He describes the beauty of Jeffrey realizing that vulnerability is a gate you must cross through to fully live.[11] He purports that acceptance of loss is necessary to value what you can gain. He is appreciative of the growth that came from learning he was actually stronger than he ever imagined. He expressed gratitude each step of the way and still looks back on it with an impressive recognition of all that it took from him and all that he gained before, during, and after it. He credits much of his handling to the work he did in therapy throughout the ordeal. He was honest about inevitable loss from the beginning and began to grieve with each passing day. He didn't avoid or deny reality, and he asserted he was a more complete person because of it, even though it fundamentally changed him and continues to reshape him as his life progresses. He cites the experience as all the proof he needs to believe that there is a God out there, as he saw him at work through this process. Again—I am filled with so much awe in that I can just as easily conclude that there isn't a God because of the cruelty, pain, and suffering that AIDS brought into this world, and into Uncle Tom and Jeffrey's lives. No one is right or wrong; we are all entitled to our own beliefs, and there are a multitude of explanations. What I can't argue with is his conviction that his life with Jeffrey and the death of Jeffrey were the best and worst experiences of his life. He learned what unconditional love is and how love persists when everything else is stripped away from you. He learned more about who he was and who he could be. Perhaps that is the true depth of life that makes it beautifully painful. And he was never the same again.

4

SKID MARKS AND BANISHED TEARS

My great-uncle Ernie's death on September 13, 1965, stands as the main event that changed the budding landscape of my dad's life. To understand my dad requires an exploration of the stories of the men who came before him. His father, Teddy, is the younger brother of Ernie, and one of the most complicated figures in our family's story. It is unfathomable to imagine the heartache of losing your older brother, your idol, at the ripe age of sixteen and in such a tragic way. But it was Teddy's reality. Ernie was killed in a one-car accident when he was just eighteen years old due to drunk driving. His death was a tragedy in itself, but it's even more ironic that cars were a fixed staple in the lives of the men in our family. They made their living working on cars, soaked up any and all information they could, and marveled at the beauty of the machines every chance they got. They can take them apart and put them back together again with ease and know every feature and fact just by a quick glance at any vehicle on the road. Yet, these machines also tore irreparable holes in the fabric that held our family together. How do you reconcile such passion for the very same thing that brought you your most painful wounds with no sutures big enough to mend?

Ernie worked nights at the Diamond Horseshoe, pumping diesel fuel for the semi-truck drivers passing through. He got off about midnight but often stayed to socialize with his cronies until 1 or 2 a.m. At the time, Interstate 80 was in the process of being built, meaning there was heavy construction, and the road surfaces were not prepared for the speed highways encouraged. He left work and was traveling home in his 1955 yellow and white Chevy Bel Air. As he rounded a corner on the westbound bypass where four lanes of traffic merge to two, his speed was too much for the unpolished road underneath him, and he slammed into a pole. The story published in the local newspaper reported that his car traveled 413 feet on the right side of the road's shoulder, where it subsequently smashed into a barricade, side-skid for 77 feet, hit another barricade, skid an additional 113 feet, and was finally stopped by a power pole. During the crash, a concrete base was uprooted from the road and the pole was sheared off. At this point, the car was bent into a horseshoe formation that rolled over 1.5 times and slid an additional 40 feet before landing upside down on the east side of the highway. The engine was completely torn from the car, and the pole was mangled. Ernie died instantly from his neck being snapped as a result of an absent headrest, a dangerous characteristic of cars at the time. The wreckage lay peacefully uninterrupted through the early morning hours, just minutes away from his sleeping family, unaware of the devastation they'd wake up to. A truck driver reported the crash to the local police approximately one hour after. The death certificate notes the cause of death as a skull fracture due to an automobile accident. However, the police report noted that Ernie's BAC level was recorded at .11, a detail never told to anyone who wasn't alive during the tragedy.

Waking up early in typical fashion to get ready for work about 5 a.m., my great-grandpa Bonnie noticed Ernie's empty bedroom and realized he hadn't made it home from work yet, an unusual occurrence. Bonnie was confused but left without expressing any concern. Within two to three minutes, he merged onto the highway and saw commotion surrounding a hardly recognizable vehicle destroyed in the ditch across the desolate lanes of traffic. At some point, he must have realized how familiar the car remnants were, and it's possible he saw Ernie's lifeless body trapped inside. Unfortunately, while he was alive, Bonnie never openly shared what he saw and felt as he came up on the investigation of his son's accidental death.

It is unclear what happened between Bonnie arriving on the scene and his return home, but once he arrived, he informed his wife (my great-grandma Vi) and youngest son, Teddy, that Ernie had been killed. He was robotic, completely void of human emotion, and overcome with shock. Without staying around to hear details other than where the accident occurred, Teddy quickly raced to the scene. As he drove up, he could see the car still flipped upside down and his brother's body, bloodied and disfigured, suspended inside. He took it upon himself to get a closer look but was apprehended by police. He was told he couldn't be there, whether the deceased was his brother or not. Unresponsive, he obeyed and drove home, marking what would be the first of many days plagued by unasked questions and lonely experiences he never learned to give pitch to.

It is a painful truth that something broke inside Teddy the day his older brother died. Perhaps broke is an understatement. Better yet, something shattered all throughout his body, debris left to float around aimlessly in the depths of his sorrow. Maybe at first, the breakage could have been reconstructed, but instead, in the immediate aftermath of Ernie's death, he became targeted by his own mother, who told him that he was never the favorite and he should have been the one to die. As you can imagine, this created internal deterioration that stunted efforts toward healing. From the get-go, Teddy had no chance at supported adaptation to such a devastating loss.

Although I collected somewhat conflicting reports, the general consensus is that Bonnie was unable to work for around six months following Ernie's death. Vi struggled to take care of herself, unable to get out of bed most days or assist in any workings of the family. They were both lost in their own grief, neglecting their still-living son, who was desperately trying to hang on to anything familiar. Teddy knew their lives had to move forward, but he couldn't fathom how, and he had no support to help him in the vital sense-making process of deep pain.[1] So, instead of connecting with his own humanity and learning to process the true range of his suffering, he worked. He created an airtight routine, a solitary regimen of chasing exhaustion to avoid pain, anger, and uncertainty. Overnight, he inherited immense responsibility and unnamed pressure. He became fixated on and anxious about the reality that he would soon have two households to care for: his parents' home and the home he was building with his soon-to-be wife. He didn't have time to acknowledge or sit with his grief, as his life became about survival. All he could do was breathe and work.

Bonnie and Teddy had a surprisingly loving father-son relationship. I say surprisingly because, for the most part, I am told by the women in my family that Bonnie was a mean, harsh, and opinionated man. That things were always his way or the highway, and that he demanded a lot from the people around him, showing little appreciation or kindness in return. Some of those iterations, along with seeing for myself how Teddy has been throughout my life, made me assume that he had had a problematic, perhaps even abusive, relationship with Bonnie (this reminds me I need to check my assumptions). The comments about Bonnie have created major riffs in my dad's relationship with both his mom and my mom over the years because he so vehemently disagrees with their assessment. This conflict illustrates how unique each dyadic relationship in a family can be, and how skewed reality can become when experiences don't match. It also speaks to the varied sides of people we may or may not be privy to for any number of reasons. Throw grief and family secrets on top of all that, and it's the perfect concoction for generations of unnecessary deceit and heartbreak.

Fast-forward a few years, and Teddy had a steady job, married Becca (his high school sweetheart), and had two sons, my dad being the oldest. From the beginning, my dad and his Grandpa Bonnie had an out-of-this-world relationship. My dad credits Bonnie for being the most influential and reliable father figure in his life. From day one, it was a relationship unmatched and irreplaceable. He taught my dad what to value and find joy in and how to work, hunt, fish, and build a relationship with nature—the only thing that grounds him to this day. My dad describes Bonnie as a calm and peaceful man who always abided by the law, was conservative and fearful of risks, and often preached about the importance of making good decisions, avoiding drugs and alcohol, and working hard to earn your keep. I wonder if, in a way, my dad served as a sort of replacement for Ernie. Perhaps it was as if Bonnie felt he had another chance, another son, and he needed to go above and beyond to ensure my dad's survival in a way he wasn't able to do with his own firstborn son.

Pretty early on in his childhood, my dad developed a habit, for better or worse, of relying on Grandpa Bonnie to protect him. There had been invisible barriers the size of boulders between my dad and his own dad, Teddy, since the day he was born, designed in large part by grief. When Ernie died, Teddy's emotional tolerance and development seemed to freeze. The pain of loss was overbearing, and he carried it in silence. He didn't have examples of appropriate support and scaffolding that must occur during adolescence. He didn't learn how to express himself, much less how to treat a child trying to learn the same things. Anger was the only acceptable emotion. It sent a message of strength, stability, and stamina. Other vulnerable emotions were off limits, a consequence of stunted grief and failed attempts to evade his own pain.

My dad always knew the boulders were there, but he remained puzzled by just how dangerous they were. He tried to find and study them, to memorize their shapes and anticipate how they might fall and affect the family operations. But grief's imprint can be somewhat invisible to the naked eye, oftentimes disguised in discreet undertones of personality. With Teddy's unwillingness to speak to his experiences, my dad was forced to learn how to be independent, how to scan his environment for trouble, and how to be self-sufficient. He developed an approach to compensate for times when he couldn't see a boulder drop out of nowhere to punish him, just or not. He quickly learned that the only person who could ever talk sense into Teddy was Grandpa Bonnie, which drove them closer. When my dad needed immediate shelter and relief, he busted through the chain-link fence that bordered his childhood home and sprinted across the street and two houses west as fast as he could. Once there, he could finally breathe. He waited in the shadows while Bonnie trotted over to restore safety and screw Teddy's head back on straight. My dad trusted Bonnie with everything he had. However, he knew the intervention was only temporary and that the boulders, even if stymied, could gain traction and chase him once again if given the right elements.

Grandpa Bonnie and my dad never spoke about the obvious issues they saw in Teddy. My dad recalls that Bonnie knew about some of the demons Teddy fought, but he never addressed them head-on, to his knowledge. This trend of sweeping the obvious under the rug laid the foundation that only further perpetuated emotional reinjuries. I wonder what it would have done for my dad to have someone explain his father's grief to him. To give him context and understanding of the tragedies he had lived through.[2] Over the years, my dad tried asking curt, subtle questions, trying to better understand Teddy and the history of our family, but Teddy's responses were always shorter than the questions that preceded them. He asserted that he had to become a man quickly and take on a needed role to hold the family together. I think about the pressure and undertaking that would be for a teenager, and it saddens me to no end. As angry as I was a few moments ago, now I am heartbroken. Teddy was wounded too. What a lonely and isolating existence, with little to no nurturing from the ones who are supposed to take care of you in your most debilitating moments. Not that extra information would have made Teddy's eventual behaviors acceptable, but maybe it would have helped my dad better understand why he couldn't dodge the painful boulders that landed abruptly on top of him.

Fast-forward to my dad's early twenties: he had grown up, not unscathed but in one piece, and had married my mom and had Dalton and me. He worked alongside his dad and grandpa every day, their worlds continuing to revolve around the car industry. At the age of seventy-one, Grandpa Bonnie remained a healthy, active, and ever-reliable man. Only in hindsight can my dad say that he was probably the first to observe that Bonnie's heart had started to give out. The Friday before he died, Bonnie and my dad had been called out together to handle a job fixing four skidder tires on the outskirts of town. A defining feature of Bonnie by that stage of his life was a bottle of Tums tucked inside his shirt pocket. He popped them on a regular basis to curb heartburn, but he was taking more than usual that day. Bonnie shooed away voiced concern. He huffed and puffed but stayed true to who he was, not faltering from his responsibilities, and completing the job without additional support.

The next day, my dad went to work early, as he usually did, while

Teddy and Bonnie spent the morning together fishing. Typically, Saturday nights were spent planning trips to the mountains to get firewood if either household was getting low. If they needed to restock, my dad was always a trusted passenger and had accompanied them for every trip since his early to mid-childhood. If no call came, the plan was such that Sunday mornings were spent getting up early and going to have breakfast at my dad's favorite diner. This particular weekend, he didn't receive a call, so we all got ready and headed to Foster's. As we pulled out of the driveway, there were sirens going off in the distance, seemingly heading west. My dad noted the noise, telling my mom it sounded like they were headed down Highway 230. This moment in time captures how utterly clueless we can be with regard to how our entire world can change in an instant. It is wild to think how the simple noise of a siren can mean absolutely nothing in one moment and signal the most devastating moment of our lives in another. The sound itself doesn't change at all, but the meaning it takes on can vary so greatly. When we got to the restaurant, we exchanged the usual pleasantries and made our way to the back. The staff knew us well, had our orders memorized, and prepped a spot for our arrival.

For reasons none of us can name, for the first time in nearly two decades, Bonnie and Teddy decided to get wood on Sunday morning but chose not to invite my dad. Instead, Vi had been invited to go, which was also rare (and yes, this gives me goosebumps). It was obvious from the start of that day that Bonnie was not in good shape. As Teddy cut the wood, Bonnie gasped for air as he tried to lift and stack it in the bed of the truck. Not long into the usual routine, he sat down on the truck bed and asked for a minute. Teddy obliged and continued until Bonnie declared that he needed to get off the mountain immediately. Without debate due to growing concern about the pallid nature of his dark skin, Teddy put the saws, gas, and wood away, closed the gate of the trailer, and jumped into the driver's seat. With warranted recklessness, he began the descent down the mountain, and as he was doing so, he tried to gauge what was happening on the other side of the truck. Vi splashed water on Bonnie and gently swatted both sides of his face as she spoke aggressively to him, trying to keep him alert and upright. It didn't work, and instead, he lost vigor and fell over toward the middle of the truck. With one hand on the wheel, Teddy leaned over and tried to prop his father up again, but as soon as he let go, the same pattern repeated. It was clear Bonnie was no longer alert or breathing at all. Speeding up, all Teddy could do was drive as quickly as he could to Woods Landing, where he knew he had phone access to call for an ambulance.

He slammed the truck into park and raced into the building, noticing for the first time that he hadn't secured the trailer properly and the gate was wide open, now woodless. He was shocked and confused that he hadn't noticed huge pieces of wood flying out behind him, but he couldn't focus on his absentmindedness. "I need a phone! I need a phone now!" he screamed as he walked inside. He promptly made contact with 911, saying, "My dad is having a heart attack. Send an ambulance to Woods Landing now. I will leave and head toward town. You need to hurry!" He gave a description of his truck so the ambulance could meet them to make the exchange wherever they happened to intersect, and he sprinted out of the building. He could not just sit and wait. After what felt like an eternity, just outside city limits, the ambulance's lights and sirens were finally spotted. Teddy stopped the truck directly in the middle of the road, blocking both lanes of traffic. He got out and waved his arms to flag down the ambulance and police cars. As the paramedics removed Bonnie from the truck and got him situated on a stretcher, their movements began to slow as they assessed the full extent of the situation. Within moments, he was quietly pronounced dead as Teddy watched, unable to process their lack of urgency and the words he just heard. The local police nodded solemnly and then escorted Vi into a cop car to follow them to the hospital. In disbelief, Teddy headed home to get Becca and a change of clothes before heading to the hospital.

Meanwhile, we sat, totally oblivious to what was occurring across town. Not long after placing our order, our waitress came to the table empty-handed and made concerning eye contact with my dad, explaining he had a phone call. Thinking nothing of it, my dad walked to the front counter where the spiral, long-corded, dark brown phone hung on the wall. While Teddy changed his clothes, he tasked Becca with calling both of their sons. He couldn't bring himself to do it. She phoned our house first but was unable to locate us, so she called Tim's house. His wife (Amy) answered, and she relayed the news, asking her to find my dad. When my dad greeted the unknown caller, it was Amy on the other line who notified him that Grandpa Bonnie had died and was taken by an ambulance to the hospital. Unable to respond and aghast, my dad hung up without finishing the conversation and ran back to our table, already starting to fall apart. He bellowed, "My grandpa just died!" his voice cracking more with every word. He bolted toward the door to the parking lot and kicked it open, nearly shattering the glass and causing a commotion that startled the entire restaurant. He jumped into the car and started it, shifting the gear angrily into reverse as my mom sprinted after him. He yelled, "Stay here and finish your breakfast with the kids," as he rolled the car backward.

"You're not leaving me here. I'm coming with you," she said, climbing into the passenger side of the car as he was peeling out of the parking lot. Dalton and I stayed to finish breakfast with Aunt Tammy, totally unaware that our dad's heart had just shattered in front of our eyes.

They dashed across town and entered the emergency room. As soon as they set foot in the building, they could see right into the room where Grandpa Bonnie had been taken. He had a sheet over him already, a silent yet deafening marker of no return. Becca and Teddy stood in the waiting room off to the side, motionless as they watched their son crack. Enraged and overtaken by grief, my dad simply lost all sense of his rational mind. He started yelling, directing his rage at his dad. "Why the fuck did you have him up there? Why the fuck didn't you call me? What the fuck were you doing with him?" As his tones of anguish elevated into a tragic crescendo, hospital staff in other patient rooms got up and proceeded to shut the doors, trying to mute his pain so as not to scare the other patients and their families, shielding them from the drama of raw suffering. My dad continued to scream, blaming Teddy for what had happened and cursing his dad for not inviting him to the mountains. Ironically, my dad had just taken a CPR class, and in these initial moments of shock, he felt he could have made a difference and potentially even saved his grandfather's life. A desperate plea of the mind to try to control what cannot be controlled.[3]

After a relatively brief time and for understandable reasons, someone on staff called security to intervene in the conflict. As security removed my dad from inside the hospital, he continued to lash out at Teddy. His wrath was insatiable, and it was obvious to the staff that one security guard was not going to be enough to sustain the pain erupting in fits of rage; thus, someone called the cops for backup. Once pushed outside, my dad continued his tirade of destruction and took his anger out on the inanimate objects that bordered the building. He attacked the railings, trying with all his might to rip them out of the ground. He shook them ferociously, believing that if he used enough force, he could will his grandpa back to life and get out of this nightmare. My mom tried to find a happy medium of keeping a safe distance for her own protection but also trying to calm him down. "Troy, please, please stop, please calm down!" she pleaded, terrified his likely misunderstood emotion would land him in jail. She had never seen him this way before. The memory continues to haunt her.

As the police arrived, something in the logical part of my dad's brain told him he needed to use all the strength Grandpa Bonnie had ever taught him to calm himself down and speak appropriately. He watched the cops cautiously walk toward him and noticed for the first time that Teddy had also made his way outside and was pacing back and forth by the automatic sliding doors that marked the entrance to the emergency room. The exchange between my dad and the police officers was perfunctory. They were kind and compassionate of his grief and plainly asked him if he could keep himself and others safe. They did the same with Teddy and promptly left after assessing that the heightened emotion had escaped enough for the crisis to be over. They had averted the obvious boulders, but others were preparing to tumble.

My parents eventually left the hospital and went home. My dad stormed out to his detached shop behind our house, alone, and continued his solo combat battle on whatever he could get his hands on. He threw items from one side of the garage to the other. He took a hammer to a bench, crying out in enervating pain with each strike. He destroyed everything in sight; he was a human tornado leaving physical traces of insurmountable emotional rubble. Those moments served as his breaking point, with nearly two decades of hidden pain, suffering, and silence finally coming to a head as he felt the absence of his protector. Even though he was an adult and no longer ruled by the reign of his dad, he couldn't fathom how he would manage life without his Grandpa Bonnie. He became painstakingly aware of how much disappointment would consume him as he adjusted to only having his emotionally unavailable, traumatized, and cold father.

A couple of days later, he and Teddy reconnected for the first time since the mess at the hospital. Teddy started off the conversation. "You know, Troy, you should consider yourself lucky that he didn't die on you. What would have happened if he had died on you on Friday?"

My dad stared at the floor, speechless. In that moment, something clicked for him and he realized he had placed blame and responsibility on Teddy in a way that was completely unfair, unjustified, and just plain wrong. Shame struck him like a falling brick to the skull. Even though Teddy had never truly provided support and care for my dad in the way a father should, in that moment, he was trying to say that he had finally protected my dad, and if Bonnie had to die on someone, he was glad it was on him instead of my dad. My dad felt a hard slap of reality in admitting there was likely nothing either of them could have done differently to have saved Bonnie. A notable calamity is that my dad never acknowledged his own wrongdoing in this particular conflict. He didn't apologize and didn't relinquish the initial blame he had placed on Teddy for his own father's death. In fact, he said nothing and walked away.

The first test of reliability Teddy brutally failed came a few days later at the funeral. Because of his struggles with addressing emotion and death dating all the way back to Ernie's death, he chose not to attend. Instead, he stayed downstairs in the basement with us kids. At some point, Tim tried to convince him to at least go see Bonnie in the coffin, explaining that he looked good and it could potentially bring him some closure[4] or peace. But he refused, asserting that he would not have one single memory of his father's dead body in a coffin. He refused to remember him like that. Perhaps his insistence was sparked by vivid images of his brother's mangled body in a coffin all those years before. Regardless of the root of his stubbornness, my dad had hoped that Teddy would lead the family through the service but was instead forced into the role himself. This was another hit to the throat that convinced my dad that the one man he could count on in his life was gone, and he was thrown into the fire from that moment forward without an oxygen mask. I can say without a doubt that both of these unresolved conflicts surrounding Grandpa Bonnie's death have added to their great divide and have strengthened the stench of pain, ripe with no communication.

I reflect on each of these men and realize one of the hardest things for me to think about is how lonely each of their stories appears to be. Through my admittedly biased eyes, I have the softest heart for my dad. It's safe to say that my dad grew up living in a lot of fear that turned into anger, resentment, and moments of hatred toward his dad over the years. But, as these complicated situations typically go, I know that he loves him too. After all, he is his father. Even so, the critical and abusive manner with which Teddy approached being a husband and father ultimately did more harm than good, demons our family still tries to fight off in the present. In some ways, my dad's childhood mimicked a military environment. Things had to be done exactly how and when requested. If things weren't up to par, my dad paid a great price, sometimes with his body and almost always with his mind. His mom often walked on eggshells and encouraged her boys to do the same. He has tried to spare me by exiling many of his stories surrounding these issues. Consequently, I don't know the ins and outs of his physical abuse or the verbal and emotional abuse he witnessed, but I know enough to better understand the boiling emotion toward his parents that he has buried throughout his life. It is the same emotion that slowly seeps out in the quiet moments of peace he infrequently allows himself.

Now, conflicted and multilayered relationships between my dad and his parents churn disconnection and dudgeon thick enough to swat away when they're in the same room together. His relationship with his mom is equally complicated. This isn't meant to paint an image of her as a bad mother, because she wasn't. She was susceptible to fear and stuck in the expectations and boundaries of what it meant to be a good Hispanic, Catholic wife and mother at the time. She tried her best and positively contributed to who we all are, so much of which I am ardently grateful for. I love my grandparents. *And,* I am angry with both of my grandparents for not protecting their child and doing their own work to be better parents, to shield my dad from unnecessary trauma and emotional absence.[5] At times, it's hard for me to have respect for them and the role they played in creating some of the more difficult-to-digest parts of my dad. The inner conflict I experience while I write this speaks to the necessity to address the duality we all possess. You cannot really know any of these people without seeing both their bright and dark sides. Nonetheless, all of this trauma only served to strengthen my dad's detachment from his emotions as a means to survive[6] and pushed him closer to Grandpa Bonnie, making his death even more earth-shattering.

At the time of Grandpa Bonnie's death in 1998, I was seven and Dalton was four. Our dad had two very different father-son relationships in his life: one he idolized and one he despised. As I review how these dynamics impacted my own development, I am most puzzled by the fact that, in many ways, more so with Dalton than with me, our dad chose to do nothing but repeat some of what he hated the most in his own upbringing. I am the first to admit that my relationship with our dad is completely different than his relationship with Dalton. I have a way with him, as many daughters do with their fathers. His soft spot really only exists for me, and I can call him on his bullshit and demand respect from him in a way no one else can. I am not complaining, but at times, this privilege is a boulder of its own. I often try to make sense of this, as it continues to impact our day-to-day functioning and takes up a lot of my own mental space as I navigate and try to support the most important men in my life equally and respectfully.

A key factor here is the ideas of work ethic and relentless loyalty to family[7] because these concepts represent values that define the relationship dynamics of the men you just learned about. What I mean by this is that both admirable and passive qualities exist in my dad. It is in some ways shocking that, despite his emotional struggles with Teddy, my dad shows up and does what needs to be done, always being the bigger person and ensuring the security of his family. At times, I'd go as far as to say that he goes over the top to ensure they are taken care of, even when he shouldn't (or perhaps when I wouldn't). I wonder if this is part of a fallacy he has created in which he believes that if he just continues to do the right thing, maybe at some point, Teddy will express acceptance of him and allow the type of father-son relationship he has always yearned for. Or, perhaps he does it to honor what he thinks Grandpa Bonnie would have been the proudest of. Whatever the reasons, this has always been his approach: to work hard, steer clear of any sign of laziness, and push through any and all pain to accomplish goals and be a provider (ironically similar to his own father, as you can see).

One thing Dalton and I learned early in life is that laziness is our dad's absolute biggest pet peeve, and this has contributed to the conflict between the two of them. It is curious that Teddy appraises work in the exact same way, a confusing spin on how the sameness between them drives them further apart. As much as I struggle to admit this piece (because the sexism makes me recoil), I know that my relationship with our dad is partially different due to the simple fact that I am a woman. I am my dad's daughter; thus my role and what he perceives I am capable of are different than what he expects from Dalton. This infuriates me, but it is a reality interlaced by strong and rigid Spanish gender roles. Another part of the differential treatment is that I truly operate at the same speed as our dad and always have. He often talks about how there has been no point in his life when anyone has asked him to get up and do anything. The same is true for me; no one has to motivate me or tell me to work. A 7 a.m. wake-up time is too late, an hour-long TV show wastes too much time, and the money isn't going to make itself, so we get out and hustle from sunup to sundown, my dad using his physicality while I emphasize my intellectual flex. I know part of that is our natural temperament, but I also think his urgency was created as a result of the fear, discomfort, and unpredictability he lived in as a child. Dalton and I were not abused and did not grow up in an environment where we were fearful of our next wrong move. Sure, our dad got angry and yelled a lot, and sure, my parents fought more than we care to remember. But, productivity was not a vital component of survival for us like it was for him, and it shows through in some of the disagreements between my father and my brother.

I am disheartened by the shattered fragments of a promising relationship between my dad and Dalton, muddled by the assumption that Dalton is indolent. But the thing is, Dalton isn't lazy. His work ethic is different than my dad's, and he is bullheaded enough that he straight-up refuses to do things asked by our dad because of the manner in which demands are made. He confronts our dad in ways that our dad never did with Teddy, and thus, the cycle of unhealthy father-son relationships has continued. Neither one sees from the other's perspective because the views have been too skewed by years of painful verbal exchanges and uncalled-for physical altercations (although different from what my dad experienced).

As you read these words and start to visualize the complicated nature of what it means to be a man in our family, I hope you can see both the good and the bad in each of these damaged and beautiful men. From the moment Ernie died, my great-grandparents were unable to support Teddy. A broken man learned to break other men and then taught those men to break other men for decades to come.[8] It is harsh proof of my family's reality, worsened by a collective inability to move through grief in constructive ways and an unwillingness to lean into the vulnerability needed to console aching souls. It's saddening to see how Teddy has responded to pain over the years. For instance, while interviewing him, his most frequently given answer was that he didn't remember anything. He didn't remember what his relationship with his brother or parents was like. He didn't remember how he or his parents reacted or changed in the days and weeks following his brother's death. He didn't remember his brother's or father's funerals or his most traumatic fights with his oldest son. Although I was annoyed and angry at first, I find it partially brilliant as well. Has his brain starved off connections to painful memories in order to prevent trauma from impacting him? Has he actually forgotten? Were the years of forcing his tired body to exhaust itself through manual labor a way to erase the hardships of his past? Was it easier to focus on the excruciating monotony of chopping wood or changing tires? Or, was he simply lying and just unable or unwilling to access the words needed to answer my questions? How much of not remembering is within his control, I don't know, but I can see that he has spent much of his existence fighting against the inevitable human experience of unbearable pain.[9] In doing so, he has caused himself and others much more pain than he likely intended or was necessary. His incessant pacing has moved him nowhere.

Interviewing my dad was polarizing in comparison. Asking him to elaborate on aspects of his past was one of the hardest conversations I've ever had with him. Seeing him break down and show emotion in small bursts was often too hard for me to take. I don't know how to respond to a man who is always so unwavering in his pursuit to appear emotionless. I noticed how restrained he was as he approached these topics. You could both see and feel the reserve with which he tried to tell his stories. He fidgeted, cursed, shifted his eye contact rapidly, and moved to block his face from being seen. He paced, stormed off, threw things, and slammed doors and cupboards shut as he managed to express vulnerability to the daughter for whom he always strives to be strong. He cried. He showed emotion, even though it was hard, which demonstrated he is miles ahead of the men who came before him, a feat in and of itself that needs to be praised. It's a small glitch in the merry-go-round that maybe someday he can jump off of.

He fights his pain and sadness so strongly, never having learned that it's actually okay to just feel them. Teddy made him into a hardened, well-oiled machine but didn't realize that no matter how much he put him through, my dad was still a human being. But being a human was never an option for him. I feel helpless as I observe the emotional stunting that never seems to get better, no matter how much I address it. There is a distinct and obvious cringing that occurs when someone tries to hug him, and he is intentional about maintaining the tough-guy image he portrays to others as a form of protection. Ouch. I see fragments of such independence and self-reliance but also recognize that so much of who my dad became is because of him putting his head down with the hopes of being accepted by a man who can't even accept himself, much less anyone else.

My dad possesses much beauty as well. He is loyal to a fault and values and respects history. We share in common an insatiable appetite to hear the stories of our family's past. Aside from being taught a strong work ethic and how to fix nearly everything on the planet, my dad's favorite aspect of his relationship with Grandpa Bonnie was being able to hear the stories of his life. The stories that evolved our family's DNA and molded the man he idolized so dearly. Hearing about the importance my dad places on quality time reminded me of when I am happiest in this world: sitting around a crowded table, relatives of all generations present, talking over one another, telling stories, and reminiscing about better days. Talking about people they've lost that shaped who they became, laughing about memories that have made their lives worthwhile, and teaching us the values that have carried generations of us through this life. I learned that my dad talked to Grandpa Bonnie every single day of his life until the day he died. I share this, too, but in my case, it is with my Grandma Pryde. Even though I have no memories and no direct personal connection with Grandpa Bonnie, realizing that my dad looks at him the way I look at Grandma Pryde gave me a blinding perspective on just how much this man meant to him. It built insight into how much his death has impacted my own relationships because of how much it changed my dad.

I am in awe of how much my dad has continually overcome, and I want to thank my grandparents for helping him build those skills too. It's an uncomfortable conflict that gives my heart a good beating each and every time I think about it. Case in point: When I was ten years old, my dad started a business that has evolved over the last two decades into a multimillion-dollar annual success. Even more astounding is that he has done this with no college education and no mentors to lead him. He is relentless in his dedication to provide for his family in a way he could only dream of while growing up. And he has. The privileges he has created have shifted the financial stability and resources for generations to come in our family—and he did it with only the undying support of my mom. Success aside, I know he has paid a significant price for all the pain he has endured and the repetition of emotional neglect he has inflicted on us and cannot undo.

If you haven't noticed, I love my dad fiercely. He has both more and less flattering parts of himself, which is not uncommon for any of our caregivers. I encourage you to look more deeply at your own. You will see both light and darkness. I have tried not to make excuses for the men in my life but rather to look at objective experiences they've survived that have influenced their abilities and inabilities to show up in healthy ways. Despite his flaws, he is and always will be the number one man in my life. I am his everything, and everyone who has ever met him knows it. The only part of weddings we both cry at is the father-daughter dance. I couldn't listen to country music the entire time I was getting my PhD across the country because the moment it came on, I felt a painful yearning to be in his presence.[10] I never feel physically safer than I do when he is around. I feel blessed and grateful to know all sides of him and to understand why he is the way he is. It is exhausting to hold such admiration for what he has overcome yet such heartbreak and confusion regarding why he hasn't been able to kill the very things that have harmed him the most. He recognizes there is no benefit to the way he buries his pain and the disrespect he shows those around him when demanding things be his way or no way. Dalton is the main casualty in this cycle, creating tears in our family that I don't know how to patch. His stubbornness has led to many heart-wrenching and difficult conversations and a stinging sense that I have, and continue to, let him down because I haven't taken the exact path he had planned out for me. He hoped I would marry early, live in our hometown, and take care of his grandkids while he got to watch them grow up. He has and will continue to send strong messages about what he thinks is right, inserting his opinions whether solicited or not (and they're usually not). I have accepted that and can take his words with a grain of salt because I know his intentions and heart are pure, even though the impact can be brutal at times. He is much harder to swallow for others, and despite my best efforts to help open his eyes, the cycle of destruction still persists in us all, in one form or another. Admittedly, I share with him my own struggles with vulnerability and strive to hide any sign of the human that resides within me. I can't blame him for not breaking the cycle when I have the knowledge myself and can't seem to do so either. Perhaps my efforts in documenting these patterns are at least a start for both of us.

I wonder what it would have been like if Ernie had never died. I wonder what it would have been like if Grandpa Bonnie had lived longer. Once a death occurs, it isn't just over and done. People don't just move on intact. They move *forward*,[11] but the overbearing shadows cast by the footprints of that loss change everything. And not just for the days or weeks following a death but for generation after generation. The scars influence how we show up, who we become, and what we instill in those who come after us, and that's why this story is important to tell. Something I learned in the process of putting this chapter together was that there was a major gain from Grandpa Bonnie's death that none of us ever knew. It turns out Grandpa Bonnie was frugal and did not like taking risks, financial or otherwise. My dad reported very matter-of-factly that had Grandpa Bonnie still been alive, he never would have started the business because he would have been encouraged not to, and he would have listened. I think about how our lives wouldn't have changed at all, and what opportunities and experiences I wouldn't have had. It reminds me that with all loss comes gains, in small and big ways.[12] Sometimes they are obvious right away, like when someone dies and no longer suffers, but in many ways, gains after such agony take months or, in this case, years to acknowledge and understand. And maybe sometimes, there truly aren't any gains at all.

Although Uncle Ernie died years before my dad was even born, the severe losses resulting from his unexpected death changed many people's lives. These changes permeated several generations of parent-child relationships in traumatic ways, led by insatiable dolor and suffering. Throughout my dad's life, he has seen the skid marks of Uncle Ernie's accident and been hurt by the boulders too fast to outrun. His life was forever impacted before it even began, by a person he never met. And through his suffering, he has grown. Grown into someone who is learning that he must talk about his demons and confront his pain in ways other than busting tires. He has built a gorgeous family and security for us that will allow us to live out a future much different than he ever imagined. He is respected and reliable. If you are lucky enough to be loved by him, you will always be taken care of. His learnings of what it meant to be a man were stained by grief that circumvented our family, always outwitting us, always rearing its ugly head without any surrender that could help us move through suffering to nurture connection and healing. Yet he is trying. And he was never the same again.

5

LOSING THE ILLUSION: SHATTERED PERFECTION

Strong. Bossy. Sassy. Independent. Opinionated. Leader. Confident. Funny. SMART. These are some of the most common descriptors people who knew me in childhood used to capture my essence. More than anything else, my aptitude for intellectual stimulation and unabating drive for success have been how others have viewed me. It's safe to say that I have always had a strong appetite for learning. I was an inquisitive, observant child from the beginning. There's no doubt that my flight for life influenced that, but the sheer size and often obnoxious manner of my family also planted the seeds for an insatiable desire to take in every morsel of knowledge I could to fully comprehend all that existed around me. I've never been able to stop trying to understand, to know all the answers. Unfortunately, no one warned me of the false security curiosity can breed and that no matter how much I study or seek to understand, some things are simply beyond even the most perfectly concocted strategy to know. But even so, I have never backed down from a valiant fight for information and likely never will. Although much success has been born from this labor, it has also come at a cost that has created an ongoing grief process within me. I have suffered varied losses at the hands of my own discomfort with vulnerability and struggle to accept that perfection is an illusion I've chased my whole life.

My mom's parents are paramount in setting the stage for my intellectual debut. Grandpa Bill often told me that no one can ever take away my education and that being able to read is a privilege in life to never take for granted. I began reading with assistance, mainly from Grandma Pryde, when I was three years old. She would spend hours with me, consuming book after book and watching Disney classics on repeat. She paid attention to every question I asked and took her time to scaffold the wisdom she could share with the solutions she knew I needed to learn on my own. As a sidebar, I have struggled to broach the subject of my own demons more than any other topic in this book. Addressing the double-edged sword of perfectionism turned out to be one of the top three hardest chapters of this book to write (can you guess the other two?). Partially because the content is solely focused on me but also because of the abyss of pain stirred up by not being able to quiz Grandma Pryde on what she remembers of me and my childhood. I spent more time with her than anyone else, and I have known and been forthright from an early age that my academic pursuits and success would not have been possible without her support and encouragement. Besides that, it's safe to say she knew me better than anyone else. Although I struggled to be vulnerable even with her, I took the most self-exposure risks, which were met with unconditional positive regard and an undying optimism and belief in me. Night after night through my athletic and academic journeys, she was the lone recipient of my summaries: dissecting my accomplishments for the day, talking through my organizational strategy, and thinking out loud to help me best redistribute my energy to efficiently cross off the varied items on my never-ending to-do lists. These nightly check-ins that began in elementary school were carried all the way through my final day as a doctoral student. I am in awe of our mutual dedication to our sustained routine of refining my craft (and frustrated by my clear selfishness). Sometimes, I would read my papers out loud to her or, especially as they got longer, I would email copies that she'd print, take notes on, and call to help me hone my strategy to ensure a perfect grade.

But way back when I was a toddler, the goal was just to enjoy the quality time as I learned the ropes of phonetic and semantic etiquette that would turn me into an avid lover of language. Sadly, I don't remember any books that were our favorites and can't recall what my go-to requests were, but I know there were always piles of books close by and that she would often take me to the library or surprise me with slick, shiny, uncreased pages of new stories for my mind to absorb with surprising ease. People commented on how well-spoken and cognizant I was of the world around me, often referring to me as a miniature adult. They marveled at the big personality and budding sophistication in such a tiny, medically fragile little girl. I had a maturity about me and a comical, no-nonsense attitude that made me stand out from other children. Don't get me wrong, I still blended in well and got along with kids my age; I just seemed to have a duality about me where I could converse with my peers and also throw out vocabulary and knowledge of topics that made adults gasp with disbelief (this description of myself actually annoys me).

I am a September baby, meaning that when it was time for kindergarten, I was right on the cusp of uncertainty for enrollment. In the mid-1990s, they often left it up to a combination of a standard kindergarten screening and the opinion of a child's parents to either hold them back or allow them to start, warning that there could be some risk in being the youngest (or oldest) in the class over time. As conversations began to take place about my aptitude for school, there was no question whether I was prepared to start. I could not wait to begin my formal education and was committed to the pursuit of knowledge. My excitability swayed my family to take action. My mom and Grandma Pryde took me to my kindergarten screening. Unsurprising to them, I shocked the test administrators and received a straightforward recommendation to enroll just before my fifth birthday.

From the moment school started, I was enthralled. I never complained about having to go to school and never needed direction or discipline from my family to complete homework. I was more of a teacher's pet than a rebellious student (again, *so* annoying). I wanted to impress my teachers and be seen in a positive light, and boy, was I. I had a bit of a sly and sneaky streak and could use my intellect and demeanor to manipulate adults to get what I wanted. This was when the self-imposed pressure started to build as my identity morphed around what it meant to be the best and brightest pupil.[1] I remember overhearing conversations between school personnel and my family discussing my potential as a student and my emerging intellectual gift. I internalized this idea of *potential* that started a never-ending marathon centered around achievement as the foundation for self-worth.[2] The gains and losses of this are complicated and multifaceted. On the one hand, I developed an impressive amount of self-confidence in my abilities as each new goal provided evidence upon success that I was capable of nearly anything I set my mind to. On the other hand, I began to form unrealistic expectations and standards for myself to meet the pressure I was creating from this *potential* I heard about so often.

Potential. Potential is an interesting concept. It is defined as having or showing the capacity to become or develop into something in the future. Let me lay this out. Following my flight for life, I became keenly aware of my *potential* for illness and death. Yet at the same time, to the surprise of my doctors and family, my *potential* allowed me to beat respiratory failure. Doctors cautioned about the *potential* for relapse and insisted that I take precautions to avoid setbacks. My identity was expanded to include chronic medical ailments that emphasized the *potential* for disaster. On the flip side, in the few years following my flight for life, I naturally fell into activities that propelled my brain development and athleticism, which led to a sharpened focus on my giftedness and *potential* success. Now, don't get me wrong. I recognize my brain did not have the abstract reasoning nor cognitive precision to come to these conclusions in elementary school, but I believe that these experiences, along with my innate desire for control, manifested the impeccable training plan for perfection that would run my life for decades.[3] Not to mention, because of my awareness of death, I refined a belief that my time on this earth was limited and that I had to work tirelessly to be sure I didn't die with untapped *potential*. If I were going to die young, and I believed (and still believe) that I would (will), I could NOT allow anyone to speak to my *potential* posthumously. Instead, I needed to provide a list of accolades that could be referenced. I had to accomplish, no matter the cost.

Once kindergarten started, the ultramarathon had begun. I was focused and driven, and I continued to be my confident and sassy self in and out of the classroom. I tended to lead the group regardless of the activity. I was a naturally gifted athlete and developed a passion for basketball. I loved competition with myself and anyone else who would dare challenge me. I did not mess around. Emotionally, I appeared even-keeled and apt at identifying and expressing my emotions to get my needs met. I didn't get into trouble much other than an occasional redirection for my salty mouth (I am appalled at some of the rude things I said as a child, and I appropriately got lectured for them). I truly loved life. Who wouldn't be excited to get up every day when there was constant mention of all the *potential* within you just waiting to be unlocked? Once first grade came around, though, I showed the beginning signs of emotional distress that, only in hindsight, I can say was a precursor for raging perfectionism.

In first grade, my teacher, fittingly named Mrs. Reid, made the developmentally appropriate decision to build non-academic playtime into the weekly curriculum. She called this time "centers," which consisted of different activities strategically placed around the room to foster socio-emotional growth and simply let her students be kids. From day one, I did not buy into the decision. When it was time to play, I developed a habit of having an emotional breakdown, mimicking what I imagine was like a mini anxiety attack. Uncharacteristically, I cried and struggled to communicate my needs and emotions. After a predictable meltdown a few weeks in a row and Mrs. Reid's growing stress in navigating this challenge, my parents were called in for reinforcement. It is unclear who got it out of me, but I eventually explained that I was in school to learn, NOT to play. I had my parents, grandparents, brother, and a slew of cousins when school was over. I had NO time to waste by ignoring all there was to be learned in the first grade. Realizing the cause of my pain had to be somewhat humorous to the adults around me (again, I am rolling my eyes right now), I am grateful they were willing to put their heads together and figure out the best way to accommodate me and encourage my passion for growth, even if it came with unforeseen costs. It was decided from there on out that when it was time to play, I would be escorted down to the other end of the school where the fifth and sixth graders welcomed me in to complete literature circles during their scheduled reading blocks. I didn't miss a beat socially in either environment, and now that I reflect on it, this is probably why, to this day, most of my best friends tend to have several years on me.

As elementary school continued, so did the pattern of being challenged with more advanced coursework and accommodations to keep me stimulated. As my identity solidified around being a strong student-athlete with a bright future, unbeknownst to all of us, I was also developing a lack of self-compassion[4] and a belief system that more is always better, required even, and failure is not an option. It is my best guess that perfectionism really took hold somewhere during this time. I'd like to explore what I mean by perfectionism, as it can be a topic that is misinterpreted and often not well understood. The empirical literature has tried to capture its crux in a multitude of ways,[5] so I will describe how it manifested for me. First, it involved setting incredibly high goals and expectations for myself. I struggle with using the word "unrealistic" to further define this aspect because I have achieved a lot of the goals I set for myself over the years that others assessed as unrealistic. However, the unrealistic part for me comes with *how* I try to execute each goal without any sign of flaws and at the cost of basic human needs like sleeping and eating. Second, a focus on extreme self-criticism and analysis of wrongdoing became an automatic cognitive process. I learned to be quick to dismiss the positives and only dedicate time to ways I could improve. A third, less impactful aspect was the evaluation by others of my achievements. Given that people thought highly of me and expressed this, I felt a mounting pressure on my shoulders to maintain this image. My self-critical nature was more harmful than any constructive criticism I could have gotten, but nonetheless, once you are conditioned to receive praise and be seen as near-perfect, it ignites a pretty uncontrollable fire to keep those impressions warm.

I also want to explain a confusing relationship within me in terms of confidence, self-worth, and perfectionism. I do not want to send the message that I grew up as an insecure and diffident child. Due to a combination of my early achievements and my family's teachings, I had (and have) plenty of confidence in my ability to be successful. Perhaps even more powerful than that, I was fortunate to have a family that taught me how to value and trust myself and how to appreciate and acknowledge my abilities. Grandma Becca is the most pivotal figure when it comes to my self-confidence. Not only did she teach me affirmations to know my true worth, but she also demonstrated confidence in how she showed up in the world. She told me stories of moments in life where she realized how much she loved herself and recognized how important it was to value herself in a world where others would not do the same. I have voicemails she has left me over the years where she called just to remind me that she is a beautiful person both in and out, in case I had forgotten (watching her look at herself in the mirror is also a one-of-a-kind experience all on its own). It is astounding that she is able to hold herself in such confidence without coming across as arrogant or condescending to others. It's a true gift and one that makes me laugh and appreciate her dedication to passing it on to me. It's hard not to want to care for yourself when you witness how far a little self-love can take you. Or, a lot of self-love, in her case.

Despite the strong defense to guard me against a sense of inadequacy, perfectionism somehow entered with a rapacious quest for more. I could always do more. I could always be better. Everything I chose to do needed to be extra. I turned everything into a competition with myself and pushed myself to the limits, always gleaning what it would take to go just a little bit further. My continued success was never enough for me, and as my self-criticism[6] fine-tuned how to pick out and capitalize on any flaw, big or small, I learned to gloss over my strengths and quickly move on from success. Instead, I would hyper-focus on what needed improvement and devise what mission I needed to complete next. The pressure mounted, not from others, but from me, myself, and I. I see perfectionism as a form of loss because so much was stolen from my ability to just be a kid. No one did it to me but me, and I figured out how to suffer silently, which was easier because my image oozed greatness and *potential*. Yes, that word again. *Potential*.

My favorite year of elementary school was fourth grade, primarily because it embodied some of the most formative memories of my academic success. I met my favorite teacher, Mrs. Sheaffer, who is now just Jen to me. She has become a second mom and someone I speak to regularly, even as an adult. She was a magnificent teacher who saw something in me that she nurtured, despite her ongoing frustration with my regular stubbornness and, at times, complete lack of adherence to her rules. By then, I had set a goal for myself to read at least one book a day from cover to cover and had developed a no-excuses routine to be sure I kept the promise. (If you're wondering if this borders on compulsion, the answer is likely yes). I was able to absorb information and complete work at an alarmingly fast pace. For example, she assigned an activity, and I would hustle ahead and complete it all, oftentimes before she finished going over the directions. Once done, I pulled out a book from under my desk and got to devouring the pages, ignoring the environment around me. I cannot tell you how many times she tried to redirect me, asking me to put my book away and pay attention (as I was distracting other students or unintentionally encouraging them to misbehave with my developing leadership skills). I would momentarily comply to oblige her but only long enough for her to turn her head, and then there I was, with my nose in a book again, disregarding her efforts to keep my attention. She got to the point where she no longer had me stay in the classroom for reading time and would instead excuse me to go to the library, where I would wander through the shelves, selecting books I hadn't read and encouraging my librarian to order more I couldn't find. I am both elated and shocked that my teachers found a balance of allowing me to socially connect with my same-aged peers while also providing my mind with the tools it needed to thrive. I feel a sense of indebtedness to their curation of my skills, and I hope each of those teachers knows how much they positively impacted the course of my life.

Although it was my favorite year, fourth grade was also my most embarrassingly nerdy year. There was a long-standing program called Accelerated Reader designed to encourage kids to read through healthy competition. Books were assigned a certain number of points based on their difficulty level, and upon completing one, you had to take a multiple-choice test to assess overall comprehension. The computer kept track of the scores, and all fourth-grade through sixth-grade students were encouraged to participate. At the end of each school year, the top three scores were announced, with the first-place recipient getting schoolwide recognition and earning a brand-new bike. A fourth grader had never won the award (something I didn't know at the time), but as soon as I learned I was eligible, I knew without a doubt that the prized bike would be mine. I was also obsessed with basketball and had practice every day after school, so I had to figure out how to create a routine to master all the trades I was pursuing. I stayed up as late as I could until I either finished a book or until my parents would come in, take the book away, and turn off the light. If that was the case and I wasn't done, I would ask my parents to wake me up early the next morning, picking the time I estimated I would need to finish the task. I was the first fourth grader to win the program and rode my new pink-and-black bike with pride. Academically speaking, fifth grade was no different except for two distinct factors. One, I had read literally every book in my school library and had to ask my librarian to order more books. And two, I repeated the Accelerated Reader champion feat but chose to give the new bike to the second-place winner. Barf, I know.

The rest of elementary school was focused on preparing me for the next series of academic milestones. My teachers arranged for curriculum from the junior high to be delivered so I could work at my own pace and not distract others. I opted out of recess in the afternoons during my last two years of elementary school so that I could instead visit Mrs. Sheaffer's class and help her students who had reading problems or grade assignments with her smelly fine-tipped markers and impressive sticker collection. I never once received less than an A, and my only negative socio-emotional evaluation came in sixth grade when I had to spend a half day in in-school suspension due to getting caught writing a note with one of my friends using curse words and making fun of another girl in our class (not my proudest moment, yet I did respectfully write F*** instead of spelling out the word, so a mini-win). Even though I had a self-destructive mindset brewing internally, I continued to exemplify emotional stability, social intelligence, and evolving leadership qualities. I didn't exude signs of distress unless a mistake was somehow made on the basketball court or on an exam or assignment. I was savvy enough to insist I could problem-solve my way out of future missteps with my confidence intact, quieting any would-be concerns about my self-perception. It was during this time that I adopted the phrase "I'm fine" as my primary tagline.

You can and should now pause to make fun of me. It's okay. Even I have to make fun of me. Even though I seemed to be a rising star in the eyes of those around me, I have a feeling I was, at times, a point-blank nightmare as well. It is a surprise in some ways that I even had friends at all! I know that my attitude made my family want to knock me around from time to time too. Just ask Dalton. For the adults in my life, I must have been an odd mix of impressive, comical, and downright confusing. I seemed to be the full package and to have it all. A great family, amazing friends, an above-average balance of brains and athleticism, and of course, endless *potential*. No one considered that I struggled with much of anything. But boy, were they wrong.

I want to be clear that I had an amazing childhood filled with remarkable amounts of unconditional love and encouragement. I am privileged in so many ways, from physical, emotional, and financial security to steady social and emotional support and outlets. From day one, I seemed to be the golden star of the family and was treated as such. I felt intense adoration and knew how lucky I was to have fierce supporters. When I reflect on this part of my life, there are many gains and much to be thankful for. But, as with every life event, there are also losses. *And*, some of the losses I dealt with (some self-imposed, some external) contributed to an unhealthy desire to control myself, others, and the world around me. And by control, I mean control perfectly, with no exceptions. I somehow managed to assimilate that because my image was centered around perfection, there was no room for mistakes, failure, or even a slight admittance of struggle. I was perfect, inside and out, for all intents and purposes, and I had to continue to craft and control my life to ensure perfection's survival.

I would argue that the control piece likely came about long before fifth grade. Being the oldest child who had been born into a near-death experience and survived my own flight for life, a lot was naturally out of my control. Innumerable doctor's appointments, the persistent anxiety from my loved ones, and at times, even my ability to breathe voluntarily was compromised. I hated that. I still hate that. When your body turns on you and you aren't afforded the same experiences as other kids around you, it changes you. I hated my body for how it acted sometimes. How it stole time away from my friends and from school when I was sick. How it sounded and moved when my lungs were infected and inflamed. How it made me stand out and separated me, not for my accomplishments but for my flaws. How I always had to use an inhaler before activity. How it made me imperfect. I tried hard to hide this about myself, and I lied through my teeth about my pain. I ignored doctors' recommendations, skipping or throwing away my medication in secret. I vowed to myself and required that my coaches insist that I never cut corners in my training or took breaks my teammates didn't. I loathed the control my respiratory system had over me and the worry it gave my parents. How it dictated how my days would go and what the conversation would be centered on. Having such severe lung issues reminded me that I was human. And humans are not perfect; therefore, I wasn't much interested in being one.

There was another side of humanness I tried to scoop out of myself during this time too. Fear. My home was, at times, a tumultuous and unpredictable battleground between my parents. They sometimes had explosive fights, frequent enough that I developed yet another perfect strategy to shield Dalton and me from the fallout. They bickered constantly throughout the day and in front of others, but the nights were when things could really get heated. It was mostly just verbal assaults on one another, complete with cursing, name-calling, and threats to leave. I knew how distressing the fights were for me, and I assumed they were probably worse for Dalton, so I did my best to protect him. Even though I tortured him on the regular (there are plenty of home videos of me smacking him down when I thought no one was looking, followed by the camera shutting off momentarily and turning back on to my post-discipline tears), I was firm in my belief that I was the *only* one who could harm him. So, when the brawls began, I sprinted across the hall to his room, pulled him out of his bed, and walked him over to my room. If I was in a good space or not yet too tired, I talked loudly while reading or telling stories. When I felt like I couldn't handle the emotion, I would wrap his head with blankets to shield the noise and hold his hand so that we could both go to sleep and let their fire burn out without us.

There were a few times when my mom would go as far as to pack our bags and try to leave the house amid the conflict. One memory in particular that remains vivid in my mind is when Dalton was still in a car seat, so I must have been about six or seven. She had gotten us down to the foyer and was trying to get out into the garage so we could go to our grandparents' house. My dad blocked the door with his body and wouldn't let her through it, exclaiming that she would never take "his" kids. Perhaps this remains so crystal clear to me because in the moment, my intellect briefly compelled me to want to correct his improper grammar by saying that we were "their" kids (yes, you can laugh; again, I was an odd child). But I knew better than to get involved. Instead, I looked after Dalton and covered his ears and smiled at him, doing my best to assure him that things were fine.

As I got older, I deflected more of these altercations (which also stirred up intense sadness and an acknowledgment of unfair responsibility). With my invisible shield wrapped in emotion-repellant, I have stood in between them, momentarily becoming the parent and scolding them for their Neanderthal ways and traumatizing approach to conflict resolution. My verbiage in those moments proved to do the trick, which led to a parental mediator position I never officially accepted and desperately wanted to relinquish. I feel compelled to defend both of my parents here, as I know that their intention was never to cause any harm to Dalton, me, or each other. I understand that they weren't given all of the tools necessary to build a relationship that could adaptively withstand disagreements. They were also children when they solidified their commitment to one another. Nonetheless, intentions do not always equate with impact. Even though these intense moments were rare, their impact was heavy, particularly in how it deepened my desire for control. I did not accept that I could not control them. I assume another part of why I was so hell-bent on my academics was that it was something I was in full control over. I did not need another soul to assist me. It was quick and easy satisfaction that quieted my worry in an often unpredictable and seemingly powerless world. Not to mention, there is nothing in the world like being able to get lost in a good book (hopefully you don't know your way home right now).

I am attempting to fully capture how perfectionism took hold of my brain and tried to shake out all remaining human components. When you understand some of the lowlights of my past and then toss in the influence of what it meant to be a woman in my family (gender norms), strong Spanish cultural underpinnings, and heavy tendencies to avoid, deny, or bury feelings and problems inherent in a family structure, then you have the propellant that led to a strong yet silent part of my formative identity. Inevitable family losses, both death and non-death, also contributed to my budding belief system. Dating all the way back to my own medical trauma, I learned that I needed to be strong for those around me and that showing emotion contradicted what it meant to be sturdy and reliable. I learned that expressing any sign of weakness (a.k.a. emotion) led to more emotional instability from the adults around me because they didn't expect it or know how to assist. This awareness led my perfectionism to become a mighty apparatus powered by a ravenous need to control. The outcome was more loss— a loss of flexibility, vulnerability, genuine connection, and the child part of my childhood. But, because I remained a human through it all (much to my dismay), I needed to find a way to deal with my stress. A way to keep my perfect identity intact but let some of the emotion within me percolate quietly and in solitude.

I have racked my brain for years, thinking about how all of this led me to regulate my emotions through a system of silent and self-sabotaging punishment. Trigger warning: I have no idea how cutting first came to me, but it began in fifth grade. I don't remember any of my friends doing it or seeing it on TV. My best guess is that I most likely read about it in a book. Go figure. Remember, I was a child of the 1990s, so we didn't have cell phones and computers to Google the unknown or social media to chase circles of belonging. Cutting myself became a regular habit with a routine that I put great care into perfecting. I learned to make ultra-fine changes to my way of being in the world to keep it concealed. It happened with intermittent frequency over the years until my early twenties, with some stretches of complete abstinence and some periods of daily occurrences. At first, I was creative and chaotic in my approach, but over time, I graduated to more serious and reliable methods. I developed a pre- and post-performance strategy, like any dedicated athlete would do. I will not go into great detail here because it is not something to be glorified, nor do I want it to serve as a how-to for others in distress. I have scars as reminders that are hard to look at and require an ongoing effort to hide from the world around me.

The point of confessing this is that I let perfectionism take away the permission I didn't think I had to be human. I had to remain an exception in order to be exceptional. The result is a grief process that has had multiple waves as my life has progressed. I had a faulty belief that striving to do away with emotions was the optimal way to live life, and self-injury[7] was a multipurpose means to achieve that. Over the years, I accumulated evidence that supported these beliefs and more deeply ingrained them into my psyche. Self-injury was my most reliable and trustworthy accomplice. It was a dependable relationship and a way of connecting with myself I couldn't do in any other way. Now I know that I paid dearly for it, sacrificing self-growth, emotional evolvement, and social support for falsely secure self-destruction.[8]

I began this chapter by mentioning the many gains and losses I perceive from the illusion of perfection. As I reflect on this time in my life, I am compelled once more to assert a reminder that overall, in my opinion, I truly had a phenomenal childhood. I was privileged and lucky in ways many children only dream of, and I own that. No one ever preached or pushed perfectionism on me. No one mentioned high expectations of grades or athletic performance. No one criticized me for moments of innocence and childlike behavior. I was never once told I needed to be perfect or to achieve any of the sights I had set for myself. My desire to control and to be flawless came from within, impacted by the external. In fact, I have always been encouraged to relax more and slow down. So, I often wonder why, with all the advanced logic and reasoning I approached the world with, I wasn't able to catch the harm I was doing to myself and work to utilize the support available to me. Perhaps it was because my dad's family demonstrated and encouraged that no matter what happens in life, you numb the pain and move on with no excuses. Or, maybe it was because any time I did show even a small hint of negative emotion, it was met by my mom with a strong drive to take it away (this is not a negative critique, as it is the urge of any good mother), which somehow always seemed to turn into a pattern of me trying to make her feel better. Or, it was possibly a slightly different manifestation of the type of control my parents also sought throughout their lives, meaning it isn't just from within me but perhaps passed on from generations before me. Whatever the reasons, I simply chose not to ask for help.

Looking back, I know it's important for me to acknowledge that there were things I gained from the pursuit of perfection and even self-injury too, which contributes to why they remained a part of my life for so long. Like any maladaptive coping strategy, habits become habits because some sort of short-term gain encourages repetition, even if it results in long-term consequences. When we are craving the need to be met in the moment, zooming out to consider our future selves is much harder to do in practice than in theory. Self-injury served several purposes for me.[9] First, I could do it in secret and in isolation. The gain was that my perfect identity would remain perfect. It was a relationship between inanimate objects and myself, so I was assured my confidentiality would be kept. I didn't have to take interpersonal risks for suboptimal support. Second, I could punish myself for any wrongdoing that impeded my pursuit of perfection. Mistakes were tallied as causes for cuts at a later time, while new goals were formed to avoid future missteps. The gains here were multifaceted, as I believed that it furthered my unyielding quest to exceed all limits and allowed me to remain focused and dedicated, which was reinforced by a growing list of accomplishments and outward praise to keep striving. Reaching that *potential* was everything. Third, I learned that I could control my body and my pain in ways I was never able to do when my lungs were giving me fits. The gain here is obvious: I was able to influence my body on my terms. Being in control of my own pain while, at the same time, getting rid of negative emotions was my ticket to achieve perfection, or so I thought. Moreover, it was a way for me to punish my body for turning against me so frequently. My body just never seemed to work right, and I hated it for that.

I am equally saddened and astonished by my ability to inculcate my beliefs of perfectionism so well without anyone sensing distress (or if they did, not communicating it to me). I was, and continue to be, seen as a pillar of strength, an example of emotional balance, and someone to strive to emulate. I am equal parts ashamed and terrified to admit that this unbalanced and destructive part of me also exists, as it shatters the phantasm of perfection I have worked a lifetime to instill in myself and those who know me. I feel immense loss in this aspect of my identity being blown to smithereens with a few pages of recollections. I feel fear about how my parents and the other pivotal adults in my life may be judged for the stories I'm revealing. I am grateful for my parents and consider myself lucky to have them and also realize they, too, are human with their own sets of experiences that led to their way of being in the world. It is part of why I wrote this book, as the universal grief and loss inherent in the human experience leaves no lives untouched. It is no one's fault that I wasn't discovered earlier as struggling with perfectionism or, rather, emotional instability. I've tried to be clear that although perfectionism was more easily perpetuated by external factors, much of the flame was accelerated by me and me alone. No one can read minds or see what someone does not want to be seen. Again, with a tagline like "I'm fine" and a high level of intellect, I could talk myself out of anything and became adept at convincing others of whatever I needed them to believe in the moment.[10]

I own that my emotional development wasn't nearly as progressive as my cognitive development, a harsh reality I have only recently begun to grapple with. I tried hard to run from the shame of it all and mask it with accolade after accolade. As much as I didn't want to write about this, I cannot be a hypocrite nor create the illusion that only others in my life have hardships that have influenced me. I have my own too. I stand by a belief that perfectionism has created both pleasurable and painful parts of my life,[11] yet I know that many experts on perfectionism may strongly disagree with this appraisal. Personally, I credit its intention for contributing traits that have allowed me to persevere when things get hard. It supported my ability to take on challenges, accumulating an impressive set of achievements from a young age. *And*, I know aspects of it created neurotic and unhealthy relationships with myself and, in return, with others. Perhaps others did know a little more than I gave them credit for, but my demeanor deemed me unapproachable for feedback. I can't say for sure. I am both thankful for what perfectionism added to my life and furious by what it has taken away. I reluctantly admit that it has continued to rear its ghastly yet enticing head in waves, even after considerable effort on my part to tone it down.

What a lot of this boils down to is, yet again, *potential*. Where do you see *potential* in your life? What have you kept hidden, and is it really worth it? I urge you to consider how you measure your own self-worth and examine how your patterns developed. I encourage you to reconsider the *potential* for vulnerability to allow you opportunities to be seen, heard, and imperfectly accepted. By yourself and others. It's okay to not be okay, and we all have flaws, whether we openly display them or not. Now that I have exposed a more raw, authentic account of my imperfect side, I am faced with a choice. What will I choose to do with the *potential* it breeds? I am not sure, but I know the pros and cons of being recognized for *potential* have always been a leading force in my life. A force I will try to accept and imperfectly honor in the future.[12] I acknowledge the evolvement in such a process and the fear that screams at me to retreat back to my safety net. But I can't turn back now. And I was never the same again.

6

THE MATRIARCHAL ANCHOR

Faith. Family. Food. These are unanimously voted as the three core themes that defined my great-grandma Clarita's life. In order to understand why losing her created a domino effect of irreversible changes to our family dynamics, it is imperative to comprehend who she was and how she became the matriarch who held everything together. Not the cliché "glue" that can hold any two objects together, but a much stronger, multipurpose rope. A rope that could shapeshift into whatever was needed in the moment to get the job done. If strength was needed, she would stand tall and resist. If support was needed, she could withhold the weight of the world. And when love was needed, she could wrap you in it, securing even the most vulnerable and unsteady of hearts.

She was a full-blooded Spanish woman born and raised in the San Luis Valley in the tiny town of Chama, Colorado. Spanish was her first language, and she embraced her heritage with pride. Spanish was the norm for the inhabitants of southern Colorado, so identifying as a minority wasn't a necessary focus of her development. However, when she moved her family to Wyoming, it was quickly apparent that they were one of a few Spanish families in the area, and English was the dominant language spoken. This cultural merging forced an adjustment to the unfamiliar and challenged her,[1] yet she rarely emphasized the clashes. In time, she learned English, albeit broken, an impressive example of her aptitude for adapting and thriving. She was a picture of resilience.

It was apparent early on in her life that she was a natural-born leader who balanced independence and interdependence with ease. She grew up fending for herself in ways that were unconventional for women, a trait she got from her own mother. She learned carpentry skills and other historically masculine trades so she could help when unexpected breakdowns on the ranch or in the home occurred. She was the oldest daughter in a family of eight, so naturally, she was responsible for ensuring the health and happiness of her family. This strengthened her nurturing abilities, fostering an impressive relational skill set. Rounding out the physical and emotional parts of the self was her spirituality, which began in her childhood and centered around the importance of faith—regarded as her most important virtue. When you think of Grandma Claire, you think about devoted Catholicism.[2] So, we must begin there.

First, faith. Grandma Claire grew up Roman Catholic and remained a dedicated servant until the day she died. It was not a request but a rule that each of her kids attend church every Sunday, no matter what. Behavior in church was a serious matter. You were to be prim and proper and stay focused on the proceedings. If a misstep occurred, she would send a note to you through either a firm pinch on your butt or a laser look that pierced fear right into your body. She prayed the rosary at the dining room table at least once a day and always had a bible close by to study. In the evenings after dinner and chores, she lined her kids up in a kneeling position on the floor around a picture of Jesus, and they prayed the rosary together. This was her meditation practice, and everyone knew this time was sacred and not to be disturbed. As she became a grandma and great-grandma and lost some control over the reins of our family's beliefs, she was quick to remind the family of the expectation to take part in their faith. If a grandchild was over, they too would kneel and participate without fuss. She deeply believed faith was *the* major coping tool to handle life's ups and downs and wanted to pass that on.

She built and sustained several religious and cultural traditions that decorated the holidays. Midnight masses for both Christmas and Easter were followed by early morning pancakes. The family would then disperse for sleep and showers and promptly scurry back over to partake in overwhelming feasts to celebrate their commitment to faith. She had countless crucifixes, rosaries, scapulars, photos, artwork, and figurines of the different saints and disciples placed around her house, removing any doubt that it was indeed a very Catholic home, holiday or not. She beamed with pride any time one of us received a sacrament and was sure we celebrated with good food and opportunities to connect.

Second, family. After her relationship with her Lord, her family was everything. Growing up on a ranch and being strongly committed to the Catholic playbook for life meant birth control was not a topic up for discussion. She married young and began having children, delivering twelve in all, with eleven surviving to adulthood. The majority of her time spent as a young mother took place in Chama, not far from where she herself was raised. She didn't anticipate or desire to leave the San Luis Valley.[3] But, since the curveballs of life never really care what we think or want, after having her eighth child (Grandma Becca), her husband (my great-grandpa Rosendo) got an opportunity for a job on the Union Pacific Railroad in Wyoming. This represented a chance at stronger financial security and would reduce some of the stress inherent in running a ranch while also trying to feed a family of ten with more children on the way. As hard as it was to leave, the potential for rewards was greater than the risk, and so they went. That meant significant change for their nuclear family, moving nearly six hours from home to a completely new landscape, both literally and figuratively. Grandpa Rosendo's job took him away on the weekdays, meaning she served multiple roles as the head of the household in a new place without any support.

She learned how to be the captain of our family's ship and created a system to efficiently meet everyone's needs as best she could. She sharpened her skills as she balanced both the motherly and fatherly roles needed to keep their household functioning and figured out how her children would assist with the process. Laziness and backtalk were unacceptable. If she was cooking, you were cooking. If she was washing clothes, you were washing clothes. Cleanliness was prioritized, and she was particular. She created a schedule and expected her girls to fall in line with managing culturally feminine chores. They were not allowed to cut corners and were dissuaded from using modern conveniences as they became available. For instance, when it was time to wash the floors, no mops were allowed. Floors were to be washed on hands and knees, and she checked for satisfactory performance, oftentimes demanding chores be redone. She possessed a strong work ethic and sent the message that educational opportunities would be hard to come by (I have many questions for her about this), so it was important that all her children knew how to fall back on an ability to work hard and take care of themselves without the need for anyone else. Impressively, she also embraced more progressive roles like managing the family's finances. She allocated money to bills first, then to groceries, then to needs for the kids, with the remaining balance being split between a small allowance for Grandpa Rosendo and for herself, usually put toward materials for crafting and creating clothes.

Although Grandpa Rosendo was a hardworking man, when he was home on the weekends, he liked to let loose with his crew. These gatherings involved a fair amount of alcohol, which drew him to the neighborhood bar, where he spent endless hours joking with his comrades until he got notice that he was in trouble and needed to rush home. It was clear that Grandma Claire didn't like his drinking. Even though she never openly condemned his drinking problem, she still conveyed her aversion through her quiet yet stern demeanor, displayed by somewhat paralyzing looks, firm gestures, and facial expressions that delivered a full-blown lecture without any words. She kept her composure and worked hard to maintain her home the way she saw fit, whether her other half was off drinking, working, or at home. This carried over to her approach with her grandchildren, too, some of whom had their own struggles with substances and other mental health issues. She was not one to highlight these facts in an abrasive way. Quietly, though, she let those of us suffering know her love and support were there to propel persistence through the rubble.

She was soft-spoken unless provoked. When the time was right, she exhibited an openness with her ideas and opinions. She did not cower or hold her tongue when she felt someone was violating a norm she deemed important. In fact, she held a brawny confidence and a persuasive conviction in her beliefs. She weaved in support and encouragement by being able to explain her why, a beautiful balance of teaching both self-initiation and external discipline. This approach secured respect, honesty, and loyalty to family that shaped our decision-making approaches to align with a collectivist orientation, not dissimilar to the broader Hispanic culture.[4]

To be sure I am giving you an accurate picture of her, she had a more hardened side as well. She was *strict*. Unbending reprimands and Socratic questions to help her children connect with their values were not uncommon, and she wasn't afraid to use corporal punishment. Belts, paddles, and other creative means were all options when things escalated to this level. Sometimes, she didn't need to use words at all but could shoot a look with the narrowing of her eyes and the pursing of her lips that sent a clear and direct message resulting in immediate behavior change. For example, if one of her seven daughters was trying to leave the house in an outfit that was distasteful, she had no qualms about pointing out the expectation she held for how her daughters were to carry themselves out in the world (complete with a few choice words that could be offensive and hard to swallow). Self-respect was paramount. Similarly, she taught the importance of honoring and tending to our elders. We were to be respectful, offering them our hand and a hug, a meal, or any other comfort measure that would make their time pleasurable. She lived her life in a modest way and encouraged us to do the same. She was content with what she had, appreciated the simplicity, and expressed gratitude rather than yearning for what wasn't hers.

She was a master at demonstrating the interdependence of healthy family relationships and the delicate but vital work/life balance. As her older kids became self-sufficient, they took on dual roles as siblings and parental figures to help take care of the younger ones. Her kids were forced to become bilingual, which served her well, as she often relied on them to help her communicate when she would cross the bridge to town to pay bills or window-shop. She wanted her kin to retain the Spanish language, yet she cautioned them about the necessary safety measures needed for minorities. She often spoke about being weary of trusting anyone outside of the family and pushed for reliance only on one another for security (a well-intentioned precaution that has caused some problems with building trust outside the family unit for many of us—myself being one of them). She was not transparent about the discrimination she faced, but it was obvious that it existed, and she was not immune to its effects.

There was a mysterious side to her in that she wasn't open about how she was personally affected by hardships she faced throughout her life, making it somewhat challenging to fully capture her essence and to really know her. Because this was her way, it is hard to compose a narrative of the privations she confronted. She had at least two miscarriages. She lost a living child. She reluctantly had her own toddler move in with her parents, who lived hours away, so that she could better tend to her youngest baby, who was suffering from a grave illness. Her husband died suddenly and prematurely. She lost a grandchild. She had both children and grandchildren go to prison. Despite these darker parts of life, she remained even-keeled and able to emotionally manage whatever life threw at her.

It pains me that no one seems able to recall a true understanding of her emotional struggles and how she coped with them. It seems as though she always had things together and persisted, come what may. This was likely intentional; the anchor must always be strong. I both admire her and feel sadness in that I predict this came with lonesomeness and little space to grow from the tribulations she survived without adequate processing and support. None of us can say for sure. There is a sense of legacy in how her tendencies to hide and use silence to endure have been passed down. These traits also contributed to her authoritarian rulings that could carry a heavy burden. I feel torn when I admit that I share this trait with her, as I recognize the double-edged sword it sharpens and the missed opportunities for growth through avoiding vulnerability.

Third, food. Her cooking was renowned. She spent most of her life in the kitchen and personified mastery as a chef, able to prepare fixed staples daily or throw together an impromptu meal for unexpected guests with less-than-ideal ingredients that somehow turned into everyone's new favorite dish. She became known throughout the community for her food, which drew a lot of uninvited guests around mealtimes, all hoping there would be something freshly made to offer. She had a garden that every generation of our family would sneak into and quietly try to pull our favorites out of the earth without getting caught. For some, it was the strawberries; for others, the peas. I loved to pull the rhubarb right out of the ground because it made me feel strong (even though I hated the taste). It was important to me to prove to others I was strong, like her, and this seemed an obvious way to try. She made masa for tortillas every day, making it nearly impossible to walk into her house without there being the thickest, fluffiest, most scrumptious flour tortillas you could ever dream of, staying warm in hand-embroidered towels she had made. They were perfectly rounded, never too doughy or too burnt, littered with small brown holes from the balanced flipping she would do over an open flame with her bare hands.

As the family became more autonomous, one fixed part of everyone's life was her home as the common ground where our family came together. It was often described as the most desirable place to be in town. There was rarely a time of peace and quiet. The kids and grandkids would make their way to the house each day, her kitchen a revolving door with cousins galore, endless homemade snacks filled with love, and constant energy to turn even the most boring of games into a competition for the record books. There are memories of cookie sheets upon cookie sheets of bread on every free surface in the kitchen, fresh beans, fried potatoes, green chili, buckets of macaroni, fruit cocktail, empanadas ... you name it. Her home was a gathering place not built out of obligation but out of true passion and excitement for being able to find comfort, security, and togetherness in a way the outside world just couldn't duplicate.

As our family grew, the core tenets of her life remained faith, family, and food. One of her most prized roles was getting to be a grandma to a total of twenty-four grandchildren, thirty-four great-grandchildren, and now a slew of great-great and even great-great-great grandchildren (many of whom were born after she died). She took the job seriously and stretched her pull with her kids to spend as much time with us as possible. She tried to take the load off her kids, who were all working parents, striving to make ends meet and provide enough love and support to raise children in the way they were raised. She expressed gratitude for having a hand in the newer generations of her bloodline and was respectful to not overstep or pry into our lives. Yet, when enough was enough, she would point out the obvious and use both direct and subtle approaches in attempts to repair what was decaying. Miraculously, she seemed to have enough time and energy to make each person feel seen and loved. Her presence oozed a sense of safety in an otherwise chaotic world. She was just solid, providing such strength from the construction of her character. When you were around her, it was as though you could take a couple of breaths and feel protected from all the monsters, real or imagined.

As is the case with most families, as children transitioned into adults, there was an obvious separation from the constant need for her tender care. It bothered her that she began to see her loved ones less, yet she was quick to acknowledge the importance of her family creating their own lives and taking the space needed to find their own ways in the world. Although there were times when she would mention this heartache, she did not speak about it with resentment or mean to induce guilt or shame, and she didn't seem to let it bog her down. Instead, she expressed more reverence when others made the effort and was always prepared with a fresh, homemade meal to nourish both our stomachs and souls.[5]

Despite Grandma Claire's status as the anchor of our ship, with its foundation made sturdy through faith, family, and food, no one escapes the eventual descent from this world to whatever comes next. She battled several acute illnesses in the few years preceding her death. She fought and beat colon cancer, making it look like she escaped the ordeal untouched. Her resilience somewhat did a disservice to our family in that we came to view her not just as our matriarch but also as someone who would live forever. She bounced back from setbacks so effortlessly that it was as though she would outlive us all. No one considered what it would be like to lose her because her endurance created a false sense of security. This is, in part, what made the sudden and unexpected nature of her death all the more difficult to digest. This was furthered, in another part, due to general death anxiety, a trait that runs rampant throughout society.[6] Our family is no exception. There's a strange cognitive phenomenon where people try to convince themselves that everything will be fine and death will somehow skip over them and the ones they hold dearest. Denial at its finest. Coping with the grief that shatters this deceit can be harder to process in a space that makes no room for the obvious to be accepted.

In the last year of her life, she developed a rather grim relationship with her spatial skills, beginning to fall with frequency. Each fall seemed to somehow protect her body but consistently involved her head in one way or another, leading to balance issues and a slow cognitive decline. She likely had several concussions without direction for how to track and treat the pattern of symptoms she experienced. Following her initial fall, our family noticed brief episodes of confusion and a general detachment from reality that naturally scared everyone. These episodes led to ER visits for evaluation. When tests came back negative and her alertness was restored, she was discharged with little instruction for follow-up care. The next occurrence would trigger the same series of events, which led to a couple handfuls of hospital visits lasting four to six hours a trip over the subsequent weeks. Her pliability prevented anyone from acknowledging that perhaps her body was alerting us that it had started its final race.

She was diagnosed with pneumonia on New Year's Eve in 2000, which came as a bit of a surprise given that she was not demonstrating any difficulty breathing or other telltale signs of respiratory distress. In the preceding weeks, she began to express how tired she was from the yo-yo of rebound illnesses. She mentioned missing her parents and her late husband—signals the family tried hard to disregard.[7] She was admitted as a standard precaution given the respiratory results and her cognitive fog, a result of electrolyte imbalances and lingering concussion symptoms.

The second day of the new year in 2001 and the third day of her hospital stay would prove to be her last. Grandma Claire's final moments were spent with family crammed in small spaces near her. There were huddles of people in the hallways, exchanging worried glances but shying away from acknowledging the terror. They avoided asking questions or attempting distracted conversation to cut the tension. Seeing her in such a declined state was difficult, so everyone took turns as they tried to keep their emotions at bay and share the space so that her room didn't get too hot or overcrowded. After an attempt to get up, weakness overtook her and she lost consciousness, crashing rapidly from suspected cardiac arrest. After a "code blue" was initiated, the doctor began lifesaving measures. Two nurses tried to usher stragglers out of the room so they could continue resuscitation efforts. The commotion and sudden panic by the hospital staff alerted the family in the hallway that our future was now in grave danger. While they worked on her, Grandma Becca and Aunt Dora were afforded the privilege of staying in the room, both holding her hands, but at a distance so the medical professionals could move around them. Support staff admonished people as they shuffled in, floundering with no real intention. After a few minutes, the uproar stopped. The staff walked out and delivered a fatal update. Their attempts were unsuccessful, and our ship's anchor would no longer secure the vessel that held our family.

Personalized grief began to erupt after a surreal standstill. It was as if the whole family had entered a dazed state, a detachment from reality, as they tried to swallow the profound bitterness of death. For some, it was explosive; for some, silent; and for others, it kicked into gear a need for productivity. Several of the immediate family members were not there, so a few courageous ones walked away to make phone calls and allow the news to pull in the black clouds that would dominate our skies for weeks to come. Grandma Pryde informed me. I don't know how she found out, and I only recall that I had just gotten picked up from a University of Wyoming Cowgirls basketball game. I had a sticker on my cheek and pom-pom strands in my hair. She told me, soft and kind, and I simply said "okay" and launched into my summary of the game. My age may have had something to do with that, but I have carried around heavy guilt about such a nonchalant response and would change everything about that moment if I could, other than spending it with Grandma Pryde.

Grandma Claire's funeral was the first I ever attended. I was ten years old. The church was literally bursting with people, many of whom I'd never seen before, to the point where the intricate French doors stayed open for the duration of the service, even though it was January in Wyoming. Each pew was crammed airtight, everyone touching to squeeze in extra space. The aisles on both sides had two rows of people standing from the back of the church up to the front of the pews. The back of the church had a foyer and two sets of stairs, one that led downstairs to a gathering space and one that led upstairs to where the ensemble for live music was set up. Each of these spaces held unorganized groups of people, some sitting and standing on the stairs, some leaning against the walls, and some actually standing outside, surely unable to hear the echoes of the priest as he led us through the traditional proceedings, just as Grandma Claire would have wanted it.

As the immediate family, we entered after the other guests had been seated, walking up the aisle together as everyone stared at us, studying our pain as we marched, raw and on display. I was shocked at the auditory stimulation brought on by different tempos of tears. It was overwhelming to see so many people suffering together at once and to know that all of their misery was because of the love and connection expressed by one woman. I noticed tissues being passed around, acts of affection through the squeezing of someone's hand or shoulder, and the wiping away of tears. These sounds changed hues throughout the proceedings. Sometimes quiet sniffles would become loud wails of anguish that scared me as I retreated further into my mom for a reassuring touch. Sometimes minimal cries would progress into overly annunciated wallows of anger and denial. "No!" "Oh, mom!" "God, no!" or even just "Mommy!" or "Grandma!" The surprise of the screams of heartbreak without warning sent chills through me as I tried to make sense of the pain and the apparent finality of death.

The most gripping memory of the funeral came during such a display. The delivery of the eulogies sought to sum up over eight decades of life in just a few minutes, complete with excerpts from the bible, both in Spanish and English. As the speeches concluded and my two cousins, Mark and Jay, made their way from the podium down to the place where her coffin lay, Mark paused, seemingly paralyzed, at the side of her casket. He looked down at her closed coffin and leaned over, trying to hug it as he wrapped his face in the perfectly placed lace that draped all around it. He lost his ability to hold his weight underneath him and collapsed, crying out in agony, "Grandma, no, please, come back!"

Concurrently, new waves of grief splashed across each pew as we swam in each other's sorrow and watched its brutal embrace nearly drown Mark. Jay stood behind him, supported him back to his feet, and slowly assisted with each step to walk him beyond the pews and somewhere out of sight. Everyone needed a few moments of silence to recover.

As the service wrapped up, the funeral staff placed her casket in the hearse. The masses of guests got into one single file line, pew by pew, and made their way up to where we, as her immediate family, all stood. Each mourner walked through our wounded hearts and professed the usual meaningless phrases that debatably bring little peace or solace. "I am sorry for your loss." "How are you doing?" "I loved her so much." "I am here for you." Physical displays of support were plentiful, and although they were well-intended, I didn't see much alleviation of the missing light in most of our eyes. Those of us on the receiving end were detached from much of the bustle. The whole time, I stood right by Grandma Becca's side, pushing myself into her leg so that I knew for certain we were connected. I watched people try to console her and felt both helplessness and fierce protection in that I wanted to make her feel better and was becoming conscious of how impossible that would be. At one point, she told me, "Jita, I am an orphan now."[8] I played that line over and over again, trying to make sense of it. People live their lives without their parents? I couldn't fathom what that meant, and since I currently still have both parents, I still can't. I just knew that I couldn't leave her side and needed to be with her, so be with her I was. Perhaps this was my first true lesson in the absolute necessity of human connection, compassion, empathy, and touch to help mend the deaths within us when someone or something we love is taken. I also reluctantly admit that I have always had an odd fascination with death and the bereaved. I can't quite explain all the reasons that compelled me to be there, but I was there to stay, anchored to her and to the experience of suffering. We continued to hear echoes of cries, seeing the real-time ripple of emotions wash over each of us, taking our breath away as we thrashed around for air. After what felt like an eternity, the line diminished and we were ready to face the Wyoming winter and conclude her celebration of life.

The procession to the cemetery and the time spent shivering in the freezing cold while we lowered her casket into the ground were not any easier. As a family, we were smart to have communicated with the police department to alert them to the long line of cars that would travel to the burial. Even though the cemetery is a five-minute drive from the church, because of the number of people, it took nearly forty-five minutes to shut down the roads and allow for a slow, final last ride to her infinite resting place. Parking was unorganized, given the lack of space for a surplus of vehicles, which prolonged the quivers permeating through our bereaved bodies. They had a small tent with three rows of chairs for the immediate family while the priest said his final prayers to mark the end of our ritual.[9] Each of her children was given a skinny, long crucifix to place on top of her coffin to share one final sign of the cross. This was another moment in which the audible pitches of loss were magnified and the inconsolable pain was undeniable. My aunts and uncles cried out for their mom while others in the sea of people pressed their faces into their loved ones, trying to shield their eyes and ears from such helpless emotional destruction. I saw men cry silently, tears streaming down their faces underneath their sunglasses. I considered, for the first time, that men actually had the ability to cry at all. It scared me, seeing sides of the men I had always known to be so strong show a viscerally uncomfortable display of emotional need.

As the grandchildren and great-grandchildren, we were invited to proceed in a single file line and throw dirt into the hole they would soon fill. I took some but only a couple of fingerfuls and threw it on the grass next to the hole instead of directly inside. I wasn't sure she would be able to breathe with all that dirt on top of her, and I was convinced she would be more comfortable if she were still able to see sunshine once the clouds cleared. Someone made an announcement about the meal back at the church's elementary school to conclude the day, and people dispersed quickly to get a break from the bitter cold. Just like that, everyone turned and walked away. The final sendoff was reduced to sighs of emptiness and silent, focused steps through the snow.

An immediate family count of at least four to five dozen people at the time of her death created a lot of separate grief experiences. All individualized yet all intertwined, being forced to coexist with one another, with little space unexposed to the havoc that death creates within us. As memories and recollections began to pour in, there was an increased awareness of the plethora of unique experiences that highlighted personal dynamics with Grandma Claire, each special in their own way. Everyone learned just how much they didn't know or how much they didn't experience with her as they reflected on the woman they had lost and the lasting impact they would now have to grieve through in order to understand.

When the funeral is over and the guests all go home, the nothingness cuts through us like glass while reality slaps us in the face. Grandpa Rosendo was dead. Grandma Claire was dead. Our family was now without our leader, our pillar of moral and ethical wholesomeness. Nothing felt the same. As we continued to mourn independently and together, there was solace in knowing that the torch had been unofficially passed to Aunt Dora (the eldest of the daughters). Her house became the new meetup, and she took over as the enforcer, continuing to instill the expectations of faith, family, and food. Inevitably, many changes took place in the evolution of our family. Some shifts were instantaneous, while some took decades to come to fruition. The differences encompassed both primary losses (her death) and secondary losses (the changes we must adapt to in order to keep ourselves upright).[10,11]

Nearly two decades after her death, every person has a slightly different recollection of who she was and at what stage of her life they remember her best, a fact that became apparent during interviews to put her legacy together. Her children may remember her as a more active, strict, vibrant strong-arm, and they may picture her in her prime, say in her third or fourth decade. Her grandkids may remember her as a quieter, reserved, slightly rounder woman who always wore an apron, the beginning stages of age on her face, and the slow graying of her hair, perhaps in between her fifth or sixth decade. Her great-grandchildren (like me) remember her as a little more distant at times, seated in front of the TV watching her Colorado Rockies, turning her hearing aids down when she decided she was too irritated to entertain conversation. And toward the end, the missing hair that was shaved to allow for staples to cover her head to conceal the damage caused by hard falls, somewhere in her seventh and short eighth decade. Each one of us has a different archive of memories, a different period of her life when we connected with her the best. Therefore, we can only extract a nuanced understanding of the ways we were touched by the gift of her life. Every portrait of her we could paint would have a slightly distinct resemblance to our version of her love.

One of the biggest losses in our family is that the cultural history and Spanish language seem to have died with her.[12] When I was growing up, I heard Spanish on a daily basis. With mixed sadness and anger, I admit that once she died, so, too, did the echo of our ancestors' native tongue. As is common with minority families, there is a tendency to "Americanize" as individuals assimilate into the dominant culture,[13] with language being a primary part of that. Even as a ten-year-old, I noticed that our weekday breakfasts at one of the aunts' houses no longer rang with the rhythmic beauty of the Spanish language as we kids entertained ourselves in between quick dashes to the table for bites of pancakes or tortillas with beans and chili. This was, in part, due to my aunts no longer having to speak Spanish to be sure Grandma Claire understood the narrative, but I also wonder if it was too hard emotionally to speak it because of how much it reminded them of her.

The sturdy bond as a family unit began to dissipate as her absence became more familiar. Her house is now a lonely keeper of decades of memories left behind to live in the creaks and crannies of the aging foundation. It is no longer a priority to gather as a whole family to celebrate holidays, even those historically most important to our culture, religious or otherwise. I have vivid memories of the spectacle we used to put together to ring in the most important days of the year. With decorations plentiful and each of us dressed in our best, there was barely room to move around comfortably as we jammed copious numbers of people into tight quarters to share home-cooked meals together. The love and laughter were nothing shy of what makes up the most classic and heartwarming holiday movies. Perhaps it was a denial of our loss, an intolerance of our own sorrow, or an effort to ignore the painful absence of the sights, sounds, and smells of her virtues at play. It just appeared to be too hard to be in her space without having the physical being of her love that carried oxygen through the air and into our lungs. Avoidance seems to have beat out facing the reality of our pain. Repercussions of her death punch me unexpectedly now as I tussle with the idea of whether or not to have my own family someday. Waves of sadness overcome me when I think about how the newest generation of our family won't even meet some of the key players who were staples in my own character development. They won't see my grandma and her sisters chasing after us, hear them speak Spanish, or have them teach us the history that made way for our very existence.

This ache raises insoluble questions I often ask myself because of the way I experience loss. Why keep going? What is the point? Why keep doing anything as you once did when you are broken and alone, left to find your way without the guide you relied on to help carve your place in the stones of time? Perhaps this is normal for any family and for any generation, but nowadays, a lot of discussion takes place among our older family members about how different the values and priorities seem to be. They reminisce about simpler times when contact was more seamless, selfless generosity was second nature, and respect was a dominant feature of shared interactions. Time seems to have used its scrawny hands to scrub old ways of being from actuality. Now, more distance, less communication, and remnants of disloyalty are sprinkled throughout the morphing biology of our roots.

Part of why I struggle to understand what contributes to these changes is because I know it is more complex than any of these suggestions, and each one of us may have a different but fitting explanation. The point is, I see how it wears on my older loved ones and, in turn, me. How reminders of loss continue to show up, with sorrow and anguish not far behind. They miss the connections. Tears well in their eyes as they talk about the old familiar and expected assembly of each piece of our family's puzzle. There is so much heartache in these tears. In what they have lost. In accepting the hardships of aging and in growing up and no longer getting the luxury of being naïve to the harsh realities of the difficult world we live in. In seeing those we love and once saw as brawny and bulletproof become fragile, worn-down fragments of the people they once were.

Has love itself been lost? In some ways, yes, absolutely. Simultaneously, I also see how we continue to band together in life's darkest moments. Loss does not come without opportunities for growth.[14] When death strikes again and takes away another piece of our history, our traditions are reignited. Faith. Family. Food. Everyone is together, conflict or not. There's an air of selflessness and true altruism as we surround the most devastated with our support, connecting our heartstrings to hold up the wounded and come to terms with life's unfair lessons.

Perhaps we need more discussion about aging, dying, and what death means to us, alone and together.[15] We need to explore. How do we balance understanding our past, living in the moment, and knowing that at some unknown point in the future, death will not spare any of us? We need to accept that the waves of grief wash us out to sea both like clockwork and when we least expect it. Grief never goes away. It changes form, but those feelings and memories don't ever evaporate. The pain breaks up over time and hammers stakes in our bodies, stealing real estate and remodeling the landscape as it sees fit.

How hard should we work to remember her? It is strange how, over time, it seems our memory begins to erode, chipping away certain aspects of our pain, just like the sun does to a building left exposed to its rays. Is it always true that over time, we begin to forget? Are there benefits to that? As memories fade or feelings lose some of their strength, is that actually an adaptive, survivalist component of genetics we need in order to move forward? If we don't forget to a certain extent, do we stay stuck and unable to find purpose or move forward and salvage some semblance of happiness? If we don't talk about her, we lose her memory. We lose her legacy. Our connections die out like the end of a once-raging bonfire that has no more logs to reignite the flames that warm us.

Without her, we seem to slide on some of the values she worked so hard to make permanent. I can't decide whether that means our individual and collective values have shifted or if motivation ceases altogether without the external prize of her sought-after approval. Yet, at the same time, if we do talk about her, the emotions can be so overwhelming that it takes all the effort in the world just to force ourselves out of bed and try to keep living. To remember what we had is to remember what we lost. It's painful to bring up such pain and do nothing but simply tolerate it and surrender to its power. But we must. She deserves the sustained honor. I suppose both sides of the coin are important and deserve inspection to better understand why I am the way I am. Why you are the way you are. Why they are the way they are. Why we are the way we are. And why we were never the same again.

7

TRAUMA SHADOWS

My mom was a surprise, ten and eight years younger than her brother and sister (Tom and Tammy), respectively. Her parents (Pryde and Bill) were well into their thirties when she arrived, a bit abnormal for 1970. They were well-established in their careers and worked a lot, which was easier because they had two children who were mostly self-sufficient by that time. When they told Tom and Tammy that they were pregnant, they also explained that the baby's sex would determine who would have to share their room. The announcement brought both excitement and dread to Tom and Tammy as they anxiously awaited the new life that would change the family structure. When my mom, Lynn, arrived, it carried relief and a double dose of excitement to Tom, who would keep his room just the way he liked it. For Tammy, it brought about apathy with a pinch of disappointment. She wanted a new bike and had no interest in helping tend to the immense responsibility of a newborn baby, especially by sharing her space.

My mom made it clear during her interviews that from the beginning, all she ever wanted was to fit in with her siblings. She adored them and tried hard to be included in every aspect of their lives, always striving for acceptance. Bill traveled around the state to observe and critique teachers, and Pryde worked as a registered nurse. Consequently, they relied heavily on Tom to help care for my mom's basic needs. He did it gladly, excelling at sharing in the parental landscape that formed her early understanding of nurturance. She found the most comfort alongside her big brother. He was her protector. He was gentle, loving, and inclusive of her. They were a dynamic duo, with him providing guidance and discipline while helping her feel seen and valued. She allowed him to develop his caretaking skill set and feel accepted and loved for exactly who he was. The dynamic between she and Tammy was different. Tammy got irritated with how often her little sister would follow her around. Tammy wanted to be left alone, treating my mom as a pesty little thing. My mom did not have any cousins or siblings her age, so she had to adopt the interests of her siblings while shifting her own personality just enough to be considered worthy to hang out with them.

Her childhood was fairly uneventful in that there were no significant traumas or major life torpedoes. Yet, from as early as she can remember, she felt a sense of isolation from others. A small voice told her she was inadequate and an outsider. She hid from the start, ultimately allowing black shadows of insecurity to shield her from confronting the blinding rays of pain bred from beliefs of insufficiency. Her immediate family didn't have an overt focus on togetherness that she picked up on in other families. Even more than that, there really was no extended family. Pryde had been an only child with complicated and unhealthy relationships with her own mother and grandmother, the only two people in her family. Bill had his parents and two siblings, but they lived hours away and were not close-knit; their presence was mostly invisible.

With my mom being so much younger and coming at a different stage of life for her parents, a babysitter was necessary. The family landed on a middle-aged woman with a family of her own. While there, my mom witnessed regular, *intentional* family time with the Jetson family. Much like she felt the burning desire to fit in with her siblings, she felt the same sensation when at the Jetsons. Unfortunately, no amount of effort could change the blatant fact that she was NOT a full member of the Jetson clan and never would be. They treated her well and she felt cared for, but she also understood that she did not fully belong. She would come home and speak about the unity she observed while requesting that her family follow suit, trying to mimic the sense of belonging[1] she so desperately wanted. They would try to indulge her, typically having dinner together and then settling into the basement around the TV. They participated in other activities when able, but work for her parents and the more mature developmental stages of her brother and sister often took precedence over my mom's budding fascination with family. Thus, she developed an identity as a bit of an interloper. She covered up her loneliness by embracing an extroverted personality, complete with a bubbly attitude and hearty, successful attempts to engage with others.

My mom is brilliant, which was noted by her family at an early age. Perhaps some of this was fostered due to a need to be more advanced in order to be with her siblings. She had a knack for observing and picked up things easily. Watching them build independence made her want to do the same, but she was at a much younger age and was not yet ready. A natural separateness existed between them that she despised, even down to the physical space in their house. As they got older, the two eldest had rooms downstairs, while she was upstairs. These seemingly small details of their family's functioning had a large impact on her perceived inclusion. Feeling excluded led to a desire to be in control. She did not enjoy listening to others' demands and reveled at any opportunity to work a situation in her favor. Given that she was gifted intellectually, it was somewhat easy for her to manipulate others to get what she wanted (a trait you may see that we share).

Despite my mom's aptitude for learning, she loathed school and would often fake being sick and beg to stay home. Her hatred for school was a combination of two primary factors. One, she was bored, unchallenged by the curriculum. Getting scolded when inattentive but not given the tools for intellectual stimulation made sitting in a classroom a living hell for her. These misunderstood exchanges began her lifelong battle with a distaste for authority. Two, she was a sensitive and socially anxious child, even though she had an easy time making friends and was well-regarded by others. She was skilled at molding her personality to match the tone of whatever group she was in, so most observed her as being well-adjusted. She didn't stand out as a child who could have used additional attention because she worked hard to prove she was just like every other kid, hiding much of her true self.

In asking her to reflect on this time in her life, she recalled traumatic memories from elementary school centered on being rejected[2] within the blink of an eye. Although relatively small memories in the grand scheme of things, their significance carried the weight of the world in terms of how it led to her sense of inadequacy, cementing her desire to be accepted. It is a common conversation for people nowadays to talk about how cruel kids can be, yet it wasn't emphasized to her back then that the opinions of others are simply that: opinions that should be analyzed with caution. She was not taught the skills needed to disregard faulty evidence or master how internal confidence can create true worth. Instead, she took others' words as gospel and internalized their perceptions as fact, without any room for reasonable doubt. Judgmental comments by peers pierced through her heart, quick and sharp punctures with no hesitation. She scanned her interactions for negative feedback and clung to any inkling of criticism. Comments perhaps intended as harmless observations watered the self-conscious seeds that would grow to the size of a California redwood in the years to come.

In time, she concluded that there was a surplus of things wrong with her. She had hopped onto the self-critical train, adding extra railcars of shame, and became the conductor, constantly scanning the tracks for any signs of danger in the form of put-downs. She became so worried about what others were thinking of her that she couldn't concentrate on anything other than avoiding exclusion from the in-group. She learned to suffer in silence and to blame herself. With school becoming a living nightmare, her only solace in life was to come home and spend time with Tom and Tammy. At home, she could exhale. The once-strict authority her parents had with their older children seemed to have lapsed the third time around, making it easier to have control in a way she wasn't able to achieve around her peers. She hid her insecurities, internalizing them, creating the catalyst for shame.[3]

She was also bashful about her family. Back in the '70s, it was not common to have "older" parents, you know, people in their thirties and beyond (YIKES, by the way). This fixation added more weight to her invisible knapsack of shame. She was embarrassed by her parents, noticing that her mom had a little more gray hair, a little extra roundedness to her frame, and didn't keep up as some of the other parents did. My mom's embarrassment contributed to a lack of respect in their relationship that was made worse by Pryde's desire to be a friend rather than a parent. It is possible Pryde sensed insecurity and felt bad for creating strife without any possibility of change; she simply could not change her age. Maybe this is, in part, what allowed for such flexibility in Pryde's lackadaisical approach to discipline.

My mom's life changed for the worse when she was around ten years old. Tom and Tammy did nothing wrong; they simply grew up. Things began to shift when Tom first graduated from high school. He began college at the local university, and although he still lived at home, he was working hard to individuate from his family.[4] This meant a partial reorganization of the family structure and norms. Even the physical space changed, as my mom finally got a bedroom downstairs. Naturally, Tammy was not far behind Tom, which meant more alone time for my mom. She began to grieve their absence without understanding that's what it was: the sting of longing. She was sad and lonely, and she didn't perceive she had the support to examine the holes left in her heart by her siblings moving forward. All she knew was that she needed to be done being a kid. She felt abandoned and assumed that growing up was her only chance at filling the holes. She *needed* to grow up. So she did, with hard-learned consequences.

The first path she embarked on to grow up involved substances. My mom's first exposure to alcohol came when she was just eleven years old, at a wedding. She and a friend began to sneak champagne and consumed enough to get drunk for the first time. Not only did she like the feeling of being under the influence, but she was even more enamored with the feeling of doing adult things. This trend continued at the next wedding she attended later that year. Even though her parents were there, she found herself taking shots of Ouzo (a strong Greek liquor that tastes like black licorice). She put the shots back just like the men, providing instant gratification that she was indeed an adult. It made her feel older, cooler, and *better*. Accepted. Once she got a taste of what alcohol could do for her, she discovered cigarettes as well. Cigarettes were a symbol of popularity, and she felt that the more she smoked, the more she was viewed as a mature version of herself. Using these tools, she perfected her craft as a social chameleon. She could be preppy when with the waspy kids, nerdy when around the smart kids, and a troublemaker when surrounded by the rebels. All her attention went to blending into the crowd, sadly stunting any chance at building a solid foundation of self-esteem and a sense of self. Her time in the classroom became exponentially worse. She developed a strong repugnance of authority figures. She didn't know how to handle her boredom and was disrespectful to any adult figure who challenged her. She was going to do whatever she wanted, no matter the cost, and so began an overwhelming reign of defiance and a series of unfortunate, poor decisions. Traumatic events outside the classroom, coupled with academic opposition, became the perfect storm of an incredibly tumultuous next few years.

Trauma is the second variable that caused her to grow up too fast. When she was thirteen years old, she obtained a job at a local pharmacy. Pryde had gotten her the job and hoped it would provide structure, teach her responsibility, and keep her out of trouble. She worked there a couple of hours a day after school and absolutely loved it. It was a small and quaint space with a surprisingly diverse spread of items for purchase. She was a cashier, responsible for helping to unpack and restock the shelves and ringing up customer purchases. She thrived in this position and enjoyed the adult-like façade it provided her. She purchased cigarettes for herself and her friends without being questioned by her coworkers. At this point, she reasoned that she knew the ins and outs of what it meant to be fully grown. There was an air of invincibility about her. The healthiest part of her life was her time at Center Pharmacy, which makes the next series of losses all the more gut-wrenching.

About two months into the job, she was approached by a pharmacy intern, a man in his twenties whom she knew next to nothing about other than he was married with a baby. He asked her to accompany him down to the basement to assist with inventory. She agreed without hesitation. Once in the basement, far enough away from the stairs for noise to be muffled, he moved abnormally close to her. Before she could grasp what was happening, he began molesting her, holding her down forcefully and trying his best to take advantage of her. In only a few brief minutes, her life changed forever. Although unable to yell, she used all the physical strength she could muster and broke away from his hold. She sprinted up the stairs and out of the pharmacy as quickly as she could, but the inescapable trauma had already entrenched itself in the cells of her trembling body. The body subconsciously tallies traumas,[5] and his attempted conquest of her body took up permanent property in the record books of her soul. She arrived home shaken, immediately giving a full account of what happened to her mom. Unfortunately, it resulted in the crushing outcome of Pryde choosing not to do anything about it. Her reaction was to try to help my mom forget rather than using the moment to teach her what her true worth really was. She did not acknowledge such significant loss from being violated and denied my mom the right to grieve an abhorrent abuse of her own physical safety. Following this, my mom concluded she had no choice but to internalize the confusing anger and perpetual shame that began to follow her every waking thought. The garden grew as this secret allowed the seedlings of trauma to be watered with avoidance by way of silence and a push to ignore. The aftermath reinforced the defective narrative she had of herself. Hypervigilance and fear took over, and her natural inclination to be anxious skyrocketed, as did her need to feel grown-up. But now, the focus was on trying to protect herself by any means necessary.

The third theme in her quest for adulthood was partying and dating. About this same time, she was expanding her social network. She met a beautiful young girl named Lynette. They hit it off right away, finding common ground in their sense of humor, dislike for school and authority, and enjoyment of pushing the boundaries. Lynette was from a massive, close-knit Spanish family and quickly introduced my mom to some of her cousins. Two of these people are her now-best friend of thirty-plus years, Corina, and her now-husband, my dad, Troy. My mom and Corina became best friends immediately, initially bonding over how much they could eat in one sitting. It was not uncommon for them to crush an entire pizza on their own or visit the local McDonald's and down two sandwiches, large fries, and a large drink in a matter of minutes. They had a shared love for bad boys and were attracted to the party scene, promptly becoming each other's ride-or-dies. They were unruly and reckless, causing both havoc and heartache for their loved ones.

Her relationship with my dad got off to a much different start. They were both instantaneously attracted to one another, but to my mom, my dad was not considered one of the cool kids, so hanging out with him was hard for her to reconcile. He was a square, risk-aversive, developing workaholic who spent most of his evenings at home with his parents. They would hang out occasionally and even dated briefly but broke off the relationship due to the obvious differences in how they liked to spend their free time. Nonetheless, due to her friendships, she began to spend a great deal of time with my dad's entire family. From her first introduction, she was mesmerized by the operations of the Vialpando clan. She was attracted to their connections and consistent unity. She was captivated with hearing "aunt," "uncle," "grandma," and "grandpa" with such frequency. She was drawn back to memories of the Jetson family that used to babysit her, yet this family was the Jetsons on steroids. It seemed as though they were always getting together. And not only for birthdays or holidays—sometimes it was just for the sake of getting together, of *being*. She began to oscillate between two different worlds. One focused on belonging and meaningful shared connections that she studied with the Vialpando family[6] and the other centered on adrenaline-producing risks. Both worlds finally made her feel part of something.

Following the short-lived romance with my dad, she was attracted to the idea of being in a relationship. Along with the pattern of wanting to be older, she sought company with men much older than she. At age fourteen, she entered a romantic relationship with a local boy who was five years older. She was drawn to him because of his bad-boy reputation. He hated authority and, much to her surprise, seemed to show genuine interest in her. A nonconforming rebel who provided her with attention in a way she wasn't able to give herself was enticing. He had a car and was legally an adult, which, to her, meant great strides toward her main objective: being older. They began dating to the dismay of everyone around her. Her friends and family knew she was in an unhealthy relationship, but she could not be convinced of any idea she did not come up with herself. They were horrified watching her sink further into undeniable danger. He was abusive from the get-go, in every sense of the word. He emotionally and verbally manipulated her, making her first feel desirable, even worthy of love, and then flipping quickly, ensuring she felt as small as the mosquitos you swat away on a hot summer day. He exerted high levels of strict control over her every move, always needing to know where she was, what she was doing, and who she was with, and he insisted she follow the expectations he laid out for her. There were moments of physical threat where arguments would escalate to being forcefully repositioned, ensuring she knew where the dominance stood. Undoubtedly most detrimental, there were nonconsensual sexual experiences with no expression of genuine longing, respect, or satisfaction. Her body was objectified, her choices taken away, and she lost control. Her ability to overrule authority was not stretched to defend the supposed autonomy of her own temple, her body. She suffered in silence, grieving both the misguided belief that being grown would bring protection and the shattered realization that he didn't care about her. As is common with sexual trauma,[7] a part of her began to equate her meager worth with succumbing to men's desires, even if she didn't want to.

The fourth avenue she pursued to ensure independence was downright defiance. Coping with the overwhelming loss of trust, safety, and control and with mounting fear of every "next time," her misbehavior in school worsened. She received detention and in-school suspension more times than she could count. She was kicked out of school in tenth grade, which prompted her to consider dropping out entirely. When she was cleared to attend, getting her to stay in class was a struggle. Corina, who refused to give up on her despite her growing obstreperousness, would literally walk her to her class each morning and beg her to stay, teasing her with rewards during their lunch breaks. But the attempts were futile. My mom would watch Corina walk away, waiting just long enough to sneak out of the classroom, take her car, and waste time before promptly returning at the lunch break to pick her up. She was completely disengaged, and nothing and no one would deter her from this bitter path of self-destruction.

The only effort she put into school was doing research to help her understand the process of withdrawing entirely. She had to wait until she was at least fifteen years old or had gotten through the first semester of her sophomore year to legally drop out. The moment she crossed this threshold, she went directly to her mom and said that her mind was made up and no one was going to tell her what to do with her life. However, there was one small snag she needed help with. She would need a parent to accompany her to the school to make it official. Although terrified, Pryde was, unfortunately, more concerned about ensuring that my mom would continue to be open and honest rather than guiding her to build personal responsibility. After a few weak attempts at persuasion, she gave in.

At the end of the spring semester of my mom's sophomore year, the two of them entered the school counselor's office together. Pryde remarked years later that she was secretly hoping the school counselor would convince my mom of the terrible decision she was making. Instead, her demands were met with no guidance or support. He surrendered with devastating ease and agreed with my mom's decision, essentially sending the message that she was a lost cause and dropping out was the best option. I can only imagine the desolation that overtook both of them in that moment. For Pryde, it was realizing that her daughter would continue down a dark path, with utter terror about what may come next hovering below clouds of powerlessness. For my mom, it confirmed that she was not worthy of being fought for. It also reaffirmed that she knew everything there was to know and widened the lack of belonging that already held her hostage.

In quick succession, my mom lost almost all her friends and realized that dropping out was NOT the cool thing to do. Once again, she entered the space of feeling rejected and scrabbling to seek the acceptance she just couldn't seem to hang onto, no matter how hard she tried. This led to further self-deprecation and withdrawal into an abyss of disparaging overwhelm. As she struggled to adjust to ravaged connections, she began to realize that since school was off the table, she needed to learn to make a living. Responsibility became real in a way she had never grasped before. The only two peers by her side were Corina and, to her surprise, my boring, non-thrill-seeking, hardworking, quiet, future dad. Throughout their tenure, he could not have been clearer about his disapproval of her wild ways and disrespectful interactions with adults. He knew he was not willing to put up with that but consistently found himself gravitating toward her, silently being her biggest cheerleader.

As she grappled with what to do next, the love between my parents was somehow growing, and they both began to consider the prospect of a future together, but with a caveat. My dad was direct about his intention to start a family and exponentially change the direction of his life. He exclaimed that he would be there for her, but he wanted someone he could rely on too. Someone dedicated to the pursuit of success and who would truly be a responsible adult, not just pretend to be one. He set appropriate boundaries with my mom, the biggest being that if they were going to make something work, she needed to turn her life around. He wouldn't deal with the partying, the outward lack of ambition, or the disrespect toward others. This was not done in a dominant, forceful, or demanding way; rather, it was discussed as the limits of his boundaries to ensure that he could trust and rely on his partner. He hoped these steps would start to undo some of the false beliefs my mom had about her true worth and potential, as he was able to see past her façade in ways she couldn't. Since they couldn't deny their ongoing attraction, they began to discuss their goals for the future and realized they were on the same page. With my mom basically being at rock bottom but beginning to recognize she could be and deserved more, she decided to complete two things in order to turn her life around. One, start to make money, and two, finish her education to give herself a real chance at a future.

Simply put, my mom stepped up once she committed to my dad. She wanted to be a wife, and she wanted to be a mom. She felt that he wanted her for her, not for her body, an invite to the next party, or an "in" to get hard-to-come-by substances. She wanted the type of family she had become used to witnessing when she was with my dad's family. With traditional school behind her, she got a full-time job. She had a knack for numbers and taught herself how to budget while saving up for the things she and my dad needed to start a life together. She studied for her GED and, amazingly, completed her education *before* her class walked across the stage. Not only did she complete her own education, but she also ended up doing most of my dad's homework to help him earn his diploma the same year. Despite her trauma, her brilliance remained.

As her life began to turn around, she still had one hell of a time in the battle she fought with herself to feel accepted, which was transferred from peer relationships to my dad's family. Although they were always pleasant and seemingly accepting of her presence, she had to work hard to feel like a part of their clan, something I still see shadows of doubt about. Intersectionality[8] and the entrance of privilege, power, and oppression play a major role in this part of her life. At the time, she was the only White girl who had been introduced into the Vialpando clan as a viable familial candidate, making her stick out like a sore thumb. Although without malicious intent, they frequently made subtle comments that pointed out her "otherness"[9] and lack of understanding of their cultural norms. There were invisible hoops she had to jump through to earn her place while trying to partake in an entirely different cultural approach to life. She didn't cook, she didn't clean, and she certainly didn't respect her elders, none of which were acceptable for a woman and future wife. This fueled her already-rampant sense of being a floater. She observed the women around her. It helped that she was outgoing and inserted herself into the mix, trying to mimic the actions of what she thought would lead to inclusion. But this created an internal tug of war in that some of the gendered roles she took on she disagreed with and found to be disrespectful. She struggled with submissiveness to the men and the unequal balance of power she observed during gatherings. Yet, she quietly obeyed and morphed to fit the expectations in order to hold onto the strongest sense of family she had ever had.

Despite the internal debates from time to time, she developed a ferocious and unconditional love for my dad and his family and believed that a life together was destiny. They married when they were still children themselves, eighteen and nineteen years old. They paid for nearly their entire wedding on their own, which was no small feat, given that they threw a party for nearly five hundred people, which is, by far, the most talked-about wedding in our family to this day. Following the wedding, complete with all the best Spanish traditions, including a dance that lasted well into the early hours of the next day, they journeyed to Yellowstone National Park for their honeymoon. While there, they became pregnant with their first child. As the oldest living child of theirs, I wish I could say that child was me, but fate had other plans for them.

About two months prior to their wedding, my mom developed a superficial blood clot in her leg that was a result of her birth control method. She was advised to stop the pill and told that the issue would resolve itself, and it did. Six weeks after their wedding, she took a pregnancy test, which came back positive, bringing the purest sense of elation she had ever felt. They had two weeks of bliss, which was an abundance of time for her to begin to envision how their lives would change as they moved from a newlywed couple to a young family of three. Unfortunately, this thrill was short-lived, and another bout of heartache grabbed hold. About eight weeks along, she began bleeding slightly and experiencing severe cramps. Uncharacteristic for her, she felt so poorly she asked to leave work. When she arrived home, she went directly to their bedroom, beginning to panic as she noticed her bleeding become more severe with each passing hour. She felt mini labor pains and was unable to manage the uncontrollable jerks of her body. She realized she was losing the baby and called my dad.

"Troy, Troy! I need you to come home now. Something is happening to the baby, and I need to go to the hospital."

"What the fuck do you mean? What's wrong?" he gasped, fear mounting in his voice.

"Just get here, please, and fast." There was no response, just a lonesome dial tone.

About ten minutes later, my dad arrived and bolted inside, dashing back to their bedroom only to find her in an increasingly dire situation. She was crying loudly and uncontrollably with giant drops of grief pouring from her eyes. She was sweaty, pale, and horrified, three observations that made my dad's hair stand up on the back of his neck. Through shallow breaths and fits of crying, she explained what she thought was occurring.

"Troy, I'm having a miscarriage. This isn't good, Troy. I think I'm losing the baby."

The word "miscarriage" struck him oddly, and as he helped walk her out to the car, he could not comprehend why it would be used to describe the pending loss of a child. After securing her in the passenger seat, he sprinted around the vehicle; he was now visibly rattled. He couldn't latch onto the idea of losing a child when he was still trying to wrap his head around the fact that they would be having one in the first place. Too much too fast; he couldn't process it. He sped across town with fixed concentration. As each passing block became a blur, he accelerated, trying to race the ensuing fear and idea of a future he felt slipping further away. He stopped the car at the entrance to the ER and helped her walk inside. They placed her in a wheelchair and ushered her to a room for assessment.

After what seemed like an eternity, the attending doctor bluntly announced, "Sorry, but you have lost the baby. We will need to prep you and perform a D&C to remove the fetus."

There was no gentle acknowledgment of the loss, no words of comfort expressed, and little education given to help them understand their first unified loss. It felt more like a robotic transaction as the doctor prepped for surgery to help make way for the healing process her body would have to undergo.

The procedure was brief but painful. Unfortunately, she woke up in the middle of it and could feel both pain and pressure while she tried to make sense of the attention being paid to rid her body of a life she hoped would change hers forever. After a short recovery, they were informed they could go home. They were given run-of-the-mill condolences sandwiched between pointers that guided them through what the physical recovery might look like in the coming days. They went home, babyless, just like they were two short weeks ago, but it felt SO much different.[10] They had created something. They had had a life on the way, and even though they didn't get to meet this baby, they both lost a significant piece of themselves. For the time being, this shattered their view of what their future was going to be.

They silently tried to make sense of what led to the miscarriage. My mom focused on the knowledge she had gathered as the daughter of a nurse who worked in labor and delivery and her own research she had started to consume as a mother-to-be. My dad did not attempt to understand the biological explanation but instead focused on his fear about how my mom would adjust. He tried to bury the devastation he felt in having the life he had promised my mom take an unexpected and painful turn.[11] They didn't speak much about what they had gone through. What can you say? What would you say? Without words, they seemed to understand on a spiritual and emotional level that they simply needed a child. It was a shared goal that was perhaps the single greatest desire that bonded them together, both then and now. They couldn't do anything about the past, so they focused on the future, never talking about their current pain. They tried to move forward as if nothing had happened, as if they were both okay. But as we all know by now, losses of this magnitude are not erased with the passage of time or by ignoring their shadow.

For my mom, it wasn't just an emotional loss but also guttural. Something she felt viscerally. A part of her was cut away and stolen, with irreparable sorrow being used as the suture. The physical trauma her body endured and the psychological suffering of losing a life she carried inside her ignited fierce flames of desire on a cellular level to be a mother. As her typical coping mechanism, she wholeheartedly blamed herself and internalized shame for what she believed she had taken away from her and my dad. She felt guilt for losing the baby, for letting him down, as if she truly could have controlled it. She unfairly remembered mistakes from the past and tried to over-accommodate to make the miscarriage make sense. To somehow hold herself responsible, an attempt to clutch some fragment of control. It was easier to blame herself than to acknowledge the uncertainty and confusion behind life's unfair outcomes. Sometimes, bad things happen despite our best intentions and have nothing to do with how worthy or deserving we may be. We don't always understand why we are plagued with certain losses. What she did understand was that she just wanted a family—needed it, in fact. She was determined to have a child and sought to provide an environment for her kids that she wished she'd had herself. They had to wait three long months before trying again, per the doctor's recommendations. Within a couple of weeks of being given the green light, they were successful in their efforts to become pregnant again (*ew)*, this time with me. And I guess the rest is history, much of which is being shared with you amid these pages of lived experience.

I know she will easily dismiss these words, but my mom deserves a standing ovation with infinite encores for the resilience[12] she demonstrated and the efforts put toward changing the direction of her life. She doesn't allow herself grace to recognize that she cannot take on *full* responsibility for her tribulations. Sure, there are some decisions that she can and should take some ownership of. Yet at the same time, with many of the traumatic burns she suffered, others watched her as she played with fire and didn't insist that she step back from the heat. No one stood up to her defiance, and no one looked hard enough to catch glimpses of trauma reflected in each poor decision she made. It seems like there was a joint sense of learned helplessness[13] and no one knew how to intervene. Retelling my mom's history in this way leaves me shredded. I could feel the grief chase her and the shame fill her empty spaces. Tears flowed steadily with each new paragraph, urges to hug her stronger with each keystroke. So much isn't fair, yet her hardiness overcomes me. How lucky am I to come from this woman?

Going back to her early years, I must confront my own feelings of misplaced guilt as I think about the care and attention I got that my mom didn't. We share our intellectual capacities, but others gave us such different playgrounds for what to do with our brainpower. The lack of proper academic support and her constant worry about acceptance are two major losses she faced early on; no one identified her needs or worked to provide a more comfortable learning atmosphere for her. There were forgone chances to teach her about the cruelties of others and that true inclusion comes from within. It brings great sadness to acknowledge that so much was missed—so much that could have consequently changed the course of her childhood, both academically and socially. I can't help but think how different my life would have been if I hadn't had the teachers who stepped up on my behalf, saw that I wasn't being challenged, and did something about it. I am angry and grieve these neglected openings for my mom, and I can't help but ask myself, "Why me? And why not her?" It isn't fair, and I am certainly no more deserving than she or anyone else to have been given the tools needed to excel. What resulted is a forest of shadow losses[14] with heartbreaking consequences.

Timing has a hand in how things got so out of control. Tom and Tammy's natural separation from family to navigate entry to adulthood didn't help. I want to be clear that I am not faulting any individual, and as I described in the narratives of my dad's past, each person you just learned about has a unique set of strengths and shortcomings. It is not my intention to grade the way she was parented, but instead, it is pertinent to explain how these dynamics propelled a long series of painful events. It is crystal clear that my mom needed more structure and discipline, and her parents weren't able to implement them. By her teen years, Pryde was doing all she could to steady the family as Bill battled his own demons. The psychological issues that plagued Bill during parts of my mom's childhood took a lot of attention to regulate. His absence and disengagement made discipline seem laughable; he was not present enough to enforce rules or earn respect. Perhaps Pryde's missing accountability was also due to the fear of repeating her untold traumas and losing my mom altogether. These competing needs left no one in the home to instill responsibility for wrongdoings. It was parental absence, not necessarily in a physical sense, but in an emotional, cognitive, and supervisory sense.[15]

In a raw reflection of relationships and our ability to make sense of our lives, I have attempted to be honest about both the sturdiness and cracks in those we love that impact us in the long term. My intention is to shed light on the various parts of ourselves and our caretakers who make us who we are, not to place blame or throw my loved ones under the bus. It was a collective series of unfortunate events and reactions, a scatterplot of unevenly distributed duty, albeit with the best intentions. I know the hearts of each of these people, and I purport that they all were doing the best they could. Clearly, they did a few things right; they helped make the exemplary woman who I get to call my mom, who you now have the honor of knowing.

I can't help but draw conclusions about some of the ways in which my parents tend to share a brain, helping me better understand why they are still together after all these years. They understand each other in a way no one else ever could. As different as my mom and dad are, I noticed a striking similarity when preparing to write their chapters: how they handled talking about their trauma. They avoid. My mom took several breaks while speaking, and although she didn't get up and slam or throw things like my dad did, she squirmed in her chair, fought back tears, and left the room a handful of times, trying with all her might not to let her humanity hurt me. What weighs on me the most is how much she dismissed her own experiences as she shared them with me. At the beginning of the interview, she remarked, "Tasha, I am scared to do this. I don't think you want to use me. This is going to be too boring. I don't have anything in my background that is good enough for your writing." This quote is a shining example of the inner critic I have tried to illustrate in her story: a belief that she had nothing worthy of being added to the pages of my book. Boy, was she wrong. I am often too harsh with her in these instances. Her beliefs make me angry. Angry that she can't see how fucking stellar she really is. The anger is mixed with profound heartache. Sadly, I can't make her see her worth. None of us can. I hope these pages can help to shift her perspective just enough to realize that she is one of the strongest, most admirable women on the planet. She has fought and overcome. She has suffered heavy losses yet never allowed herself to grieve.

My mom's traumas began to be reflected in our relationship when I became a pre-teen. One of her strongest qualities as a parent has always been being vocal, honest, and developmentally appropriate in how she educated Dalton and me about the world, with sex being no exception. She never shied away from any question I had and was impressively proactive in bringing up topics I was too shy and awkward to initiate myself. Although she was open and direct, she delivered information to me about sex from a sex-negative (e.g., sex is bad, dirty, and dangerous) lens.[16] I place zero blame on her for this approach, and based on the PG version of the events I shared with you, I hope you don't blame her either. She didn't disclose her experiences, yet there was an unsaid pull that made me wonder what fueled such tension in her body language when we spoke about it. The oxygen in the room was replaced with thick fog, carrying remnants of emotional annihilation we never put words to. Although the physical trauma happened to my mom, its scars were inadvertently transferred onto me, too, in the way that I thought about sex, viewed my body, and considered what was acceptable in terms of my roles, responsibilities, and safety in future relationships. Now I can identify loss in not knowing what led to my interpretations of what relationships are, are not, or could be. I pieced things together as I got older, and with shame, I admit, I was too embarrassed to simply ask her to fill in the blanks. Selfishly, I, too, ran from the fear of the unknown and anticipated pain. Until now.

My goal has been to highlight how trauma can lead to a plethora of loss and harmful repercussions of pushing against the natural need to grieve. We all have our ways of coping with life's most difficult obstacles. Some of her initial destruction has stuck with her, making it more difficult for her to keep the tattered bones of emotional wreckage buried. Her misuse of alcohol has remained steady—an "out" from her reality, from her emotions that feel too overwhelming to sit with and too overbearing to process.[17] Escaping has encouraged her to live in the shadows of her trauma rather than stepping outside of them. This has impacted our relationship immensely, and it saddens me to admit that I have learned to be aware of what time of night I talk to her or brace myself for how she may behave when alcohol is involved. Feedback about this is not well-received, as it confirms her self-judgments. Her inner critic is a giant jackass, to be frank. She degrades herself and her accomplishments, not being able to accept and let go of her torment because she goes to extreme lengths to avoid its very existence. She seems stunted in being able to acknowledge her feats, no matter how big or small. She is quick to dismiss any compliment or will instead respond with a shortcoming that renders the positive moot. This has strained our connection in that I get frustrated with her treatment of herself and don't know how to lift her up. Admittedly, I sometimes make it worse. There seem to be too many secrets and so much left unresolved.

I have seen the repercussions of trauma play out in my mom's life every day, made worse by her unwillingness or perhaps perceived inability to feel safe enough to confront what she's been through. She is terrified all the time. Unintentionally, she taught Dalton and me to be afraid of everything, too—things we have had to consciously undo so we don't live our lives with blankets of fear and self-protection that prevent us from experiencing the world. When we hurt, it hurts her almost too much, in a way that sometimes makes it difficult to be fully honest with her for fear of how it will affect her. She struggles to let go of what she can't control. Her self-worth hangs on being a good mother, so as we have gotten older and naturally not needed as much support, she has once again found herself floundering to find purpose and give credit to herself where credit is due for a job well done in both motherhood and beyond.

Yet again, I must say that she is an astounding mother, truly. On her worst days, she is more dependable and productive than the majority of people on this planet. Everyone in our family relies on her. Every misstep she took, every trauma she suffered, every memory she has of being let down, led her to go above and beyond to create the exact opposite atmosphere for Dalton and me. And she did. We wanted for nothing. And still don't. This is something she shares with her own mother, as Grandma Pryde did the exact same thing: she tried to create an environment for her children that reflected no part of her own childhood. My mom was strict when she needed to be, being careful not to be our friend but also emulating undying support and unconditional love, no matter what we did. She instilled confidence in us in a way she has never been able to do for herself. She never missed a single event either of us participated in. She asks about our emotions daily and won't let us get away with trying to bury our insecurities or worries without a good pep talk infused with relentless backing. She ensures we have all the tools in the world to have as successful and happy of a life as possible. She means everything to me. I just wish she could turn some of her efforts toward herself. She deserves the type of confidence, belonging, and unlimited bonding she has worked tirelessly to give to us. It's there if only she would take it.

Trauma can serve as a hotbed for grief. It is painful to see how often people get diagnosed with other mental health conditions like depression, anxiety, substance use disorders, mood disorders, and even personality disorders when the fact of the matter is that they have survived trauma and they often resist the natural need to grieve the losses associated with that suffering. We struggle to call trauma what it is at times and scuffle to acknowledge when grief is present. Instead, we slap other labels on people that permeate ongoing invisibility of what led them to their maladaptive coping skills to begin with. Does any of this sound familiar? I challenge you to consider a few of the people in your life through a new lens. What do you see if you look more closely? What parts have you been missing, ignoring, or avoiding because other parts stand too tall?

My mom has needed to grieve the loss of her own identity, sense of self, personal safety, confidence, and self-esteem since she was a child. The dismissal of her own grief has led to blankets of guilt and shame that cover every window of opportunity to recover. She has done her best to cope and to overcome immense odds, and I am PROUD to call her my mom and someone I will always aspire to be like. AND, the trauma still haunts her and, at times, casts a dark shadow over our relationship. She is held captive, a prisoner in the murky waters of wounds and woe. She didn't have the support and resources she needed back then, but at this moment in time, and for all the remaining moments she has left, it is never too late to let herself surrender to the grief process. To learn to be with it and to trust that it won't swallow her whole like she fears. She deserves a chance to be with grief and allow it to integrate more fully into her life.[18] She cannot undo the past, but she has more than made up for her poor decisions. She didn't deserve many of the events that transpired, yet she must grasp and understand that the "just-world" myth[19] (i.e., the belief that the world is always fair and just) is just that, a myth. Her struggles to face pain have only led to more suffering over the years, more loss, and more repressed expressions of grief that ensured ... she would never be the same again.

8

IDENTITY'S SCOREBOARD

From the moment I learned what basketball was, I fell in love. Its introduction into my life marked the beginning of my mostly unidimensional identity as an athlete that dominated my youth. I was a basketball player. To be more specific, a point guard. It was a sport that I ate, drank, slept, and breathed competitively for twelve years, all of which were developmentally formative years. One of the first articles I ever published was targeted to physical and sport educators who worked with aspiring athletes.[1] This is the paragraph that I used to begin the article.

"For the third week in a row, a high school varsity basketball coach notices one of her starters wearing wristbands to practice every day. Although her player has never done this before, she dismisses it as a new fashion trend that will likely catch on with more players. As the season progresses, she begins to notice her player's demeanor changing. She is withdrawn from her teammates. In addition, she has increased her verbal self-criticism about small mistakes and is visibly losing her stamina and quirky personality both on and off the court. The coach approaches her to ask if everything is okay. The player quickly responds, "Yes" and declines the opportunity to discuss the situation any further. The coach conceptualizes her player's changes as a normal part of adolescence and attributes the changes to hormones. More time passes and the situation seems stagnant, yet the coach thinks nothing more about it. However, one day at practice, the coach is involved in a drill and notices blood seeping through her player's wristband. She alerts her player of the situation and the player instantly runs off the court into the locker room, looking embarrassed as tears begin to form in her eyes. The player's unexpected reaction causes the coach to become concerned. She follows her player into the locker room and discovers her player tending to multiple deep cuts on the inside of her left forearm. Alarmed and frightened by this unexpected sight, the coach gasps, sits down and tells her player they need to talk. What would you say in this coach's position? How would you react to the surprising sight of deep, self-inflicted wounds on a child you care about? What you say and how you say it could deeply affect an individual engaging in nonsuicidal self-injury (NSSI)."

I often got questions about where the story came from. I distinctly remember tension quickly permeating from the pit of my stomach to the tips of every limb of my body. My chest tightened with a growing heaviness, and my heart rate rose noticeably, suddenly becoming audible in the depths of my eardrums. I was terrified of being found out. Of admitting to having this issue, of not being tough enough to rise above the stress and deal effectively like everyone else. Flashbacks of my time in sports were like a sped-up series of snapshots of my career. Somehow, I would come back to the present and calmly assert that I had made it up based on my understanding of common ways the behavior could be discovered.

Grief and loss are inevitable parts of what it means to be a dedicated athlete, regardless of the sport.[2] Athletes commit every aspect of their lives to perfecting their performance. They make a conscious decision each day to risk their bodies and oftentimes their lives in the name of their sport. We don't talk enough about how grief and loss linger in between the banners splashed with names and dates of the champions in every arena, stadium, and field across the world. We idolize and celebrate champions in the initial days of triumph while forgetting about the majority who never taste that sweet victory as the ultimate winner. The gains of being the best are obvious and plentiful. Athletes often appear to have it all in the moment. But there's so much left hidden behind the scenes. Tough seasons bring deceiving baskets of conditional support and acceptance. Everyone has an opinion, particularly with mistakes, poor performances, or losses that can diminish worth and stability before a shot clock runs out. When it's all over, when the parades are done and the lights turn off, athletes grieve the fleeting sense of feeling on top of the world. We don't often acknowledge how every year in a sport marks the passing of major losses. Losses of graduating seniors and retirees, of injured teammates who can't play, of coaches who move on, of teammates who decide it no longer defines them, of the splitting of wins and losses at the end of each season. We work our asses off to reach our goals, and we all want to be winners at the end of the season, but most of us aren't. Realizing that the outcome may not reflect the process we poured our soul into is incredibly hard to accept, so grief ensues.

When a sport becomes your identity, self-worth can hang on the athletic highs and lows.[3] Identity formation[4] is intricately intertwined with the effort we exert to become the best. Consequently, this process warrants understanding how grief usually has a seat at the table for athletes. For me, that means I need to go back to the beginning. I grew up in a small college town. The University of Wyoming is the only Division I and four-year institution in the state. It has a women's basketball team where, at the time, attendance was so poor they offered free admission to the general public to get spectators in the seats. My grandpa Bill was a former athlete who enjoyed healthy competition and wanted to check out a game. Although I hadn't expressed interest in sports, he thought my five-year-old self might like to accompany him. It was an evening game, and we parked on the street in front of the local KFC. With time to kill, we walked inside to eat and sat by the window until game time. As we walked into the gym, we were handed a one-page program that listed the names of the players on both teams. It had a few pictures of the Cowgirls and background information about the coaches and players. He gave me the option of where I wanted to sit, so I chose the far east side of the court, close to where the basketball hoop was. From the moment the whistle blew, I was enthralled but didn't show it. Instead, I sat almost completely silent. I barely moved in my seat as I absorbed everything around me. Grandpa Bill watched me more than the game and concluded that I had a terrible time and would never ask to go again.

A couple of weeks later, he mustered up a bit of courage and asked me, "Princess, do you want to go to another Cowgirls game?"

He felt he knew the answer and prepared himself to be a little disappointed, but instead, he was met with an energized, "YES! I LOVE BASKETBALL AND I WANT TO PLAY TOO!" It took one game; that was it. I became hooked on a love I have never been able to give up, and I have Grandpa Bill to thank for that. (Thanks, Grandpa.)

We developed a routine for attending games, parking in the same place, and grabbing the same meal at KFC before tipoff. I was quick to pick up the strategy of the game and, in time, expressed more emotion as I watched. I was relentless in my hunt to understand. "Grandpa, why did she blow the whistle there?" "Grandpa, what is the ref doing?" "Grandpa, how do you shoot a three-point basket?" I had an uncanny knack for remembering statistics and recalling detailed playbacks with ease. I was locked in any time the game clock was ticking. I took a keen interest in the players themselves, too. I wanted to know everything I could about them. I memorized their names and numbers, their heights and positions, hometowns, and key stats, and I would recite them like the Pledge of Allegiance. For whatever reason, my favorite player became a tall, blond, power forward with a name I loved hearing the announcer say: Darci Arsene (R-Seen-E). She was number twenty-one. I am not sure how my young brain put all of this together, but I knew that I was short not tall, had black hair not blond hair, and was small not big. Obviously, I would never be a player like her. So, even though she was my favorite player, that meant I could never wear her number either. We were just too different. So, I took the reciprocal and became connected to number twelve. To this day, it is my favorite number, even going as far as to be sure my first book had twelve chapters—because why not?

Outside of the Cowgirls games, I expressed interest in learning to play, so my mom enrolled me in the co-ed youth league. It became obvious quickly that I had some natural talent for the game and an even more natural work ethic. I didn't hide that I wanted to be the best, and I proclaimed my goal to play in college (UW, of course). I embraced my dedication to outplay everyone around me. My urge to win was big, but I also capitalized on the social opportunities. I made friends easily even though I didn't hide my competitive side, especially with the boys. I was tiny, an unfortunate trait I never did grow out of, so I had to work harder to be seen as both capable and valuable. I had to be scrappy and prove that I was good enough to play with the boys. I expressed frustration about their cockiness and lack of sportsmanship. I would be wide open and still not get the ball, which only fueled my desire to get better. To touch the ball, I had to get them to trust and respect my skills on the court. Passing and shooting became strengths. I could see the floor in its entirety and could anticipate what my opponents would do. It was in these years that my basketball IQ expanded with the help of extra practice and solid coaches who seemed to understand the seriousness I was bringing to my game. Without conscious awareness, my identity had been solidified.[5]

One of the best things to ever happen to me was getting to be on a team with boys at such an early age. There were three boys I used to train with regularly, and one of their dads was a former college basketball star. He married a woman who happened to be from a family that was good friends with my own, so since we already knew each other, he took a vested interest in me. He invited me to spend extra time with his son and nephews. They were all older, bigger, and stronger than me, and they did NOT want to play with me. I noticed the differences in our athletic privilege right away. Their family was athletic, for one thing. Plus, they didn't experience the differential treatment on the court that I did. When they were open, they got the ball, while I had to fight for every touch I got. Luckily, it did nothing to deter me. Perhaps even more lucky for me, they all had natural talent, too, and didn't want to get shown up by a girl, so we made each other work. I am grateful for the initial rejection they showed me because it made me better. I used their doubt to learn how to let my actions speak for me. This is where my habit of doing extra began. Extra shots, extra drills, extra ladders, or whatever else my coaches noticed needed more attention. I would lag on defense so that I wasn't too tired to shoot (selfish), my shot was at times too forced, I often forgot to box out when underneath the hoop, and emotionally I struggled to reset when I made a mistake. Eventually, I earned their respect as both a player and a girl, and we remained connected throughout our youth.

During the summers, I attended individual camps that the university hosted and learned about an opportunity to join a revolving lineup of young, aspiring basketball players who could sign up to serve as "ball girls" for the home games. This was a chance for us to sit on the court under the basket and shuck balls to players while they were warming up, sweep the floor, deliver the game ball to the referees before the game, and fetch the ball if it got tossed too far off-court during play. These were some of the happiest memories of my life. I made lifelong friends, connected with the players I revered, and built rapport with the coaches. The coaching staff began to watch me more closely at the summer camps. The work I was putting in with the boys and the girls traveling team I joined was starting to help me stand out as a player. Fitting the recurring theme in my life, I once again had a group of dedicated adults who saw my *potential*.

During the off-season from the co-ed league, I played on a traveling team for extra reps and practice, building chemistry with the girls who would eventually be my high school team. The team was coached by an older gentleman who had a long, gray Santa Claus beard and drove a beat-up, light-blue Volkswagen Beetle. It was on this team that I solidified my reputation as an offensive force. I was just as concerned about getting assists as I was about scoring points. I was good at seeing the floor, reading the defense, and calling the right plays. I knew my teammates' strengths and how to get us points. I loved deconstructing the opposing team and figuring out their weaknesses. But of course, I struggled too. I wasn't as quick defensively as I needed to be, my communication wasn't sharp enough, and the lingering self-criticism could easily turn my mood, which caused me to disconnect from the moment, forever frustrating my coaches. I was mean to my teammates at times and snapped back at my coaches a lot too. I won't make excuses for my poor behavior; I was a fierce competitor and not mature enough to channel it effectively. Nothing beats the rush of winning a game, knowing you worked your ass off and outplayed your enemies both mentally and physically. It was a feeling I don't think I'll ever be able to match.

On the first day of middle school basketball, I walked into the gym for tryouts and heard that the coaches had been talking about me, asking when the "girl who could shoot" would be coming. I was subtly nervous. I knew I could shoot. I knew I had a high basketball IQ. If anything, I was grateful I was noticed and excited to show off what I could do. I craved a taste of real competition. I had much room to grow, though. I was aware enough of myself to know that if I made a mistake early, it would shift their perception of my coachability, and I was keenly attuned to the parts of my game that needed further development. I had more than committed to playing basketball in college and was invested in every aspect of getting there. Hearing those comments from my soon-to-be teammates before the tryouts even started solidified my identity as a player. They also revved up perfectionistic tendencies that had already been brewing for quite some time. The pressure was on.

It was here that I met Coach Tyson. He was a large man who was intimidating, loud, and quite serious. He played college basketball in my hometown and had been a star in his own right. He would become a man that I have immense respect for and owe so much to for his role in helping me through some of my most intense clashes against myself. He had a phenomenal balance of showing a sense of humor, allowing us to play to win *and* have fun, and being stern when he needed to be. We always knew what was expected of us, and he pushed us. Hard. He was not authoritarian but authoritative.[6] He wanted us to take it seriously and taught us how much effort it took to be the championship-caliber team we sought to become. He wanted to help us understand the chemistry needed to make it to the top and was good at reading each of us and helping us identify our strengths and weaknesses and those of our teammates. He was the first to water the seeds that I and a few of my teammates were Division I material, a dream I had my heart set on.

This time in my career combined for so many gains and losses. I loved the sport more than ever, and all my spare time outside of the gym was focused on getting better. I practiced my form for hours at home as I was doing homework. I watched films of our team and of other games, and I talked strategy with anyone who would listen. Coaches from around the state and other traveling teams started to inquire more about me, approaching my mom and Grandma Pryde about my talent. They radiated delight when they played back these conversations. I calmly took in the information, not reacting externally. Internally, though, the pressure was building. I was good. Other people knew it. I knew it. But I needed to get better. I had *potential* (yes—that damn word again) but hadn't reached it yet. My reputation was moving in the right direction, and our team was good. I had two teammates in particular who were powerhouses, both gaining status and attention. Our entire team started to be talked about as a state championship shoo-in when the time came. We could nearly taste it and were eager to see that through, not just for ourselves but for everyone else who believed in us.

You might be wondering how I managed all this, given the knowledge you now have about my less-than-optimal respiratory system. As the game became more serious, practices naturally got longer and tougher, and my residual lung issues started to resurface in ways I couldn't hide. In the time since my flight for life, I had also been diagnosed with a condition called vocal cord dysfunction (now called exercise-induced laryngeal obstruction), which amplified wheezing fits and the embarrassment and shame I tried to swallow with every forced breath. I absolutely hated my lungs. I hated asthma, and I hated the part of myself that couldn't figure out how to train it out of me. Coach Tyson saw how much this ate at me, and given his strikingly good balance of using humor and discipline to teach us, he developed a small way to normalize my experience. He chose nicknames for each of us that seemed to emphasize something that made us stand out, embracing some of the more sour parts of our game. My teammates were Froggy, Special K, Bigg Country, and Money. My nickname brought to life the audible echoes of my breathing problems that became a fixture in the gym. Wheezy. "Wheezy, get back!" "Wheezy, keep your eyes up!" "Wheezy, what did I just hear you say?!" "Wheezy, for three, I see you girl!" It was fun to say, and my teammates loved it. Although I internalized shame about the way my asthma took away from my play and made me stand out in a way I didn't want to be noticed, the nickname, for whatever reason, didn't offend me (thank you, Lil Wayne). Instead, it gave me a moment to smile. He used it in a way that lightened the situation, normalized what was obviously not normal, and redirected attention from me. Wheezy simply reverberated a huge aspect of sports for me that I couldn't run away from if I tried (and yes, I tried).

My teammates were good about my asthma. Whether it was wheezing, the notable oxygen depletion from my lips, a light-blue-and-gray tint that took over my face, or the occasional serious asthma attacks where an ambulance was called, they took Coach Tyson's lead and tried to reduce my stress. I had one teammate who also had asthma and kept her inhaler on display alongside mine so that I wasn't in total isolation. Some of my teammates would ask to use my inhaler or try a couple of puffs of my portable nebulizer, saying it looked cool and they wanted one for themselves. They took turns being the keeper of the machine and kept it hidden but close. During asthma attacks, someone was designated to bang on my back with their fist, trying to break up the excess mucus so I could get it up and return to play. Some loved this job, and others hated it, afraid that if they hit me too hard, they would do irreparable damage.

As you can see, I am incredibly lucky. They didn't show judgment, only rightful concern and support, which I almost always shunned and became annoyed by. In fact, I was both rude and callous on occasion. My words were often hurtful, and I shut several of them down; sometimes, I was unapproachable. I snapped at them and assumed that, secretly, they were judging me. I was judging myself enough for all of us. Even though their responses were nearly perfect, I didn't want to be treated differently. But the fact of the matter was that I needed different treatment. I had a chronic illness that impacted my ability to breathe normally and execute exercise like everyone else. During drills, if my breathing would start to escalate or my lips would turn a glum shade of blue, a coach would usually ask me to step out and get my breathing under control. I almost never complied, usually working harder instead. I would compare myself to others and sometimes express anger that they weren't asking anyone else to step out of drills. Although obviously, no one else was about to pass out but me.

I isolated as best I could, running sprints or standing away from my teammates. Anything to decrease the unwanted spotlight but inadvertently placing me directly in it. I saw my differences as deficits. My cantankerous and closed-off attitude impacted the team culture, and

I cringe when I admit it brought down our play and unity. My stubborn nature contributed to some of the more traumatic asthma attacks, given my unyielding desire not to be noticed. Had I just listened to my body, maybe I could have avoided some of the now-forever-remembered sounds of sirens and visuals of paramedics trying to restore my lung functioning on the floor of our high school gym (sorry, team).

I embraced standing out for my academic and athletic pursuits, but standing out for lung issues increased the pressure on myself to correct the blemishes they made on my perfect image. My mission to become perfect was increasingly more critical of my self-worth. Coach Tyson was the first to pick up on my perfectionism and started to call me out on it. After mistakes, I vocalized my irritation. "I can't do this!" Eventually, this turned into punishment in an effort to teach me the harm I was inflicting on myself and my teammates. "ON THE LINE," Coach Tyson would yell. Each time he heard me bellow the word "can't," it was another down and back, full speed. But not just for me—for the whole team. I must say, we got into shape incredibly fast, but I also got a lot of angry glares and frustrated reminders to believe in myself so we could stop suffering from my brain's ruthless solo attacks. I hung my head during these episodes, and it was difficult for me to reset and connect with my teammates in an adaptive way. The initial flare of anger would evaporate and find its way out of the gym's vibes, but internally, I was always keeping score. I berated myself for the remainder of practice and plotted my revenge against the enemy: imperfection.[7] There was no self-compassion and no room for excuses. With each mistake, I concluded I was not good enough and had to work even harder to undo my mess-ups. I never directly stated any of this, so my dedication to perfection on the surface just looked like an untamed commitment (and difficult-to-address stubbornness) to the sport. The result was consistent praise used to promote the ideal example of a dedicated athlete to my peers. But, it also sparked unease within others to confront me. It didn't help that, to most of my peers, I was intimidating and hard to read, and I built relationships on my own terms.

As with most young athletes, high school is where things really took off. A new head coach was hired to coach varsity in my eighth-grade year. We played year-round, which led to strong team chemistry. The summer tournaments were more successful and meaningful than any in-season finish. They rejuvenated us and got us ready to face another grueling season. In my freshman year, it was expected that I would be playing varsity, but it was unclear how much. The current varsity team already had a seasoned point guard, so I likely wouldn't start, which, of course, infuriated me and ignited perfectionistic cycles. I was cross with myself for not being good enough to take her spot, especially given that one of my best friends, also a freshman, secured a well-deserved starting spot as a shooting guard. Although happy for her, I had fierce envy (not a good teammate move) and vowed to improve so I never had to experience that overwhelming sense of inadequacy again. I suffered my first serious injury this year too. A severe ankle sprain that would continue to come back with a vengeance, taking me away from the game for short periods throughout the rest of my career. Getting accustomed to the life of high school sports also meant addressing the losses suffered at the end of each season when the seniors graduated and moved on. Each year, there was a predictable reshaping of the team that introduced grief, particularly at the beginning of a new season as we became accustomed to the changes. Our relationships, roles, strengths, and weaknesses shifted collectively and individually. We had to cope with the longing for things we missed from past seasons while also relishing in the joy and optimism we had for what our new team could achieve.

Basketball stopped being fun and became a burdensome job between my sophomore and junior years. I had earned a starting varsity spot by sophomore year, but my success was often overshadowed by the self-imposed stress caused by my unrealistic expectations and the pressure to please a coach I did not trust or like. Injuries hung loosely from the rafters of the gym, falling and crushing me when I least expected it. My jammed and broken fingers had to be taped together. I nursed severe bouts of shin splints and revolving-door ankle sprains. I spent hours in the training room, even learning to tape my own ankles while blindfolded. I took pride in playing through the pain and displaying the power of mind over matter. Submersing myself in ice baths became an objective token of my toughness. I could outlast anyone who wanted to challenge me. Externally, my leadership role had become more prominent, especially after I sealed that starting spot. To me, this meant showing up and working hard. I recited notes from the scouting reports and made sure people knew their roles and our collective strategy, which created a sense of productivity and readiness that quieted my nerves and the waves of self-criticism. I was not the one in the locker room screaming and jumping around to pump us up, but I was aware of who needed a little more support and tried to demonstrate the necessary mindset to defeat our immediate competition. As long as I was performing well, this wasn't an issue. But if I wasn't hitting shots or had a slew of turnovers, watch out. I, unfortunately, was more of a liability than a force to be reckoned with.

My dedication to hard work helped me cope with the disparaging teardowns that occurred any time our head coach was in the picture. He was rough. He capitalized on opportunities to break us down individually. He had favorites but was inconsistent with who they were, so we never knew who was on the chopping block on any given day. There was an abundance of gaslighting.[8] It seemed that once mistakes were made, he was quick to pull us from the game. The fear of failure with so much on the line became a strong focus for all of us. Consequently, our play became unnatural and sloppy. His style seemed to accomplish nothing but the deconstruction of our confidence. He had a way of isolating us from one another. We didn't productively communicate our shared experiences or talk about ways to handle his emotional knockouts, and our silence was likely the result of the shame we each felt, plus the fact that we were teenage girls. Like so many other stories we have heard in women's sports, our team was not spared from inappropriate comments about us as young women. During the stretching period of practices, there were a handful of times when demeaning comments were made about our bodies that left us silent and uncomfortable. They were subtle enough that we had to read between the lines. It was never a full and direct crossing of boundaries, but it was enough to render us speechless.

The mental side of any sport is important to train. The mind is a muscle too. In short, because of my perfectionism and highly secretive approach to handling it, my mental game overtook my physical potential. The thing that had brought me the most joy in life was doing the opposite. I didn't celebrate successes. I became curt when others checked in with me, never mentioning the mistakes I was ruminating on. I was hard to talk to because of the efforts used to hide the self-deprecation boiling within me. When questioned, I said I was fine and buried my feelings to maintain the façade of being the golden child. I used my intellect to talk myself out of conflict or worry.

I was known for being a shooter, so when I wasn't hitting, I was a failure. I was also known for being able to read the floor and deliver the ball. So when I turned the ball over, I was a failure. The war I waged on myself, combined with the horrible relationship I had with my head coach, made me simultaneously hate the sport and myself. In my junior year, I admitted I no longer wanted to play in college. Instead, I became fixated on figuring out how I would survive the next practice. I stopped learning about the recruitment process and started sharing with my supporters that I wasn't even sure I could finish out my high school career. I knew that I was not a quitter, but I began to resent the sport and dread the practices, sometimes feeling sick to my stomach at the thought of having to lace up my Jordans again. I knew that my perfectionism would run circles around me and once my coach started in on me, I would use his added fuel to self-destruct at the first opportunity I could get to be alone. And that's what I did. I mentally tallied my mistakes and spent more time deciding how I would punish myself than on resetting to do what was right for my team (I was clearly not the leader I thought I was). The relaxation and recovery strategies I should have been implementing after a long practice were substituted for long nights lying awake, trying to change what couldn't be changed (and didn't need to be). My identity held firm as an athlete, but I was slowly letting go of the dreams I had developed as a child, unaware of just how much I was mourning.

My junior year was the most stressful in that a compilation of aggravators resulted in the worst bout of self-destruction I had weathered up to that point. I remained loyal to my studies and was serious about the next step of my academic career. Coming to terms with the fact that I was losing my steam and opportunities for an athletic scholarship, studying for the SAT became a top priority. The self-imposed pressure to excel became worse than ever before. My home life was rocky, at best, not between my parents and me but between the two of them. I felt powerless to quiet the harsh emotional blows they would deliver to each other that somehow always seemed to leave me sore and broken the next day. Basketball had always been such a relief from the rest of the world. But it no longer served as the outlet I needed to deal with the secrets I kept. Trigger warning. The severity of my primary method of coping—cutting—escalated. I avoided changing clothes around teammates and wore armbands to cover up the damage, claiming I was trying to be like my favorite NBA player, Allen Iverson (not a total lie). It was a phenomenal excuse that never resulted in questions. However, I began needing to wear more in ways that did not set the fashion trend I hoped would catch on.

Coach Faigl was the coach highlighted in the excerpt that started this chapter. She was our JV coach and associate head coach for varsity. She was a former state champion and a total badass. Surprisingly short like me with straight brown hair that she always pulled back into a ponytail, she still looked like a baller. We hit it off from the start, and I had immense respect for her approach. She was genuine, unafraid, smart, and consistent. She became a mentor, not just in sports but in life, because she was also a teacher, something I aspired to be. She was someone I slowly learned to confide in (the limited amount of disclosure I would allow, anyway). I never directly admitted that I was cutting, but she knew I was severely self-flagellating and expressed worry about how I coped with that. She knew I struggled with hiding the tumultuous relationship between my parents and that I was stressed about the revolving door of lost and found love with my childhood sweetheart. I'd scratch the surface, dangling the carrot of vulnerability in front of her, but I stayed just guarded enough to maintain a strong sense of self-preservation. To my dismay, her discovery of my relationship with cutting was something I was not able to render invisible like other aspects of my struggles. I still experience a lot of guilt and shame for my unwanted exposure and what happened after.

Our relationship suffered as we navigated how to handle the fact that there were now two people who knew my secret. Following the detection, Faigl made it clear that she had two obligations. One was to report it to appropriate school personnel, and the other was to inform my parents. She wanted to give me some control, so she required that I alert my parents. I fought her hard, but she held firm. I can only imagine the fear she must have felt and the responsibility she was under to be sure I could keep myself safe. She reported to the school first. After an unsuccessful attempt by the high school counselor to persuade me to open up to her, Faigl was notified that I had refused intervention. She spoke with me via phone and heard me out as I spewed misplaced rage toward her.

"I refuse to talk to the school counselor or tell my parents. You don't even get it. I can't do that. I won't. I can't believe you would do this. I didn't even want you to know. How could you?!"

She wasn't fazed, though, and matter-of-factly insisted, "Tasha, I know this is hard. On your lunch break, I need you to drive over to my classroom. Your life is more important than your need to feel in control right now. We can call your parents together. At least one of them." Fuming mad but also well aware of the power differential, I knew my dad was more distant and unemotional and that I could manipulate the conversation in a way that would put to bed any further need for discussion. My anger was visceral, and I couldn't determine if I was angrier at having to disclose to my dad or because I couldn't use my persuasion skills to convince her otherwise. After a last-ditch failed effort to bargain with Faigl, my shaky hands dialed his number and ... I lied through my teeth.

"What?" he answered.

"Dad, I'm with Coach Faigl, and she is making me call to tell you something stupid. I have been really stressed lately and cut myself a little bit. It was the first time, it is stupid, and I won't do it again. It is stupid that I have to call you, but Faigl is forcing me. DO NOT TELL MOM."

His mind was a total blur, and he could barely understand what he was hearing because, after all, I was the golden child.

"Well, are you going to do it again?" he asked.

"NO. I just said that. This call is completely unnecessary. Educational formality," I snapped back.

"Okay, then. You got it handled. See you tonight."

I was shaking and couldn't look at Faigl any longer. I asked if I could leave and stormed out. I had never been so furious with anyone in my life. Looking back now, I see that it was just embarrassment and shame unfairly disguised as her perceived betrayal.

Unbeknownst to me at the time, she had also disclosed her discovery to both of my other coaches and kept them in the loop about how she assessed my mental state on any given day. She began making the call to pull me from games or separate me during practices when I seemed to be having a particularly difficult time resetting from a mistake. I spent many nights after practices and games sitting with her one-on-one. I was still vague and tentative in the way I shared my struggles, but I said enough to allow her to see a bit of my pain and guide me in the best ways she knew how.

I realized that some of my peers had caught on to my habit as well. In some ways, this pushed me closer to her because I felt a strong desire to maintain the image of perfection I had created and sustained with my teammates. If my friends wondered, they kept their questions to themselves. I don't think anyone knew how to address it or cope with their own shock that *I* could do something like that to myself. Plus, I wasn't the most welcoming of discussion, especially for something so personal. After all, I was the girl with endless amounts of *potential*. I was good at everything I did and was thought to have it all. In many ways, I did have it all; I just didn't see it.

My last two seasons were huge letdowns. We weren't winning literally or figuratively; we were just trying to survive. As teammates, we had a fierce loyalty to each other and focused on making memories that would last a lifetime. It was about more than basketball. Knowing we couldn't trust the leader gave us a chance to bond in ways that carried us through the most difficult moments. Our head coach's out-of-touch comments compounded. I came home almost every night irate and mentally defeated. I would repeat a few of his lines to my parents. My dad talked my mom down as she put her mama bear gloves on and insisted on reporting him.

"Tasha, we just can't keep seeing you be this upset. We need to say something. This isn't okay, let us help you!"

These attempts at support provoked me. I would exclaim, "No way. This is my problem. I'll handle it. I don't need my parents sticking up for me. I AM FINE."

No one was going to fight my battles for me. For better or worse, I chose to stick out this fight with basketball until the bitter end. I logically knew that I didn't have to keep playing if I didn't want to. My parents reminded me all the time. There was an abundance of encouragement and praise, and I was *never* forced to tough it out. Regardless of how I played, I was showered with positivity from all angles, especially from my mom. I could have laid down in the middle of the floor, sobbing for the entire game, and she would have congratulated me on how well I stayed still and how steady my stream of tears was. I had more support than anyone could have asked for, and I was given every opportunity to be helped. I just couldn't figure out how to support myself or let others in.

A few weeks before regionals my senior year, our head coach was ejected from a game and placed on leave for the rest of the season due to instructing a teammate of mine to purposefully injure an opponent with abnormal amounts of force because of a foul call he disagreed with. Rightfully enraged, parents from the other team followed our bus to the restaurant where we were getting dinner, and a dangerous physical altercation was only narrowly avoided. That was the event that sealed the deal on his tenure, and he was fired two weeks after the conclusion of my senior year. There is much contemplation about what could have been had we had a better leader. We failed to reach our goals. It was a hard pill to swallow but expected, given that we couldn't trust or respect our head coach. Additionally, the failures of my personal athletic goals became painstakingly visible. I didn't make all-state because I was too inconsistent. Even though I frequently led statistical categories for assists and made three-pointers, there were nights of poor production when I might as well have left the gym.

After a mistake, I became perpetually fixated on staring at the bench, just waiting for the whistle to blow and signify my walk of shame. That anticipation did nothing for my ability to stay present and move on to the next play. The perfection did not secure the external praise that would come from an all-state nod. I left empty-handed. I felt that the time and effort for the better part of my young development got me nothing in the end. I carried a surfeit of what-if questions with no way of ever playing them out. Years of effort all came down to what?

The perception of wasted time and unresolved grief.[9] The *potential* became embers that turned to ashes quickly, with no chance to rebuild a stronger fire.

In reflecting on what makes me *me*, I cannot exclude the importance of basketball and what it taught me about who I am and who I could be. Analyzing its impact on my life has to take place within the framework of gains and losses.[10] Distance between my career ending and now has allowed me to combat the conclusion I had previously come to: that it was all for nothing, just wasted time and energy. That is simply not true. On the one hand, it manufactured steadfast habits for my relentless dedication to the pursuit of excellence. Reluctantly, I admit that it exposed me to an experience of undeniable failure that is both necessary and healthy for my evolution as a person (even though my perfectionism will barely allow me to type that sentence). On the other hand, it delivered the blocks I used to build the foundation from which I have approached all of my other endeavors off the court. Once an athlete, always an athlete. My mindset toward life continues to reflect the lessons I learned in the athletics environment. Some lessons I hold with high regard and respect, crediting them for their assistance in the accolades I have scored and the confidence I have garnered. Other lessons I recognize have influenced a tendency to be a bit (or a lot) self-destructive in my rapacious quest for achievement. I fell victim to often latching onto the wrong messages of mental toughness:[11] the pursuit of perfection and an inclination to hang my self-worth on the next achievement milestone that suddenly means nothing to me once it's in my hands.

Stepping away from the sport was bittersweet. I was relieved not to have to deal with our head coach or my inner tugs of war anymore. I had nightmares for years about the first day of practice, where I doubted my ability to survive another season. I would wake up sweating, so thankful that I never had to deal with that again. Conversely, I lost who I was, and I lost my team.[12] The built-in, forced family was no more. I had no idea what to do with the free time outside of academics that was now freed up. This confusion extended beyond my own perception, which did not make things easier. Other people suddenly had a challenging time talking to me too. For nearly my whole life, I was greeted with questions about basketball and school. When my career was over, I could see people try to stop themselves in the moment or fall over their own words as they had to think about what else they could ask. It became painfully clear that no one knew what any of my other interests, passions, or hobbies were. Hell, I didn't know what they were. I had no clue what other aspects of identity made me *me*. Plus, not following through with my D1 goal also shattered my image of perfection. I was flummoxed, which resulted in me throwing myself even harder into my academic pursuits. I was grieving the loss of the athletic part of my identity, and I had no clue how to verbalize that or even begin to cope with it effectively. Being a standout student was the only other thing I was known for. My competitive nature still ran strong, so I transferred it to setting goals to beat myself by excelling at the college level.

Once again, it's crucial to repeat that no one but me is responsible for how I chose to handle the emotions I didn't want to feel. I didn't accept the human version of myself and thus felt like I couldn't put my whole self out into the world. I unintentionally harmed those who cared for me along the way, and I couldn't see it in the moment. Now, I feel much regret about that. I apologized to my old teammates and coaches, who graciously allowed me to quiz them on their memories, but I do not feel that saying sorry makes up for it. Perfectionism bred a self-absorption I am not proud of. I had a strong need to control anything and everything. I hated that my image was intricately intertwined with having respiratory issues (although I now know that my perception was exaggerated due to my internalized shame about it). I was devastated that we failed to reach our potential as a team and that I gave up on my individual goals as a player. I felt powerless over the ups and downs of injuries and having to adjust my training to heal my body. I had a horrible relationship with my head coach, and that challenged my worth. I hid the stress from other areas of life, too, trying so hard to take control of things that were out of my hands. It added up to being too much to handle alone. I craved a way to control my mind and body and to escape from the constant self-criticism that buried me alive. It is sad but no surprise to me that once I graduated, I cut off most of the people from that time of my life. The shame of what I thought I was hiding so well (and likely wasn't) was too much for me to admit. I don't believe I was ever the brunt of rumors that could have "ruined" my reputation. But I had rejected so many parts of who I had misguidedly summed myself up to be that I didn't want to be remembered by others as someone I was trying to forget. Yet again, I was zooming in on the minuscule remnants of imperfection that I thought added up to my total worth—zero. I put myself on an island, believing that I was an exception no one could understand. What a crock of shit.

There's something more to be said about the external experience of being an athlete. The pressure I added to my plate was compounded with the image I latched onto and was intensified by how others spoke about me. My reputation in my family and throughout the community was of an all-star student and athlete. The stands were packed with a huge section devoted to my ever-supportive family. My family—my grandparents, especially—have talked joyfully about this time in our lives both during and after my basketball career. These memories are some of the happiest of their lives. My mom and Grandma Pryde never missed a single game in twelve years, home or away. Truly, not a single game. They were as much my friends' and coaches' mom and grandma as they were my own. The bonds built throughout those years allowed for dynamic belonging, not only for us as teammates but also for our families. Our involvement in sports shaped their identities too. Our moms were known as basketball moms and our dads as basketball dads. I'm shocked that in recollecting all of this now, I remember very little about the statistics and objective data of the games I used to make myself sick over. Instead, I am left with the connections that carried me through those years and helped shape the person who writes these words now (some connections I am honored to report I still have). I considered myself a failure for cheating my family out of four more years of memories from a college career. There is grief in not only the loss of my identity but in how my family was forced to reshape theirs as well. They, too, needed to find ways to fill the time that used to be taken up by our travel adventures. They, too, had to figure out who they were without their star player.

It is no surprise that I didn't touch a ball for several years after graduation. It symbolized retraceable failure, its circular shape representing the never-ending rotation of intrusive regret. There were so many things I wanted to erase. The sounds of squeaking shoes and bouncing balls were unwanted reminders of the grief that comes from goals unaccomplished. The echoes of whistles and the release of the latest pair of Jordans sparked misdirected hatred for the sport. It was my choice to play, yet it brought a fierce sense of inadequacy. We had talent, passion, chemistry, and the want to, but the intended outcomes never followed. Accepting that we can engage in the process and still suffer an unwanted result was (and still is) dizzying. There is also a grieving process around my neglect of how important the mental aspects of the game were. I didn't have the emotional tools to build a better relationship with my mistakes, to practice mindfulness in a way that propelled my game forward rather than keeping me stuck on repeat with plays from the past I could do nothing about. Self-talk, moderating anxiety, and visualizing success were things I never even considered.[13] Sadly, pushing through pain and ignoring what my body was trying to tell me was how I came to define mental toughness.

Guilt and shame are the primary emotions in my fallout with basketball. Facing the guilt, especially toward what I put Coach Faigl (and others) through, led to waves of harsh self-condemnation. I am flabbergasted and forever appreciative that she gave me my first true taste of the necessary, albeit unflattering, side of vulnerability. I have mad respect for her willingness to risk me hating her forever in order to keep me safe. I hope that my ability to do this for other athletes now in my career can serve as a meager token of appreciation for what she taught me. At the same time, I am both ashamed and saddened that I was the culprit of the traumatic experiences that she (and others) had to endure in order to support me. I shudder at the pain and fear it likely caused to be powerless comrades left with no game plan of how to help me fight my own worst enemy: me. I am sorry for this. Reliving this disgust during my interviews for this chapter was excruciating but necessary. I had to acknowledge, name, and sit with the ugly sides of who I was at that time and recognize that those traits aren't fixed and don't align with my values, but I still have to face them in order to grow. I apologized and had to admit I was wrong and that I caused harm. The truth is, it was my responsibility. I cannot go back and change anything, even though there are definitely pieces that I would. Simultaneously, I can acknowledge that without things happening as they did, I would not be who I am in this moment, *and* I recognize there are things about who I am in this moment I frankly still dislike and wish to reject entirely. I am exhausted by the vacillating joy and devastation my experience as an athlete brought me. It is an identity I still hold dear to my heart and believe I always will. It's no surprise that I pursued a career path focusing on ways to help other athletes avoid some of the residue left from the avoidance of mourning the varied losses I encountered as an athlete. It's also not ironic that I still experience fits of shame when I have to admit to the collegiate, professional, and Olympic athletes that I work with that I have no idea what it's like to achieve the elite success (and failure) they have. The lessons learned in the athletics environment have made me a formidable challenger to the enemies in life, both internal and external. The connections created due to the mutual pursuit of hard-to-achieve goals create lifelong bonds that cannot be broken. It's a true chosen family, for better or worse. I still love basketball, and I still honor and respect the process of being an athlete. And after playing the game, I was never the same again.

9

THE GAMBLE OF DENIAL

At the end of the chapter that taught you about my great-grandma Claire, I mentioned that the torch was passed to her eldest daughter, Dora, to lead the family. Aunt Dora (great-aunt to me) steered the ship valiantly, keeping our seas fairly calm and no doubt making her mother proud until her own weathered body began to succumb to the inexorable. It all started with gallbladder surgery. It was 2006, and Aunt Dora (a.k.a. Aunt Do—pronounced "dough") was sixty-seven years old. Following the surgery, she was informed that she was positive for hepatitis C, a viral infection that causes liver inflammation and, if left untreated, can contribute to severe liver damage. Her modest existence was challenged by her doctor as he asked what she thought were violating questions about typical ways individuals can be infected. After a thorough investigation, her medical history revealed that she likely contracted the disease back in 1959 while receiving a blood transfusion after the delivery of her second child. Regardless of the cause, her examination results couldn't be argued: her liver was not well.

Initially, this diagnosis was met with shock, denial, and confusion. It was an equally infuriating and unbelievable diagnosis, especially because of the effect hepatitis C can have on one particular organ, the liver. The liver is an organ our family tends to have a turbulent relationship with. She had one of the strongest vendettas against it due to her husband dying from cirrhosis nearly four decades earlier at the ripe age of thirty; it was a result of uncontrolled alcoholism. She hated alcohol and hated its impact on the liver. It was an organ that left her as a young widow with four small children and a sixth-grade education. An organ that left her responsible for providing for her family with no time to protest the reality of her pain. And now, it was an organ that once again threatened her livelihood and the well-being of her family. She wasn't going to have it. She didn't drink, so how could she get sick with a disease that only heavy drinkers died from? Her inability to make sense of it served her denial well.[1] She was forever dismissing the truth of her prognosis and the definitiveness of her disease. In her mind, she was going to get better. Her determination to live was something she expressed frequently, leading to a complicated process of how we evolved as a family to cope with the plethora of losses we suffered over the next five years.

Following the diagnosis, she felt better for a while, so hepatitis C was filed in the back of her mind, never seeing the light of day in her waking thoughts. Aunt Do was a private person, and given that she was now our matriarch, she was intent on keeping her health status a secret. Consequently, there was no discussion, likely intentional on her part, of what this diagnosis might mean for her in time. For some, if no questions are asked and no information is gathered, it is easier to halt the sense-making and eventual acceptance of your own impending death.[2] Instead, she went about her life as usual, continuing to overwork herself and execute her leadership responsibilities for our family. The hardships she faced taught her that complaining was an unnecessary evil and a distraction from meeting obligations.

A few months post-surgery, the first sign that something was off came in the form of complaints of constant, dull pains in her upper right abdominal cavity where the liver sits. We could track her pain due to the frequency with which she would hold that area and show glimmers of hurt in her facial expressions. Quietly and usually when only a few were around, she admitted that the pain was intense and would not go away. Initially, the pain didn't stop her from doing anything, but slowly, it became sharper, causing unavoidable halts in her movements. The pain was inconsistent, and she was inconsistent in reporting it to us. The disturbance was slight enough that it wasn't cause for concern. There was an overwhelming group-think mentality,[3] strengthening faux security that she would overcome the battle her liver had in store for her. She was stern about ensuring that we either downplay or hide her illness altogether. She instructed her kids not to share medical updates when approached by loved ones. She even went as far as to blatantly call her kids liars (not her greatest moments) when they tried to deliver honest reporting from doctor's visits. Consequently, many were shocked at learning about her illness. The unified denial of death held our family together like weather-resistant adhesive, defying all logic.

Next, exhaustion overtook her. Even though she rarely complained of fatigue, we started to notice its effects due to the way it peeled away layers of her iron-clad routines. Her house, always so spotless and organized, began to collect dust on surfaces and crumbs on counters, an unprecedented situation. It became common to see the butter left out on the counter or food that a visitor brought over left hastily uncovered. Attempts to engage her for explanations resulted in either a brief scolding, reminding us to mind our own business, directions to remedy the situation, or being ignored altogether (a mean habit she executed exquisitely). The best we would get was the least frightening admission: that she was tired and didn't know why. We knew why, though. Her illness was having tangible effects on her, observable evidence we could not disprove. Her meticulous efforts toward maintaining her dwelling place and her self-care were beginning to falter. And it scared us. Fear made it easier to shy away from stating the obvious, and because we wanted to remain respectful, we didn't press the issue. Even so, her growing fragility didn't need verbal confirmation to show itself.

As the aches and fatigue worsened, she found herself increasingly in the role of the patient. The cared for, not the caretaker. This change chipped away at her identity[4] and led to periodic misguided resentment toward anyone who tried to help. Her career had been built on ensuring others' homes and responsibilities were well tended to. She was as good at taking care of others as she was bad at taking care of herself. The irony in how she would lecture others to take medication and downright lie to us about taking her own was not lost on any of us. She was a caregiver to the old and wealthy in the community, but taking a turn to sit on their thrones challenged her perception of her own strength. It was something she had problems managing, which, unfortunately, decreased her willingness to make the necessary changes to prolong her life. As bystanders, our complacency resulted from confusion about how to address the slow deterioration. How do you initiate a conversation with someone about their own death when they so blatantly refuse to admit its impending reality?

As the discernable pain and lethargy became unwanted companions, we began to see the illness manifest more visibly with the yo-yo-ing of swelling, water retention, and widespread inflammation that overtook the lower quadrants of her body. There were times when her legs would swell to more than double their size. She was prescribed a medication called Lasix, designed to help reduce extra fluid, but her medication compliance was atrocious. The second-best solution was compression stockings, which she fought, not liking how constricting they were. She expressed fear that her skin felt so tight it was going to tear from movement or contact, so we needed to be careful when touching her. We pled with her, "Aunt Do, you have to keep your legs elevated. You have to keep these socks on, and you need to take this medication right now!" She was too hard-nosed for any follow-through.

This was also about the time our attention became focused on her relationship with sodium, given the link between swelling and the build-up of too much sodium that is known to affect liver operations. Her doctor explained that these episodes were communicating that her sodium levels were signaling alarms of her liver's malfunctioning. His advice was a diet low in sodium, which was, essentially, a prison sentence in the food department for her. Although she didn't often opt to over-salt her food, her go-to food choices all happened to contain naturally high levels of sodium. She loved ramen noodles, bread, all varieties of Mexican and Chinese food, salted chips, and cured meats like bologna and spam. Her obdurate demeanor meant she could rarely be persuaded to test her taste buds otherwise. We lectured her incessantly about the necessity of replacing high-sodium foods with lower ones. Enter the endless stream of us playing dietician with her. This power struggle made her feel like she was losing control of her own life. No one had ever told her how to live her life. In fact, she had spent her whole life doing that very thing for all of us. Food was no exception. It was a symbol of the way she led our family and brought us together, both physical and emotional nourishment. Food became an enemy, alongside our persistent demands, and she felt it was defeating. Her reluctance to hand over her leadership title typically won out. She continued to eat what she wanted when no one was around and secretly convinced each of us to deliver the goods she was craving. She knew what she was doing, putting us in an impossible position where we couldn't be disrespectful by not following through with a demand. When she asked us to do something, we did it. It was either have her be angry with us for not giving in to her wishes or sneak her something that made us feel more connected and righteous in the moment. She conned me into several unapproved trips for an ice cream cone at the McDonald's drive-thru or the occasional chicken fried rice. It was always good to feel we had made a good move in her eyes.

The inability to sustain the necessary changes in her diet led to further irreversible damage. Enter ammonia, a chemical the body produces during the digestion of protein. It is processed in the liver, and when levels begin to rise, it signifies that the liver is officially too diseased to process the chemical effectively. To manage symptoms, she was prescribed a chalky green liquid substance called Lactulose. She was supposed to drink the equivalent of two shots to help reduce the amount of ammonia in her blood. Predictably, she hated the taste of it and would either downright refuse, only take some, or draw the process out for hours at a time, rendering the eventual consumption useless. As the ammonia levels rose in her blood, the chemical had nowhere else to go but her brain because the liver was no longer doing its job. The result was horrifying bouts of disorientation. Her eyes were open, yet no one was home. A fogginess overcame her, and although her body was in the room with us, her mind was completely detached. Her body would go limp, which made it more difficult to help ensure her safety. She wasn't able to communicate who or where she was. Sometimes, these episodes came on rapidly without warning, and other times, we had clues to prepare us. Once the disorientation hit, we had no choice but to deliver her to the emergency room to restore her cognitive capacity. There, they would give her intravenous infusions of sodium benzoate and phenylacetate to normalize her ammonia levels then discharge her with instructions to resume oral medication.

Regardless of the array of symptoms or the severity of her last episode, she remained staunch in her belief that she would get better. We would ask her how she was, and even when we *knew* she was worse, her response was consistently, "Oh jita, I'm better." During doctor's appointments, she was respectful, but when they reported on her dreary prognosis, we saw her mentally check out and stare at the wall. When appointments were over, she'd remark, "You know, that guy is nice, but he has no idea what he's talking about. I am fine." Her stubbornness was equally comical and irritating. Despite the repeated negative reports, she didn't appear to wallow. I wonder now who she was really doing this for: herself, us, or both? And was it helpful or harmful? On the one hand, it forced us to recognize and communicate that she wasn't a reliable source on her own experiences, which led to imperative teamwork to share observations among each other and her doctors. We spoke for her in a way we had accepted she wouldn't do on her own. We became more unified, which perhaps was a subconsciously intended consequence of her ineptitude to admit her mortality.[5] On the other hand, her opposition tested our patience. She was likely preoccupied, undergoing her own grief process related to the unfavorable changes in our family that she feared would follow her absence. She didn't want to die because she believed that no one would care for her family the way she did. She was right.

This pattern persisted for nearly five years. Overall, we had good experiences with the many stops in the ER and eventual longer hospital stays. Although these times shed light on the seriousness of her condition, they were also filled with a lot of laughter and strategizing. One of the most consistent patterns was how Aunt Do communicated with the hospital staff.

When they first entered for any reason, they made their way to her and said, "Hi Dora. Can you please tell me your last name and date of birth?"

At first, this was no bother to her. "Trujillo, six-sixteen-nineteen-thirty-nine." Quickly, though, this became a huge pet peeve. She obeyed without protest but rolled her eyes and got terser, executing the task with pressured speech and the smallest hint of annoyance.

The medical staff would leave the room, and she would complain, "Don't they know my name by now? What's wrong with them? Pendejos."

"Aunt Dora, be nice! It's their job!" we would reprimand through belly laughs. Countless attempts to explain that they were doing it for legal and medical purposes were wasted.

She stood her ground, doubling down on her name-calling, "Eeeee jackasses, don't they know that by now?"

The humor was helpful. We had spells of hope that would resurface, typically sparked by Aunt Do's love of gambling. As sick as she would be, if the opportunity to gamble presented itself, she magically seemed able to gather herself long enough for a quick trip to Central City (a small mountain town where gambling is legal in Colorado) to hit the slot machines. We were panicked that even the stress from the drive could send her into a downward spiral. At the same time, the thrill she oozed for these trips gave us misleading hope that she'd heal. Having something to look forward to that brings pure joy can do wonders for even the sickest of souls. When she was gambling, we could push her death further from our minds each time she felt the rush of pulling that slot machine lever. Gambling seemed to give her a leg up in coping with her pain, too, as if the excitement of what was to come provided the medicine she needed to forget her internal decay. Maybe our fears were misplaced. Did we do the right thing by trying to keep her home and safe? While we were trying to prolong her life, she was trying to live the time she had left.[6] Maybe these questionable decisions were actually a strategy on her part, moves to utilize the time she had left in a meaningful way.

But back in Laramie, she struggled to relinquish control at the hospital.

"Jita, I am so cold. They keep it too cold in here," she would whisper.

"Aunt Do, talk to the nurses. You have to tell them what you need. They can't read your mind," I remember saying.

"Oh no, they're busy. I don't need their help with anything."

Sometimes, she'd ask me, "Jita, I hurt. What can I do for the pain?"

"I'll tell them to get you something," I'd reply, eventually giving up on pushing her to self-advocate. She vacillated between giving in and fighting; her grief became prominent. She suffered much loss in the process of letting go of her autonomy and admitting that she needed help from others.[7] I can't imagine how desolate and heartbreaking this must have been for her. Collectively, fear grew in the quiet recognition that she didn't know how to care for herself anymore. So not only did she have her grief, but she could also feel ours in the air too.

Consequently, she had valid shifts in demeanor. When the fear became too overwhelming, she swatted at it. Sometimes, it was met with laughter. You could hear her comedic relief from down the hallway as she furthered connections among all of us with her quick wit, short attention span, and lifetime of smile-worthy memories.

I'd walk in, and she'd start, "Hi Ugly, how are you?" I would begin to respond but be cut off quickly by something else that seemed more pressing. "Eeee, I have so many decorations to put up for Christmas. What are you doing today, Ugly?" and the pattern continued. Other times, she batted at her fear with increased irritability and uncensored, unsolicited feedback. Although likely not intended to be downright mean, sometimes her verbal exchanges could carry a massive emotional blow.

If your appearance wasn't satisfactory, she had no problem letting you know. "Ayy jita, you don't look good today."

If food was brought that wasn't up to her standards, she didn't care who the cook was. "This doesn't taste good. I want more salt."

All those thoughts that she had previously taught us to keep to ourselves began to spill out of her mouth without apology. Although usually funny if not directed at you, when it was your turn to be struck, it really knocked you out. Grief can pack a punch.

In the last year of her life, she had three terrifying ambulance rides. The first came about a year before she died. Observing the pure terror of her children as well as the seriousness of the medical professionals tore down a few bricks from her avoidance wall. The second time played out eerily similar to the first about six months later. Reluctant agreement for more help came only after our begging and pleading; a few more avoidance bricks tumbled to the ground, producing grief debris that contaminated the air. Fear of her falling and the intensity of each disorientation episode became harder to manage, so it was decided it would be best for her to stay at the home of her middle daughter, Bev. She wasn't there for more than a couple of days before another crisis struck. She tried to get out of bed on her own and took a hard fall, a combination of her physical fragility and confusion. The ER promptly admitted her, expressing concern over her grave condition and giving no mention of a return home, a stark difference from previous interactions with ER staff. This time was different.

After they made her comfortable in a room, the hospitalist asked for a family meeting with the key medical decision-makers, another first. Aunt Do's four children and her three oldest grandchildren were present. The attending physician was a stern, older gentleman with a thick gray mustache who wasted no time beating around the bush. In simple and direct terms, he began.

"Dora's condition is declining rapidly. There is not a chance that she will get better. I want to be clear with you about your options. Prolonging the medication will sustain unnecessary suffering, and there's no chance it will reverse her condition." He paused but didn't wait for any response and shared two options. "We can stabilize and release her, but it will only rinse and repeat the same cycle. She will be back in the hospital quickly. Or, we can move her to hospice. I will leave you to talk and come back soon. Are there any questions?"

It is unclear who asked what, but he doubled down on his point that hospice was the most humane and compassionate decision the family could make. He informed them, "Once we take her off the medication, it is possible that she could rally, but this would be deceitful reassurance. Although you may second-guess your choice, her improvement will only be temporary. I suspect she has at most six to seven days." With no questions asked, he left them to talk amongst themselves. Just like that, one conversation led to the heart-wrenching need to make a life-changing (and ending) decision no one ever yearns for.[8] They were faced with a crushing ordeal. Do you accept defeat and allow your parent to go comfortably, or do you keep fighting, trying to salvage as much time as possible?

No one was ready to say goodbye, and frankly, they all had been living in various levels of denial until the doctor burst their bubble of delusion. The decision would come down to her four children, all in different places with their own grief and unique family desires to consider. A giant hindrance in this process was that because of Aunt Do's unrelenting denial of her own death, she never spoke with her children about her wishes if she couldn't communicate them herself. There was no will, no DNR, and no informal preparations to guide them. Now, they had to make ambiguously rushed decisions for someone who may or may not regain consciousness. They had hefty doses of shock piercing through their veins, so the realization that her life was coming to an end was an unexpected kick of reality to the gut. The wind was knocked out of them, making it nearly impossible to orient themselves to the task at hand.

What would you do in this moment? Would you keep providing potentially life-prolonging medication with harsh side effects, or would you accept death for what it is and move to make your parent comfortable? And, how would you begin to talk about that decision with so many hearts and opinions to consider?

With Aunt Do's inability to participate, they ultimately decided comfort care and a transition to hospice was the best decision given the circumstances, though none of them felt secure in this choice. To make matters worse, there was some pushback about the decision by Aunt Do's siblings, further illustrating the mental bargaining that overcomes the heart. But the decision was made. To accommodate for the size, strength, and auditory prowess of our family, the medical staff were kind enough to move her into a room with an adjoining leisure room where we could comfortably fit the constant rounds of visitors. Once she was settled, the family made phone calls to loved ones. Selfishly, there was some hesitation about spreading this update due to what it would mean for the quality time we had left with her. We had to juggle competing needs not just among ourselves but also with our large extended family, as many of them arrived to say their goodbyes.

The arrival of extended family was another sign of death knocking.

As the doctor suspected, once the medication was stopped, she did rally for a while and was mostly coherent over the first four days, only somewhat gliding in and out between our world and that which comes next. She was able to have full conversations, laugh, reminisce, and even assure us she would get better. She delivered orders, insisting that all of her visitors were well cared for, especially in the food department. "Corina, make some more enchiladas and invite everyone over. Make sure there is enough for everyone," we all remember her asserting.

Sadly, in her moments of lucidity, there were never any follow-up conversations to ask her about her final wishes, likely born of fear, discomfort, and devastation. She made quick and quiet comments, showing some awareness of her imminent death.

I recall her leaning over toward her granddaughter, Sarah, and asking, "Am I dying?"

Sarah paused, taking a deep breath, only being courageous enough to admit, "Grandma, you're really sick. We don't know what's going to happen yet."

I sat frozen, my body screaming as it tried to run away from my breaking heart. I was so glad she didn't ask me; I had no blueprint for how to answer.

Another time, she launched into problem-solving mode with her youngest daughter, Corina. "You need to keep the family together and do right by what I taught you ..." Then, turning to me, "Jita, how was class today?" Just as quickly as she'd whisper the words, she'd refocus on something else, pretending as if the exchange never occurred.

Sometimes while a bit more befuddled, she spoke about conversations she was having with our deceased loved ones, a chilling foreboding.[9] For instance, she once told Sarah, "Eeee jita, I talked with my mom today." She paused, looking through Sarah as if something else was happening in the empty space behind her. "Who is that man behind you?"

Sarah looked around, never able to register a human form matching her description, and reluctantly tried to set the record straight. "No one is in here, Grandma."[10] No amount of heat could quiet the chills we felt in these moments.

As predicted, her last two days she was barely conscious. Her mornings were spent with her sisters and cousins praying the rosary around her. When she was unconscious, the family played music, prayed, and carried on as if she were just taking a nap, trying to be as natural as possible so as not to scare her with our own death anxiety and existential dread. There is some peace and comfort in knowing that although she was private, she needed and felt our presence strung together with the comings and goings of the people she dedicated her life to. In fact, those days provided us with some of the most quality bonding experiences we have ever had as a family, a gain in the face of great loss.

We received education to help us better understand what to look out for in her final moments. It was a huge adjustment, for me in particular, to shift my focus from insisting more bloodwork be taken, asking for updates on her lab values, researching what they meant, and exhausting my resources for answers on what could lead to positive change. We were well past that now; the numbers no longer had meaning. At the time, it felt like giving up, and I was livid, but in hindsight, perhaps it was instead a genuine display of mental toughness. There is strength in admitting the eventual finality of life.[11] Instead of numbers, our only markers became what we could monitor with our own eyes and hearts. The most memorable observations were how cold her hands and feet felt and the shallow breaths with prolonged time in between them. We could track when her ammonia levels had skyrocketed by increased periods of disorientation. Her eyes would dart about or stare blankly into nothingness. Her head swiveled back and forth somewhat uncontrollably, similar to a real-life bobblehead, but not the kind that made you laugh. What looked like an alert, conscious woman was really being driven by involuntary movements that let us know her body was finally shutting down.

The night of August 3, 2011, dozens of us were gathered at the hospital. Games were played in the adjoining room amid both heartfelt and lighthearted conversations. Corina, Sarah, and Brittany (her granddaughter), volunteered to make a run to grab some late-night Taco Bell. As they returned, they all glanced up toward Aunt Do's room, looking to see who they could spot in the windows. Sarah was the first to break the silence. "Who is that guy?"

They noticed a man sitting in the window and squinted their eyes as they tried to place him. He had his back to the window, and they could see that he was wearing a white, short-sleeved T-shirt with the sleeves crisply folded and what looked like a cigarette pack securely in place. He appeared to have a full head of dark, curly hair, and he seemed to have a darker complexion and broad shoulders. They came up blank, unable to remember who was wearing a white T-shirt.

"No clue ... I've never seen him before," they all agreed. A bit confused but otherwise unaffected, they dropped the matter and carried the food upstairs. As they settled back in, they took a look around both rooms to try to figure out who the mystery man was in the window. The three of them asked about him but were met with nervous glances and blank stares, most of us finding it equally funny and bone-chilling. At first, we challenged their spatial skills, suggesting that they were looking in another patient's room. They countered that they saw others they recognized and even pointed out the same artwork that hung on the walls. This man was in Aunt Do's room; they had no doubts about it. Corina persisted, giving a more descriptive account of their visual recollection.

"I am telling you he was here! Short, broad shoulders, dark skin. White T-shirt with something tucked in his sleeve. He was right here!"

Suddenly, our Aunt Ruth's heart dropped to her toes. With goosebumps rippling through her body but willing to take a risk, she began to explain who she thought it was. "Ayy, jita. That sounds like your dad. I think your dad was here to come and get your mom." She was referring to Aunt Do's husband, now deceased for forty years: Uncle Clarence. She continued, "That's how he dressed, creased to the hilt with the sleeves of his white T-shirt folded over to hold his cigarettes." She stopped, needing silence to steady herself.

Because of his untimely death, neither Corina, Sarah, nor Brittany ever knew him. Corina had been just fifteen months old when her dad died and had no conscious memories of him.

In the moment, this event wasn't given the attention and contemplation it likely deserved. Most of our heads were elsewhere, and to be honest, the potential of what that could have been had us facing the reality of Aunt Do's death and our own spiritual beliefs (or confusion) in a way we were trying hard to avoid. But we knew time was running out.

The next morning, August 4, 2011, the priest visited early and gave her last rites, the final sacrament of anointing of the sick in the Catholic religion. Around 11:00 a.m., Aunt Do's two oldest daughters, Bev and Gloria, decided to run home to shower. They had attempted to leave several times before but couldn't bring themselves to depart due to anxiety that she would die while they were gone. Gloria obsessively felt the limbs of Aunt Do's body, checking to see how cold they were, and whispered into her ear, "Mom, I'll be back soon. Please don't die."

They asked the nurses, "Do we have enough time to go shower and come back?"

A nurse responded, "We can't say for sure, but an hour or so away should be fine."

Around 11:30 a.m., Corina was scrubbing the floor in the adjoining room. She was interrupted by Aunt Terry (one of Aunt Do's sisters-in-law), who aggressively told her, "Jita, hurry, you need to come in. It's time." Corina's stomach dropped, and a wave of nausea overtook her as she took a deep breath. Woozy and unsteady, she got up off her knees and rushed to Aunt Do's bedside. Her brother, Dino, took his position on the side opposite of her, oblivious to the hurried movements of the others in the room. Frantically, the family delivered orders that someone call Bev and Gloria.

Across town, Bev heard her phone ring and immediately felt a stabbing pain in her chest. Her hand was tottering, and her voice was shaky as she answered the call. She heard streams of tears and stuffy noses followed by the agitated elevation of a voice she could not place. "Bev, your mom's taking her last breaths. You need to get back up here now, jita." Bev wanted to plead for her mom to hang on, but instead, she hung up and dialed Gloria while sprinting back out to her car.

Gloria was brushing her teeth when the phone rang. She brought it to her ear, not expecting what was waiting on the other line. Bev's speech was pressured and loud. All she could get out was, "I'm coming back to get you right now! Mom just died." Gloria angrily reacted as she tried to make sense of what she heard. She ran outside to wait for the car, screaming, "No!" over and over again, uncertain if she even ended the call or how her legs had carried her outside.

Meanwhile, Dino and Corina tried their best to turn off the outside world and simply be with their mom in her final seconds. Corina looked over toward Dino, clutching his mom's hand tightly, and exclaimed through tears, "We have to tell her it's okay to let go." Out of respect, several extended family members quietly made their way out of the room to allow her to die in peace, surrounded only by those in her immediate family: two children, one grandchild, two sisters, and one brother. Through clenched teeth, they squeezed her ice-cold hands and told her their goodbyes. Silent waterfalls of tears soaked their faces, and the family all sat together, watching her leave this world, trying to display a united front of undying love and support, both for her and each other. They watched her take one last breath in. Her chest ceased movement, followed by the obnoxious machines announcing the obvious. Corina then instructed Brittany to go get the nurses.

It was only minutes after they announced her death that Bev and Gloria returned. They stormed into the hospital room, Gloria so visibly distressed it sent new waves of woe piercing through the helpless bystanders. She began yelling while running over to the bed, full of anguish, proclaiming, "You promised me, you promised me!" She wrapped her arms around her mom, almost leaping into the bed, trying to pull her up, as if the jolt of human contact would somehow will her heart back to beating. Dino and Morgan (a brother of Aunt Do's) physically intervened to place Aunt Do back in the bed and help move Gloria to another area of the hospital. Heartbreak had overtaken her and was on full display. They knew she meant no harm and encouraged the other women in the room to move toward her with consoling arms. Dyads and triads were formed from the larger group, with one another embracing each other's pain. Echoes of sorrow etched trails of grief through the hospital, with nearly the whole building expressing compassion and heartache as they helplessly watched our family fall apart.

I received the call from my mom as I walked to my car about 11:45 a.m. The second I heard her voice, I knew. I froze and glanced at my two friends, who, just moments ago, I was laughing with about something I could not for the life of me remember anymore. It all seemed too trivial and pointless now.

"Tasha, your Aunt Dora just died. I am so sorry." I grabbed the wall to stabilize my wobbly legs. "Okay, thanks Mom. Are you okay?"

I remember telling myself not to indicate any signs of weakness, to stay strong and not to cry.

"No, I'm going over to Sarah's to watch the kids. Are you okay?"

Of course I said, "Yes, I'm fine." What a fucking lie. I hung up quickly to avoid any faltering of the guise I was trying to maintain. I swallowed for the first time in what felt like hours and told myself that Aunt Do was gone. I had no idea how to move myself through the next moments of my life. I stood in the hallway with the dead phone up to my ear for what felt like an eternity, almost paralyzed. I don't remember what happened next.

Aunt Do's children and siblings got together right away to plan the services. Much of our family from out of town had already arrived or were en route, so it made sense to solidify arrangements quickly. The couple of days following her death were filled with visitors bringing boatloads of food, expressing their own mourning, and simply being present in attempts to ease our aching hearts. Planning proved to be challenging. One of the only things we knew about Aunt Do's death wishes was that she didn't want to be viewed postmortem. Unfortunately, her wishes competed with the needs of her survivors. With little additional knowledge of her wishes, much of it was left up to debate.[12] Tensions ran high. Some wanted a viewing; some didn't. Some felt that having one was needed to aid the rituals that allow for adapting. Some wanted her to be buried; others cremated. This, in particular, brought about serious conflict, given that, at the time, cremation was highly frowned upon in the Catholic faith. Although Aunt Do had briefly admitted her desire to be cremated, it created overwrought conflict among the living. Some wanted the typical long chain of condolence exchanges; some didn't. There was no way to please everyone, and the heightened emotions led to superfluously heated arguments, even for an already passionate family like ours. In the end, a viewing at the funeral home, a closed-casket funeral, cremation, and a condolence line won out.

In their planning, a decision unanimously agreed upon was that they wanted *me* to give the eulogy. I remember being asked by Corina and feeling immediately sick to my stomach but beaming with honor for such an important task. I wanted the job and felt like I was the best person for it, but I was horrified that I wouldn't be able to do her justice and would let the family down. Of all the wishy-washy decisions that occurred with her death, this was not something I could allow them to ever second-guess. As our family put together posterboards of physical pictures, I created a virtual slideshow that we could play following the funeral. Assembling this allowed me to view hours of her life in tandem and sparked conversations for me to gather tidbits of information that would help me form as concise of a story as I could to capture who she was. It was here where it became painfully clear that our matriarch was gone, only this time, there was no security in who might be next to pick up the torch and relight it.

Aunt Do's rosary and funeral services took place five days after she died. They had an uncanny resemblance to Grandma Claire's nearly ten years earlier. The church was overflowing with people packed in like sardines. The front of the church had been converted to a makeshift greenhouse, as plants and flowers covered nearly every inch of visible space. I sat in the second pew at the very end due to the responsibility I was given to speak. The task was enormous, having just a few minutes to ensure every attendee was able to feel her spirit, say that they learned more about who she was, and honor her legacy all at the same time. Until my name was introduced by the priest, I was mostly unable to register what was happening around me. I had been told by one of my great-aunts the day before that it would be better if I didn't cry while delivering my speech (ridiculous, I know). To meet her demand (that I unfortunately agreed with), I recited mantras of bogus mental toughness, trying to rid myself of all vulnerability.

I looked out on the sea of faces, mostly tear-soaked with specks of Kleenex littering the areas in between bodies. I didn't want to make eye contact with anyone, so I found three points I could fixate on in the back of the room to be sure my head moved appropriately in between reading my words and acknowledging each corridor of listeners. I said to myself, *Aunt Do, I love you and hope you like my tribute.* Loud weeps and belly laughter filled the air right on cue. People embraced and consoled one another at just the right moments. At the conclusion, I scanned the faces of those closest to Aunt Do and felt their silent approval. I whispered to her one more time, *I hope I made you proud, Ugly,* and returned to my seat, using every ounce of energy in me to wrestle the tears I wouldn't allow to fall.

We did not bury her right away due to a conflict about the best way to close out the rituals that would commemorate her life. Instead of the cemetery, we gathered for an enormous meal. We took extra care to be sure that every person in the place left feeling overly stuffed and satisfied, just as Aunt Do had taught us to do. In the days after, the food began to dwindle, our out-of-town family made their way home, and we were left to face our new reality. Her burial plans loomed ominously in the distance. Resistance and sidestepping played a strong role in the continual procrastination. It took nearly two months to solidify a date. It was a closed, private burial for her immediate family and a few of us extended loved ones—an invitation I am grateful I received. It was a snowy, bitterly cold day, quite fitting for the way our hearts remained iced over from the storm of her death. What I didn't quite have figured out then was that just as the hurricane-force winds carrying grief drenched us throughout her illness, the same weather patterns were continuing in the aftermath. The wreckage was just as unpredictable and breathtaking. Her loss was (and still is) always right around the corner, waiting for the gusts of reminders to force evacuations of pent-up tears and admissions of sadness, loss, and suffering with no end.

Hepatitis C wasn't discovered until 1989. In 2014, the cure came, but it was three years too late for our family. I was a second-year graduate student when I began to consume research indicating that a new medication was approved by the FDA that could be taken orally once a day for eight to twelve weeks. It had minimal side effects, and it improved the survival rates of hepatitis C to upward of 90 percent. My conflicted feelings were so difficult to decipher. I read and reread the news for days, unable to put words to the visceral experience equitable to high-magnitude earthquakes all throughout my torso. Grief started all over again. I was equally furious she wasn't able to hang on longer and that the scientists behind the breakthrough hadn't sped up their process; clearly, I was looking for someone to blame. I remembered her sadness. There was always bewilderment about the fact that it was her liver. She did not understand how that could happen, given that she never had a relationship with the bottle. And now, so soon after her death, there is a cure?! It wasn't fair. It isn't fair. And then I was (and still am) reminded: life isn't fair.

Aunt Do's illness was long, and although her death was expected, it somehow still felt sudden. There are endless debates that could take place about the effects of sudden versus expected death trajectories.[13] Is a sudden or expected death "easier"? Would you want to intimately befriend fate or be blind to the progression of what may happen with a certain illness? Do you prefer time to process, make sense of, and learn to cope with an inevitable loss, or would you rather the Band-Aid be completely ripped off without warning? Everyone will have unique inclinations, and no one is more right or wrong than anyone else. This is a personal set of needs and likely looks different for every situation, even in the same person's life. What does it look like for you? Slowly watching her decline and dealing with the severe shifts in prognosis was an exhausting emotional roller coaster. The game of denial became an art for most of us, led by her attempts to dissuade us from absorbing the obvious. She tried so hard to keep the secret of her own descent, but were those attempts to appear bulletproof helpful or hurtful? To see her rebound instilled undying hope in a complete recovery, but it was false. To see her suffer led to undeniable truth in death, and it was painful.

Our collective grief was made more difficult because we lacked vital information about her death wishes that could have helped us better prepare. This is a major sore spot for me and something I am known to reprimand my family members about. As I've said, my family tends not to ask questions of providers, perhaps due to discomfort over the stark power differential in the room. This usually leads to sub-par reports after doctor's visits, filled with "I don't know" and "I'm sure it's fine," giving us no strategy to act upon. Cultural barriers and educational oppression also contribute to the difficulty in navigating the medical space for my older relatives. I am not faulting anyone or suggesting that had different questions been asked, her life could have been spared. It couldn't have been. There was no cure for her disease at the time, and her death was fate, just like it is for all of us. However, I do think more communication could have led to helpful shifts in the unfinished blueprint that led us haphazardly through her care. It was a brutal tug of war: a pull to encourage the courageous display of toughness, and a push to honor the inescapable fragility of what it means to be a human.

Not being able to speak fluidly and honestly about death had huge consequences for our family. The decision to move her to hospice care can't be reversed. The impact of the decision continues to instigate questions embodying spiritual, religious, moral, and ethical conflict. Did her children make the "right" decision? Can you ever truly answer that question in a direct and objective way? Since they were raised as devout Catholics, the choice put them in a compromised position to play God in a way that was juxtaposed with their understanding of how the world works. Their internal dissension haunts them. While interviewing them, I saw regret and uncertainty flash across their faces. They were tasked with a horrendous choice with no way of knowing what the future held. They did the best they could with the information they had at the time, but the pain of loss is reignited all over again each time it crosses their minds. The precariousness was visible by violent head shakes, hung heads, and forced admissions of surrender to grief. Questions of whether they made the right decision send haunting chills down their spines. This piece could have been avoided, though. Her death requests could have been addressed before it was too late.[14] No one escapes death, and if our family could have understood the benefit of communicating about it, perhaps their regret wouldn't continue to inflict such deep wounds during the recollection of their decisions.

I often wonder if I could have done more to be helpful in this process too. Although I was frustrated with Aunt Do while it was happening, her lack of communication with the doctors meant she relied more on me, something I reflect on with appreciation now. She knew I had every intention of becoming a doctor (although she struggled to separate psychologist—PhD—from medical doctor—MD. During our daily visits, she'd ask me questions that she should have been asking her actual physician. I never knew the answers outright, but I would figure them out. I spent hours researching her questions, talking with my mom and Grandma Pryde, and consulting with my boss, who was an internal medicine physician. I'd report back in the most digestible way what she needed to do. She'd shrug her shoulders, roll her eyes, and quickly change the subject by interrupting me mid-sentence when she no longer liked what she was hearing. Sometimes I pressed, but her glances were honestly very powerful in achieving her desire to halt the conversation. She did not like what I had to say, yet we both knew I was doing the right thing by her. Sometimes, the most painful thing we can choose to do is still the right thing. I didn't realize it at the time, but she was telling me she trusted me. I was forever annoyed at her ineptness at following through, but she was strengthening my confidence and giving me precious moments with her to bond in emotionally vulnerable ways. I don't know if that was intentional or not, but I know being trusted by her was no small feat. It was hard to impress her and rare to have her outwardly express approval, yet in those moments, she showed me that I mattered to her. And that matters to me.

I want to address something that is delicate and perhaps taboo, but necessary. Watching someone wither from a chronic illness brings terrifying thoughts we reveal to ourselves but never utter out loud. One of the main themes reflected while I was interviewing our family was how frequently we all had unsaid moments of wishing her suffering would stop. In other words, admitting that death would bring relief.[15] Not wanting it but understanding its purpose. For those of us who are religious, that meant praying for God to take her. For those of us who aren't religious, it was just wishing her peace and an escape. Through discussion, I learned that these unspoken invitations of death were met with intense guilt, shame, and embarrassment for even thinking such a thing. But watching someone slowly waste away and watching your grief-stricken family decay are challenging. Naturally, some silent bargaining develops. Isn't it humane to have thoughts of just wanting your loved one's pain and suffering to stop? Even asking for a bit of reprieve for yourself is understandable, as it was exasperating to watch her make poor decisions, sometimes just to prove a point that she was still the boss. The reality that to live also means to die transcends our emotional inclinations, and we must give in to the universality of death. Much of the guilt around these thoughts is common yet manufactured; it is not as if our thoughts really have the power to will someone's life to stop (but I guess that depends on what you believe). Perhaps trying to prove we have control over the inevitable is easier to make sense of than admitting the painful reality that all human bodies eventually cease to exist. We are all on borrowed time.

Our family changed irrevocably when Aunt Do died. Don't get me wrong; our family is still a mostly connected unit with a lot of love. Nevertheless, our collective identity as an impenetrable family was shattered. The branches of our once-strong and healthy tree emerged from the storm, weathered, severed, and repositioned by the winds of despair. It was as if the unity we had prior to her death passed over with Aunt Do into the unknown. Over time, our family has evolved to embody more conflict and both emotional and physical distance. Grief has manifested misplaced priorities and a fixation on materialistic possessions that can never replace the holes we arbitrarily try to fill from her death. Her strong arm, both verbally and nonverbally—that used to keep many of us accountable to the values we were built with—has evaporated. People say and do things many of us believe would not occur if she were still around. It's hard to know if these dynamics were always bubbling under the surface or if some of the instability was born as a direct result of our permanent grief.

Aunt Do died over ten years ago, and the losses persevere. Time does not erase the imprint of grief. Cumulative losses of her absence have modified personalities and reformulated identities.[16] For example, Aunt Loretta (one of Aunt Do's sisters), once fearless, a social butterfly, and the family historian, now lives in the past, bound by the constraints of the four walls surrounding her home. Chronologically, she should have been the next sister to take the reins as our matriarch. Though her heart still beats, she seems to have stopped living the day Aunt Do died. The loss of leadership over our Vialpando clan is painfully obvious. We have become hardened and stronger, perhaps made more resilient by the idea of loneliness and interdependence being unwanted but unavoidable companions as we age. The grieving process is unique from person to person in the immediate aftershock of death and over time. How one person responded at first is unrecognizable to how they react to the loss now. Some needed medication, some reacted with isolation and social withdrawal, and others with fits of outrage and mislaid irritability. With the passage of time, reflection allows us to question some of the decisions we made. What do we each regret, if anything? I regret remaining hidden and freezing in moments when I could have facilitated productive conversation. Moments when I could have acknowledged the hard things. I regret my stubborn resistance to cry at her funeral. To be disingenuous and again use my intellect to push people further away.

A part of each of us is gone. For me, it lives in my chest, a hollowness that only her presence could fill. Right away, I had to reconsider how to spend part of my day, given that I rarely missed a day of visiting her, whether by phone or in person, especially toward the end of her life. I questioned whether I was strong enough to go through death again because I was more cognizant of the eventual fate of others (I still question this with every major loss). Now, I often contemplate this conflicted idea: I do not want to outlive my family members. The pain of loss is so excruciating at times that I crave my own death before theirs to avoid my own suffering (selfish AF, I know). One of the pitfalls of a giant family is that as you begin to see them all age, you begin to envision a future with each of them being plucked away, one by one. However, this awareness has also made me appreciate, stay engaged, and be intentional about keeping my priorities in perspective. I use this realization as a guide with my decisions. Will I regret NOT doing something if it were to be my last opportunity? When you really come to understand that there is no remedy to death, does it make you want to live more or cower away?

Our handlings of grief run the full gamut of adaptive to maladaptive. The conscious recognition of the finality of her death hit us all at different points in time, further complicating the collective grief experience and clogging the pathways to adjustment. Thirteen years later, she is referenced more frequently now, perhaps because, on some level, we have become used to living with the pain of her absence. More laughter and happy references are mentioned, and a sense of heartwarming recollections and her presence fill the air. Her legacy is still visible in each of us, though to varying degrees and with different components being emphasized: her work ethic, her dedication to family, her cooking, her natural ability to bring others together, her raw honesty, and her compassion toward caring for those who can't care for themselves. Even her stubbornness, famous eye rolls, and obnoxiously loud nonverbal communication. She was the first of her eleven siblings to go, but she will not be the last—a harsh reality I hope we all are working harder toward accepting. Some of us have learned our lessons about the importance of talking about our own and our loved one's deaths, and others still try to hang onto the fallacy of escapism and play the undefeated game of avoidance. Either way, our family will never be what it once was. And we will never be the same again.

10

AN UNRAVELED STORYBOOK ENDING

Have you given much thought to the construction of the family photos displayed in your house? In your parents' houses? Friends' houses? Who decides where each person should be placed? Who made the call on clothing, lighting, scenery, and poses? What is the motivation for such a photo? Were there certain images the people involved wanted to portray? How did their understanding of relationship norms form the decisions that led them to that very moment? What are the belief systems that have no physical form in the picture but embody a large presence over how it all came to be? The family photo, both real and imagined, symbolizes deep meaning for how we learn to envision our future from an early age.

It was the first day of kindergarten for Yolanda's last child. Her two eldest, ten and eight years older than Lorenzo, were basically grown. Walking him to the door to start his academic journey was bittersweet because he was her baby. He still is. As she walked with him from the north side of the dirt road toward the kindergarten doors, vibrantly decorated with colorful stickers exemplifying adventure, she spotted me and came to an abrupt halt. I was walking hand in hand with my mom, full of excitement for learning. She was drawn to my porcelain light skin, huge blue-green eyes, and perfectly straight bangs lying just above my eyebrows. I had long, jet-black hair down to my waist that was half-up, half-down, secured in place with a big scrunchy, the color no longer memorable. Petite and polite, I greeted her when introduced, then stood quietly. She didn't recognize my mom and wasn't familiar with what family I was a part of. As our moms made small talk, Lorenzo and I seemed to instantly gravitate toward each other. He was a doll. He, too, had delicate, fair skin and jet-black hair, combed perfectly. He was dressed "to the nines." He had big brown eyes and a bit of a crooked smile. He was outgoing, talkative, and hilarious, an absolute blast to be around that made it easy for us to become fast friends. And we did.

Eventually, with more chit-chats between Yolanda and my mom and grandmas, who alternated picking me up from school, it was made clear that I belonged to the Vialpando family (the granddaughter of Becca), and Lorenzo belonged to the Flores family (the son of Yolanda). Our families had a history of friendship dating back decades. Both families were close-knit, hardworking Hispanic people who grew up on the west side of Laramie. Their lives were fairly simple. They knew family, faith, and food and shared most of their values and experiences. The familiarity over the years led to several long-term friendships, mutual support, and admiration. Our families just understood each other, making affiliation natural.

Lorenzo and I inherited this comfort, and because we got along so well, we made it simple for our families to begin the narrative that would define the next two decades of our lives. It is common and expected in the Hispanic culture, particularly in our region of the country and within the families we grew up in, to find your one true love early in life. The typical story is that you find love as teenagers and it is quickly transferred to a focus on building a life together. You marry early, begin a family soon after, and deal with one another until the end of time, happy or not. Family is everything, nuclear and extended.[1] Historically, men are the breadwinners and the women stay home to tend to the children and household needs. By the time Lorenzo and I came around, this had shifted slightly in that most couples were working parents, a trend that has continued. It seemed as though everything in the universe aligned perfectly that day in early fall as our association with one another began. We moved the fairytale along in that we instantly had a crush on one another. Something intrigued each of us about the other, drawing us in. A bit unexplainable, really, especially for young kids.

In elementary school, our relationship was easy. We had many shared interests, and our lives were eerily similar. We had stories of time with cousins, aunts, and uncles to share, which reinforced that our experiences were the "normal" way of life. We didn't have to ask questions to make sense of the dynamics of our lives when we weren't at school. We knew the same Spanish phrases, saw the same rituals of food and faith being executed day in and day out, and looked forward to the same massive parties to celebrate the milestones in life. We were both competitive and extremely stubborn, so with a shared love of sports, recess was pure entertainment. My talent for basketball got me invited to spend more time with him outside of school. I was better at basketball than Lorenzo from the start (and yes, he knows the truth and gave me permission to say it), so I loved showing off. It frustrated him, but he pushed me to be better. Unbeknownst to either of us at the time, this is likely when the inadequacy seeds were planted for some of the differences we had as we got older, seeds that often made him feel more at a deficit than just simply separate from me.

I loved Lorenzo by the third grade. As embarrassing as it is to admit, I distinctly remember this because I had notebooks where I would write "I love Lorenzo Martin Vigil" or my name with "Vigil" at the end of it with my gel-tipped pens, insinuating that I was dreaming of a future for us. I was left out of games my friends and I would play, where we would do tricks with paper to help us determine which boy we would marry, because we all assumed Lorenzo and I would be together. Our families spoke of how cute we looked together and how well we got along, and they joked with us about "liking" each other. We even walked down the aisle together when we got our first holy communions in second grade. Again, maybe it was another sign from the universe, showing us concrete glimpses of our future. It is hard to tell which came first: actual attraction or the planted story of how it was supposed to develop. Did we truly like each other and they picked up on that, or did they impose such conviction in their beliefs that we truly fell into the story, head over heels?

He asked me out for the first time in fifth grade. We were on the kickball field, and I was waiting in line for my turn to kick. He had written, "Will you be my girlfriend?" on a piece of paper and had a couple of his friends deliver it to me. I knew what it said before I opened it. I had butterflies in my stomach, and without giving it a second thought, I told my friends to start the game of telephone with my answer: a calm and collected yes. Neither of us knew what that really meant, so nothing changed, except that we would occasionally hold hands and we told our friends we were boyfriend and girlfriend. He told me that he couldn't tell his mom because he wasn't allowed to date until he was twelve. But, as an eager eleven-year-old, he asked me anyway and said he would keep it a secret. I, on the other hand, rushed home and announced it right away to anyone who would listen. It didn't surprise my parents. They had an even-keeled response. I wasn't told no; I wasn't told yes. It honestly just made sense to them. My mom helped me understand what it meant to date and tried to get me to open up, but of course, I didn't have much to say. I mostly felt proud of how grown-up I sounded.

Our first attempt at being together was short-lived. In about a week's time, Lorenzo felt so guilty about holding a secret from his mom that he broke down in tears and told her. Although she loved me, she felt we were too young and reinforced that he was not allowed to date yet. Although irritated, he obediently marched to school the next day and said, "My mom says we have to break up until seventh grade." I replied, "Okay," and that was it. Young love! Despite it being a relatively short union, it was plenty of time for the news to spread among our loved ones. This is when the scheming started between our dads. Although our moms were thrilled, they were a little more in tune with promoting developmental appropriateness, whereas our dads reacted like giddy schoolgirls. They would cheer about how excited they were and would "jokingly" make plans for our wedding. This fantasizing continued for the better part of our adolescence and young adulthood. The Spanish food, the Spanish band, how many grandkids they were going to have; they had it all laid out for us. Both sets of families thought we were perfect for one another and simply couldn't picture any other outcome. I was part of his family, and he was part of mine long before any verbal or legal commitment bound us. That's a lot of pressure for two preteens with very little experience in the dating game. Yet there we were, just trying to figure out how long we were supposed to hold hands, unconsciously internalizing the spoken arrangements dictating our futures.

We dated for the second time in seventh grade, pretty soon after he was given the green light from Yolanda. This time, he asked me out himself. We were on the south side of the wooden bleachers in the big gym at the Civic Center, my home away from home. We sat on the bench next to the visitors' locker room, the aging black stickers peeling off from years of neglect. His question led to an easy decision for me once again. This time, we held hands at school and wrote letters. We even made lovey-dovey mix tapes based on the romantic songs we heard from our older family members. We had a shared love of oldies and Spanish music, and he tended to throw in a little old-school R&B, filled with romantic insinuations way above our heads.

Our middle and high school years were fraught with ups and downs as a couple. We broke up and got back together often, usually over silly things. I was convinced we would end up together, so the breakups didn't matter much in the grand scheme of things. The rhetoric picked up in our families, extending well beyond our dads. Aside from questions about basketball and school, Lorenzo was now attached to me, so he was often brought up. We were known as a unit, even when we weren't technically together. There was mounting pressure, both direct and indirect, especially when we were separated. Since our story was "so cute," and the idea of us was pure bliss, no one paid much mind to our conflict. There was unanimous blind faith that we would work out the kinks in our relationship. However, we were becoming notably different. I continued my advanced progression toward maturity, always presenting many years older than I actually was. I constantly thought about the future: my goals, *our* plans, and how to best achieve them. I infrequently allowed myself fun, but only when my work was done. In contrast, Lorenzo was perfecting his gift of comedy. He lived in the moment, loved to relax, and was content with exactly where he was. He didn't care much for the future and wanted to have fun, with work being an afterthought.

A major difference in the way we spent downtime emerged, and that was our relationship with substances. As you can imagine, I maintained my goody-two-shoes sentiment; there was no giving in to peer pressure here. I didn't drink, I didn't smoke, I didn't party. My routine was entirely focused on perfecting myself, with substances having no place on my list. He experimented as most high schoolers do, and at the time, it wasn't something that bothered me. I wished he was as driven as me, more focused on fostering his *potential*, but I didn't see his experimentation as something to be concerned about. The norms in our families also made it so this wasn't anything to gawk at. It was common to drink and smoke. Although it was normalized, it quietly began to drive a wedge between us because I didn't understand all the hype, and he didn't want to feel tied down or made out to be a bad guy for enjoying himself. Both sides are valid, and neither of us was wrong. I didn't attempt to articulate my concerns in a productive way that he could have heard, a way that may have propelled our relationship forward. This is all hindsight bias,[2] of course, but I often question that if I had been vulnerable with my fears, maybe it would have made a difference in how our plot would eventually twist.

During our adolescence, when we fought, it ate at me, but no one usually knew that, including him. I was used to succeeding at anything I tried, so relationships could be no different.[3] I kept my feelings mostly to myself. Sometimes, I shared my distress with friends, and they tried to be supportive, but they didn't understand our dynamic. The expectations and pressures within our families were foreign to them. They responded by questioning why we were still connected, as it was becoming clearer just how different we really were. Exchanges with friends left me feeling invalidated and hopeless, reinforcing that I was just too different to seek support from others (fuel for my exception mindset). But I should have been talking to Lorenzo; it was a gross misstep on my part.

Lorenzo and I had opposite approaches to how we coped with our grief during times apart. One key dynamic stands out, and it comes back to the family photo. I almost never dated anyone else in my youth because I was focused on figuring out how to make our relationship work. Dating felt like a waste of time. I didn't let myself like another person for too long or too deeply because it felt wrong. My heart was with Lorenzo, so I chose to push people away before anything else could blossom. No other boy was supposed to be in my story. It didn't fit the family photo. However, Lorenzo had no problems dating other people. We both agree that the difference can be explained by the fact that he wasn't as invested in our future as I was at the time. He didn't have the same identity in his world to uphold, and he didn't take life as seriously. Not to mention, he was a teenage boy. He was (and is) naturally a more emotional person than me, so when he was able to connect emotionally with other girls in ways I wouldn't let him with me, he took advantage of that, sometimes even in front of me. This part was painful, but I sure as hell wasn't going to give him or anyone else the satisfaction of knowing that it bothered me (which was part of the problem).

Once we graduated, I went to college, declaring a double major, continuing my over-the-top approach to every corner of my life. He chose not to pursue higher education and instead worked and partied. We would intermittently check in, but we were on entirely different planes. Our lives led us to a crossroads we didn't take together, a first for us, which was hard to reconcile given our already colorful past. Even when we were not talking for months, we always seemed to find our way back to one another. We decided to give it another go during my sophomore year. This was the biggest test of our relationship to date. We were adults now, with jobs and responsibilities. Since I had been so focused on our future and the idea of us, I embraced the opportunity as our time to finally shine. We fell back into our routine smoothly, and I had committed myself to balancing my time more evenly so that he felt like a priority, but I didn't excel in the way I had envisioned, giving life to his stubborn insecurity of not being good enough.

Unfortunately, soon after we made the commitment, my Aunt Dora's health started to decline rapidly. As you already know, I took a big role in being present for her. I was not a stranger to death, but Lorenzo had only experienced close deaths through my eyes up to this point. This harsh reality of life hadn't yet struck him in such an earth-shattering way. As I prepared for her death, I was trying to juggle working full time while taking a full course load in order to complete my double major requirements in four years. I grew distant as she got sicker. Naturally, he tried to pull me closer, but I pushed back even harder. I felt misunderstood, and although he was trying his best to support me, he was also trying to get his needs met in a way I wasn't capable of. Conflict was heavy, and a clear distance was between us, yet the durable hope of a better future somehow kept us attached like a jumper to a bungee cord. This was when the silent internal shift in my commitment to our future began. The relentless investment I had had for us since childhood started to fade while simultaneously beginning to blossom more steadily for him. Despite the emotional shift, my logical brain still clung to the expectation that we needed to make it work. *The family photo.* Predictably, I practiced my expertly orchestrated talent: disregarding my feelings. We stayed together through Aunt Do's death, but my grief was the final straw this go-around. He couldn't handle the isolation (understandably), and I didn't care enough to try anything different. I know this crushed him. Even when we were physically together, the detachment was tangible, as if you could grab the frayed segments of string between us. Overcome by feelings of powerlessness and hopelessness, we decided we couldn't do it anymore.

This breakup was particularly memorable because of the influence of our families. Lorenzo had a habit during conflicts of reaching out to my mom for guidance on "how to deal with me." For context, I am similar to my dad, and Lorenzo has some striking resemblances to my mom. They are both emotional creatures, wearing their hearts on their sleeves, with a sensitivity that can be easily compromised with the frequent dismissal of feelings and the fear of vulnerability that my dad and I have mastered. After breakups, I demanded time away from him. Any time this occurred, I would be, let's say, nudged by my mom. She tried to teach me lessons by explaining how my actions could be harmful and not helping myself or Lorenzo. It wasn't that she took his side, but she tried to get me to understand the effects I was having on the relationship by shutting down (she never used these words, but she could have said I was being selfish, egotistical, and a total asshole, and she would have been right). She shared fears that I would wind up alone or unable to compromise enough to make our relationship (or any relationship) last.

On point with my typical demeanor, I was tight-lipped, making it difficult for her to help me and to offer her support to Lorenzo. The sprouting differences between my mom and me were made clear during this time. While she always felt her true calling was to create our family, I now felt trapped by that premise. I didn't subscribe to the same storyline anymore. I wanted more for myself. I felt stunted, now able to see the world from other vantage points and consider a future that maybe didn't include Lorenzo. My guilt was overbearing, so I stayed quiet so as not to disturb the decades of stability I was threatening to jeopardize. Despite our families' attempts to meddle, we parted ways yet again, but with one unique change to our story. I left the relationship truly questioning whether or not we were right for each other, an idea that had never been given enough consideration in the past.[4]

The next two years went by with very little communication. I thought of him often but remained diligently committed to my studies. If I'm being honest, I was relieved not to have to deal with the pressure to show up in ways that no longer felt genuine or beneficial to me. This internal warfare ripped my heart apart because I felt like it was the wrong mentality. I believed something was wrong with me. Our story was just too good to end now, regardless of my emotional uncertainty. He continued to party, so I would occasionally show up somewhere I knew he would be with the hope of being reunited with him. You know, nonchalantly checking in to see how his transition from boy to man was going. It was undisputed that our pastimes were vastly different. I was equally proud and disappointed in myself. Proud that I did what felt right for me but disappointed because I was disappointing him and our families. It brought up mild insecurities about my true capabilities to be the eventual wife and mother that he wanted and that I was supposedly destined to be. These unfulfilling encounters left me unsteady on my feet, but I felt I had a mold I needed to fit, so I forced myself to keep pondering how I could fix my broken pieces to make us whole again.

As I transitioned from undergraduate to graduate studies in 2013, Lorenzo's family suffered a devastating loss, his first significant experience with death. I was his first call; he believed I would bring stability and consolation to his aching heart. Without hesitation, I attended the services alongside him and was invited to the post-burial celebration. The night was oddly magical. We were inseparable, singing old country songs together, laughing, crying, and showcasing our revived love for all his family to see. His sister sang at the top of her lungs about our reunification, giving us all something to smile about. Alongside the pain, hope was born that finally, we were mature enough to figure it out. Fleeting comments through conversations of sorrow embodied renewed excitement for our improved relationship on the horizon. We were back together by the end of the night, with a mutual determination to finally play out the vision prognosticated upon us. We were picture-perfect that evening. Mutually vulnerable and supportive, a beautiful display of love, both inside and out. Yet again, we just made sense. In all the pain that accompanied the loss of his uncle, the gains his family was witnessing with our reunion served as an important forward progression to hold onto for all of us. It brought strength to approach the future and something to cling to while feelings of despair and loneliness bounced among them.[5]

There was one glaring barrier I wasn't sure how to say out loud, though. I was contemplating the idea of moving away to pursue a doctorate degree. As a master's student, I had built a strong relationship with my department head and now lifelong mentor and friend, Dr. Mary Alice Bruce. She opened my eyes to my *potential* in a way none of my other cheerleaders had ever been able to do. She was well-versed in academia and saw that I would limit myself if I were to stay in Laramie for another degree. She introduced the option of pursuing a PhD at another institution out of state. At first, the idea seemed bogus. I questioned her sanity and reminded myself that culturally, she just didn't understand my family, my values, and my responsibilities as the golden child. The possibility of leaving seemed even more dire when I considered what that would mean for my relationship with Lorenzo. He had no desire to leave Laramie. Not to mention that our forward-thinking conversations about getting married and having a family had only ever been set in Laramie so that we could capitalize on the luxury of having our families help us take care of the kids, just as we had experienced. We felt that it was not only the best way to raise children but the only way. Plus, he was banking on the fact that since I was almost done with my master's degree, he would take first place in my priorities. Needless to say, another four-year degree, a move, and exhaustive hours to make that happen seemed to fit into our plans about as nicely as an opera singer would be received at our pre-determined Spanish wedding.

To add further complication, that faint knocking of uncertainty about what was meant to be was getting louder, rattling my sense of identity. For most of my life, I seemed to know what was coming next for me. I wasn't indecisive. But now, I questioned my commitment. Whereas before, it was hard for Lorenzo to fully commit because we were so young, now he began talking more about our future together. Others compounded that, using words like "engagement" and "marriage." In the past, these words induced stable euphoria. But now, my stomach felt like a giant knot, left hopelessly tangled by the intense waves of nausea eroding the strength of the once-durable ropes connecting our hearts.

Another part of the discrepancy was my never-ending unease about his substance use. I had started to vocalize it more, but it was often out of frustration and pitched to him as something I just wanted him to change about himself. "Can you just not?" was probably my most frequent question ... not very helpful for productive conversation. Expectedly, it never went over well.

"I just want to relax and have fun. I'm not doing anything wrong," he'd shoot back, only reinforcing my waning investment in what was supposed to be. Consequently, I chose to step away because it was a feeling I couldn't shake. I thought I needed to get my schoolwork out of the way once and for all, and then I would be able to be the woman he desired. I hoped that I would be more loving, more free, and more spontaneous and that I could meet the guidelines set forth for me as a woman in our families and in our culture. But now, I needed to put myself first, so I did. I made the bittersweet move across the country to pursue my PhD without him, much to the dismay of my family, who were upset by the undertaking because of the postponement of the family photo. There was sadness because this move delayed the duties everyone was anxiously awaiting me to fall into: those of wife and mother.

My time in Indiana to pursue my doctorate degree was enlightening. I had never been so far from home and was completely alone for the first time in my life. Although difficult, in many ways, I thrived. I met people from all corners of the world and learned about infinite ways relationships can exist. I realized Mary Alice was right, growing my gratitude and love for her eternally; I truly owe her so much (thank you). Perhaps I was too big for my small town, and maybe I was limiting my possibilities by trying to fit into the mold my family assumed I would fall into perfectly. Right before I moved, I agreed to take another uncharacteristic risk for me: dating someone new. I met a good man who showed me a completely different perspective on what a relationship could be. Yet, my previous beliefs about what my path was supposed to look like and my lifelong comfort and familiarity with Lorenzo simmered in the background. We would take steps as a new couple, and it often felt wrong, as if I were betraying my own destiny. I was honest about this, and although he tried his best, I wasn't able to let myself give that relationship a fair shot. I couldn't listen to my conflicted feelings; I just knew my heart was still messily intertwined with Lorenzo.

Two years into my program, I got a call from Lorenzo in the fall about his desire to try once again. I felt a rekindled sense of hope for our future. It felt like things were coming together as they should. I distinctly remember asking how he was handling his substance use, and he said he had it under control and was focused on work and building a life for us. It was music to my ears, assertions I had been waiting for him to say, and mean, since we were preteens. We began a long-distance relationship, skipping most of the "getting to know you" phase (even though we had barely spent time together for years) and instead focusing on having him move out to Indiana so we could move up our timeline for marriage and babies.

In December of 2016, I went home for winter break. Right away, I was alarmed by how much I saw him drink. I believed him when he said that he had gotten to a better place with his use, yet I was seeing red flags. I debated the best way to proceed. The energy I used to contemplate my options exhausted me. It was difficult to muster enough energy to show up and be the fun girlfriend he wanted me to be. This struggle was intensified by the fact that I knew I would only be home for a few weeks, and I didn't want to spend the time with him arguing. *I'm not here twenty-four seven, so maybe I'm inferring or seeing issues where there aren't any,*[6] I'd remind myself. To make matters worse, I was completing clinical rounds at a community mental health center, spending several hours a week treating patients with substance use disorders. I noticed similarities between my patients and my boyfriend, and it scared me. I struggled to be in the moment and was instead fast-forwarding our future to what problems I may have as a wife in this situation. I was horrified at what our future kids might see. I couldn't bear those thoughts but also couldn't make them go away. Lastly, I was preparing to take my comprehensive exams. The exams carried a heavy weight and were the only barrier between me being a doctoral student and a doctoral candidate, a title change I wanted so badly I could taste. I allocated at least half of every day to studying, casting a huge shadow over this trip home, not just with Lorenzo but with everyone. I was maximally stressed and, no surprise, wouldn't let anyone in. I needed to convince myself and everyone else that I had it all under control. Yes, we were the perfect couple to everyone else, fitting the bill and making everyone proud, but the differences between us were overwhelming. I didn't feel a partnership but somehow still believed I could take control and make it happen. I just needed to be perfect.

We had no solid plans for New Year's Eve. I was just a few days out from my exams and didn't want to deal with the drunken stupidity from pretty much anyone we could have been around that night. The night before, we made a plan that I would go to a party with my mom, and then she'd drop me off at a local bar, where I would meet up with Lorenzo to hang with friends (I would likely be serving as the designated driver, although this was not explicitly decided upon). As the night went on, I became increasingly anxious about my exam, and I just wanted to go home. I was replaying notes from my study guides over and over to the point where I couldn't be present and enjoy myself. When we left the party, I told my mom and Lorenzo that I had changed my plans, confusing them both, but I just needed to be alone.

Meanwhile, Lorenzo decided to leave the bar and head to a different area of town at about 1:00 a.m. He and three friends piled into his 2000 black Chevy Camaro, two in the front, two in the back. As they pulled out of the parking lot to merge onto the main street, he took off too fast and hit a patch of black ice. The car spun and struck a light pole on the west side of the street. As it came to a complete stop, the light pole was severely damaged, now hanging over the car at about a forty-five-degree angle. The Camaro was mutilated, particularly on the driver's side. Right away, his two friends on the passenger side of the vehicle appeared coherent and able-bodied enough to remove themselves. The driver's side sustained more damage and needed reinforcement to remove Lorenzo and his friend who was stuck directly behind him. As the authorities arrived, the cops began to conduct their investigation once Lorenzo declined the need for medical attention. Two of the passengers were transported to the hospital for treatment, and one refused altogether. As the driver, Lorenzo was put through a sobriety test, failed, and was transported to the local jail without incident. As he sat in jail, the initial pain from the accident became worse, so he was taken to the hospital for evaluation. The results were concerning; they recommended a handover to a better-equipped hospital in the next town to ensure appropriate medical care. This transport took place about the same time that I was notified of the accident, in the early hours of the morning.

I received a panicked call from his sister, TC, screaming and crying on the other end. I could barely comprehend what she was saying as I tried to piece the puzzle together. Through unnatural pauses to try to calm herself, she informed me, "Tash, Lorenzo was in a bad car accident. He was drinking and driving. They took him to the jail, but now they think he has head trauma, so they are taking him to Cheyenne." My heart sank to my feet. I had an abnormal reaction to what I was hearing in that there was so much chatter in my head I could barely put words or thoughts together. I am usually calm, sturdy, and resourceful in emergency situations. But I was being pulled in so many directions at once and wasn't sure what the most important priority needed to be. TC knew about my upcoming exam, and the shakiness in my voice seemed to reverberate more chills down her spine. "TC, oh my god. What? Is he okay? What do I do?" It was as if she could see my shield of protection disintegrating through the phone. I told myself that whatever she recommended was how I would proceed. I sure as hell couldn't identify my own feelings in the moment, so my plan was to show up for his family in the best way I could.

"Just stay put, Tash. I know you're studying. I'll keep you posted. I'm going to get my parents and drive over now."

"I love you, TC," was all I could reply.

"I love you too, Tash." And with that, a dial tone snapped me back to reality.

I obeyed only in the sense that I stayed put exactly where I was. Immobile but bursting with nervous energy all over my body, I yelled out to my parents, "MOM ... DAD ... COME HERE NOW!" When they arrived, I was matter-of-fact. "Lorenzo was in a car accident. I don't have any details other than he was drinking and wrecked his car. He got arrested but got sick at the jail and so they have to take him to Cheyenne to check on his head."

My dad said nothing while my mom started to cry. "Oh my god, Tasha, what do we do? Are you okay? What do we need to do?!"

"I just need to be alone and keep studying. TC told me to stay here, and she'll update me soon. I need to study." I gave them zero opportunity to support me, once again acting like a self-absorbed jackass. I sat huddled in my room for hours, staring back and forth between my blank phone screen and the binder of notes. I held pages in my hands as I tried to turn my focus elsewhere, but it was obvious that no retention was happening. I read the words out loud and tried to remind myself of the relevance they had to my life, unaware of the vain attempts my brain was making to find some sense in all of this.

Eventually, I received two calls from TC. The first was to inform me that the moment he woke up, Lorenzo's emotional state was inconsolable, jumbled between guilt for his actions and the fear of losing me. The first word he uttered was *Tasha*. He was prematurely displaying the grief that was to come, even though we were completely unaware of it at the time. Hearing this made me feel weak in my knees, and an instant ball in my chest welled to a massive size. I didn't hold back the silent tears while she spoke. The second was the relief call that he had been cleared to come home with no diagnosable injuries. I met them at his parents' house as soon as they returned midday. I was mostly speechless and unable to engage with him in a meaningful way. By the evening, I had become angry. Irate, actually. I fought every urge not to scold him but instead to hold him, to be supportive, and to manifest that future wife everyone told me I was supposedly going to be so good at. I wasn't good at it. I cringed at every movement and had no idea how to connect as we lay with each other, mostly in silence. I stayed in my rational brain, checking on his physical state every few minutes and tending to his requests as they came up. Eventually, I couldn't handle it any longer and excused myself to walk upstairs. There, I sat with Yolanda and had the most intimate and raw conversation I have ever had with her. We were devastated. She named it first—that he would be charged with a DUI with serious bodily injury. Two of the passengers sustained life-threatening injuries that would require months of rehabilitation and likely lifelong repercussions.

Yolanda and I tried to pinpoint what was occurring, not just for us in the moment but for our families, our lives, and our future. There were many apologies between us as we both tried to take responsibility for the ways we had failed Lorenzo. I expressed guilt that, had I gone to the bar like I said I was going to, nothing would have happened. She was dismissive of this falsehood and instead provided unconditional love for me. She expressed confusion about her decisions as a parent and what she could have done differently. I also discarded this tale, as I stand by my belief that she is one of the most loving, supportive, and responsible mothers I have ever met. She brilliantly executed undying support and protection for her son, complete with acknowledging her deep gratitude and connection to me at the same time. She told me how much she loved me and recognized the toll this relationship was having on me. I expressed fear at what our future could look like and about bringing children into the mix. She advocated for both her son and me as best she could, demonstrating a gracefulness I do not believe many mothers could achieve while talking to their son's girlfriend while he lay downstairs motionless, lucky to be alive. She saw both our sides. She saw both our needs. And she encouraged me to do what was best for me, even if that meant not being with Lorenzo, something we both knew she ultimately did not want. I will forever be in debt to her for the way she handled that conversation. There was no blaming me, no pushy attempts to persuade me. She simply exposed her grief and sat with mine as we struggled to make sense of the tragedy we were now living. To say I am grateful to her is an understatement. I love this woman deeply and always will.

Before I went back to Indiana, I recommitted myself to Lorenzo, letting him know that I would not leave him because of the accident, but I needed to see change in order to move forward. I was still livid. I could feel my own iciness that made us both want to put on a coat any time I walked into a room. I flew back and completed my exams, nailing them and not sharing a single word about what had happened over the break. I have no idea how I was able to do that, but I can only assume that I had fastened extra protection to my invisible armor and guarded it like I was at war. The next month or so was incredibly stressful. Lorenzo was trying to be positive, to find himself and ways of coping that would get him through. I was critical and fixated on the logistics of it all. I would talk to my clients all day about their court dates, discussions with the judge, and boundaries of probation, and then call my boyfriend to ask about the very same things. I was devastated and bitter. We both made each other miserable. I realized that, above all else, I was only dedicated to one thing: I was NOT going to be the one to break up with him. Although my investment had essentially evaporated due to my hopelessness in trying to see a realistic path to an idealized future, I downright refused to be the one who ended our relationship. I was terrified that if I did, his family would be angry and reject or disown me, and I loved them too much for that.[7]

The tables turned in other ways I had not anticipated. My family, always so invested in the security of our relationship, now questioned their own predictions. My dad, in particular, inserted doubt about our future in a way he had never expressed before. He didn't question Lorenzo's love for me but shared mounting fear, admitting that he was no longer comfortable with the premise of me being with someone who had a problem with substances. He voiced concern about Lorenzo's ability to be a reliable and solid provider for me, holding fast to his stereotypical cultural viewpoints of what a nuclear family unit was supposed to be. Unfortunately, he shared his reservations not only with me but also with Lorenzo, without my knowledge. I understood, but even so, it still makes me hurt. I am my dad's everything, and he just wanted to protect me. Although coming from a place of love and concern, his overstep served to exacerbate Lorenzo's already strong feelings of deficiency. It wasn't just my dad, though; other family members echoed similar sentiments, new conversations I could barely believe I was hearing. The emerging unforeseen insight and doubt from my family shredded my heart in new ways, ones I wasn't able to protect with my typical defense mechanisms. Eventually, it was all too much for us, and I got my wish. Lorenzo chose to break up with me. The future I had envisioned since I was a little girl crumbled in a matter of weeks like a soft cookie smashed into unrecognizable ingredients that were no longer appealing or appetizing.

This final breakup was completely different in that the destruction seemed to carry a new sense of failure; I could not come up with any solutions to remodel what had been eroded. Our future seemed demolished, nearly incinerated beyond recognition. It cut through us much deeper, shattering the glass that protected our family pictures. He and I had both clung to this foreshadowed family photo of the two of us with our children above the fireplace in our someday home. We had imagined it for years, yet now the smiles were broken and the children's faces faded and blurry. We focused too much on this family photo. On what should be, not what was. The grief process of what could (or should?) have been crushed me under the weight of not only my pain but all the hurt we caused our loved ones on both sides. This was a separation that broke dozens of hearts all at once. We not only lost each other, but we also lost plentiful relationships with one another's families.[8] Major changes occurred despite the mutual love never wavering. Personally, I was unable to put myself in a situation to be reminded of how much I had failed (how much we had failed?) at making all of their dreams (and mine?) come true. Therefore, I could no longer be around his family in the same way. Seeing them and remembering the reality that we didn't survive the accident was overbearing, a subtle teasing of the unity I was so close to having but never able to fully grasp. I was still attached to them, yet that attachment cast too bright a spotlight on my shortcomings. It was easier for me to completely disconnect, as any time we were still in contact, the soft spot

I had for him would take over, and there I was again, instantly strategizing, trying to determine how to finally make it work this time.

It has taken years for me to process and understand the many steps we attempted in the dance that was our relationship. Ultimately, we didn't last for several reasons, and it has been difficult to fully face and embrace the parts I played, many of which I am not proud of but some that I am. Let's start with me. I was always striving for perfection, and since the narrative of Lorenzo and me had been burned into my brain as the most perfect outcome possible, I was wholeheartedly invested in making it a reality, no matter the cost (or what was actually best for me). My vulnerability was frequently absent, but part of this was because I so vehemently tried to deny my honest feelings as I got older. It was an odd dichotomy to know each other so well yet force him to have so many questions about me. To be unavailable and mysterious to him, even though we had encountered nearly every major event of our lives side by side. My steady focus on the future took us out of being able to truly connect in each moment and build the relationship that could have sustained the ups and downs we too easily dealt with by repeated sterile breakups until our feelings had subsided. There wasn't room nor opportunity to discover who we were as individuals or as a couple because the family photo had already cemented our responsibility. We jumped to what we saw and tried to live out the roles we observed from couples decades older than us.[9] Many of the couples weren't optimal role models, but nonetheless, they stayed the course together because that is just what you do in big Spanish families. Yet the two of us just couldn't seem to fall in line with this prescription for success.

As I expand the discussion outside of myself, there were notable pressures that, even though well-intended, negatively impacted some of the opportunities we could have had.[10] Pressure for me, Lorenzo, and us as a unit. The pressure I felt often came from my dad, who was a steady meddler in our relationship in its entirety. He was focused on the family photo and wanted me to fall in line with the roles and stories he had visualized since the day he had me (he still does). I wanted to please him, to maintain the perfect image of myself that he had come to expect. I didn't want to let my mom down, either, as I knew she was always rooting for us. She often talked about her beliefs of fate and destiny, and I think she saw some of her and my dad in Lorenzo and me, and she wanted that for me. I fundamentally believed in this idea of destiny when I was young, that our story was predetermined and we just needed to keep growing up in order to make the fairytale ending come true. Our extended families doubled down on these beliefs as well, through both their words and behaviors. I wasn't given an alternative to consider, as it came at us from all angles, which made me more bullheaded in my quest to simply put the puzzle together correctly, once and for all.

For Lorenzo, his unsteady identity and the engrained struggle with paltriness was a major thorn that poked at our stability on a regular basis. Lorenzo once told me one of his biggest hesitations was that he knew he would always be able to feed my soul but not my brain. He did not feel good enough for me and hadn't since childhood. My hunger for intellect and his attachment to simplicity often came between us, not because he was incapable or I acted superior but because our differences just put us on different paths to satisfy our most instinctual cravings. He questioned whether he could connect with me or fit in with the people I chose to surround myself with. He felt like he was always coming up short because I was constantly striving to make myself better. He felt bad because he didn't always want to focus on bringing his potential to light; instead, he wanted to simply enjoy being alive. The intellectual stimulation I needed and the physical touch he needed left us always feeling derisory, a recipe for disaster when it comes to confidence and security in a relationship. The cultural expectations of gender roles only worsened this. There was constant pressure on him to figure out how to be the breadwinner. Even though I never mentioned, expected, or cared about this belief, self-doubt was added to the pressure cooker of concern. Additional fright about being able to meet our distinct needs was added, constantly stirred by comments from others about our happy ending.

The points mentioned are included because of the losses I perceive within them. Perfectionism, an unwillingness to be vulnerable, living through someone else's expectations, struggling to be still, a lack of confidence, letting outside pressures rock your foundation, and not questioning what you really want for yourself has resulted in grief for all parties involved. The grief process seems to hold particular relevance in our story in that loss appears to have a dual, sneaky role of being a connector for the two of us. It is not just something that tears us apart. Lorenzo and I possess genuine care and concern for one another, so naturally, we were drawn back to each other during times of distress. The things that brought us back together are intricately tied to the uncanny similar values we were both raised with. The compatibility in this regard is, no pun intended, essentially perfect. It is both fascinating and comforting how other losses we have suffered, unrelated to one another, have reinforced some of the natural closeness we never had to work at. For example, actual death always seemed to initiate a new spark to our waning flame. We tended to always be each other's first call for such distress, and it was soothing to sit in the collective loss without having to explain it. Because there was also so much mutual love for each other within our families, it was almost expected that we would show up and support, just as any other bonded couple would do. I wonder if that tradition will carry on in some form in the future.

In time, we have been able to break away from the fixed story. We created history the way we needed it to play out for us, not the way it was anticipated before we were old enough to grasp the true meaning of love and the difference between what it means to have it and be in it. It has been nearly eight years since our last true breakup. As is the case with grief, I am not sure the process will ever truly stop. I wonder if we will always be in the back of each other's minds and those of our families. There is no way to erase the marks we have left on each other's souls. I know that I will always love him and have a connection to him. I know I have always felt particularly sorrowful when allowing myself to consider the thought that I could have children who had family members besides my own and Lorenzo's. To envision my kids not calling his brother and sister "aunt and uncle" or his parents "grandma and grandpa" brings heartache. To know that his sister can no longer be a bridesmaid in my wedding leaves a gaping hole no one else can fill. Again, the family album has morphed altogether, littered with embers of sadness all around us. I have immense respect, love, and admiration for the man Lorenzo has become. He is a good man with a heart of gold —something I never questioned. There are things I love about him that so easily bring ease and relaxation to my life, just as there are things about him that would drive me absolutely crazy had our story not unraveled at the seams. I am confident he feels the same. It is safe to say we both can fully see the ways in which our relationship would not have been healthy had we stayed together. Simultaneously, I know there's a hypersensitive part of me that still mourns it. For instance, I always root for the original couple in any TV show or movie I watch, just so that someone gets their storybook ending.

We both agree that many people would still love to see us together, and it continues to hurt their hearts that our story didn't end with Prince Charming finally sweeping up his happily ever after. That reality is painful. During interviews for this chapter, Lorenzo's family mentioned that they no longer try to dwell on it and that they'd welcome anyone whom their son loves into their arms, but they still echoed a familiar sentiment: "But you're Tasha." That burns. Both our families suffered from the unwanted dividers they had to put up to deconstruct some of the closeness we had because maintaining that sense of unity was too hard for us to witness while trying to move on. They mourn the children we never had, those souls they already deeply loved but had no faces for. I know both of our families just want us to be happy; it's just difficult to reframe the decades of assumptions about what that happiness should look like. I know we all still wonder about each other often and fumble over whether we are supposed to do anything with the strings we can't completely cut.

There is meaningful growth in all of this for our families too. Our reality has forced them to consider that maybe their own perspectives aren't the only way to go about life. Just because I didn't follow what was normal doesn't mean it wasn't what was best for me, him, or us.[11] Yet, the fact that I haven't repeated the same cookie-cutter timeline of life has left my family both saddened and confused. Some even feel guilt, pondering whether some of the dysfunction I observed led to too much hesitation on my part to fight for any relationship to be taken to such a serious level (I, however, disagree and have guilt for inducing such questions). Yes, they want me to be happy, but they believe that happiness is defined through a lifestyle I have yet to live (and perhaps don't want to) and may never live in the way they see it; thus, finding resolve for their uncertainty is a challenge. As a result, we have to think about right versus wrong in new ways and contemplate other ways of life, which is ultimately a good thing. There's a multitude of ways to live a meaningful life, and they are just now beginning to see how true that is. It is okay to live in the gray, which I have to remind myself of when my perfectionistic fits remind me that I haven't played the roles they all want, inducing a burning sensation that my time is running out (or already has).

I consider both of us incredibly lucky but not unscathed. I was able to call Lorenzo out of the blue and ask to deconstruct our entire relationship, and he didn't bat an eye. We still hold a mutual love that now has boundaries. While we talked, we tiptoed around one another at first, questioning if there were any holes in the wall where a family photo could easily be placed. But getting up to inspect it no longer carries urgency. In fact, we gave each other advice and tried to console one another with the ways our hearts have since broken beyond each other. It is a rarity, and I am grateful for the way we have consistently overcome our differences and continue to support one another. Our families have done the same. As for the casualties, we still carry our wounds within us and sometimes unintentionally infect those who have come after. It's worth acknowledging that we have both found loves we strengthened to depths we were not able to achieve together. Finally, we have both been able to let go of the image of us to see what other pictures we can bring to life of our own volition with people we found on our own, which has been liberating.

No family photo hangs in our home the way we had assumed it would. The blemishes on the wall paint their own story. The fairytale, as it was once understood, is no longer. The story is tainted, forever changed, with the stench of loss more powerful than the distinct yet attractive smell old books carry. I know now that there are many ways to define happiness, and I no longer subscribe to just one way to be successful in a relationship. The family photo as it was originally taught to me is not the centerpiece of my fantasies. Not that it is wrong or bad;

it just isn't my photo—not now and maybe not ever. The wall above the fireplace is blank, void of plans, expectations, and pressures to fit any plan made for me without my conscious endorsement. Perhaps in the debris, there is also untapped opportunity for both of us to gain more than we ever could have together. Our connection will always remain, although its shape takes up different space now, as our hearts are no longer bound by the same chains. And we were never the same again.

11

THE SHAPESHIFTS OF BECOMING

Although I've tried to make each story that came before this one as complete as possible, there are irreplaceable gaps in each chapter's composition, repeatedly missing insight from interviews of my one and only, Grandma Pryde. Grandma Pryde died on December 13, 2020, after becoming septic due to an infection that was not treated properly. The complicated grief I feel in writing this book comes from a variety of sources. The recognition of her death, the absence of comforting rituals because of the circumstances of her death, and the ongoing losses in not being able to hear her perspective of these narratives crush me. When I come face-to-face with these losses, a bone-cracking weight encapsulates my upper body, knowing that she can't answer my questions. Somatic grief at its finest. She is a main character, not just in these stories but in most of the stories that make up my life. Sadly, I can only infer her perspective using my knowledge of her and our collective memories as a family.

It's time you get to know Grandma Pryde a little better so you can adequately understand how profound our love and loss of her are. Her story will be about illness and medical decline, yes, but the bigger theme is about the various transitions her identity underwent as she moved through the stages of her life with an intent to follow her heart and live out her values. I invite you to consider the bidirectional influences of how her identities morphed in reaction to the natural changes our family underwent. A change in one part of the system often results in unavoidable changes in the rest of it. I urge you to think about your most prized humans and how this plays out for them. I would argue that you will find a confusing interplay of both celebration and disappointment as you recall the ways we grow and shrink alongside one another, a natural and universal part of the human condition.

Her osteoarthritis is the only thing I can tell she inherited from her mother, genetically or otherwise. An unintended but final fuck-you to the daughter whom my Great-Grandma Georgia took for granted and unnecessarily belittled. I never met Georgia, but I know for certain I would not have liked her. She was the complete opposite of Grandma Pryde in nearly every way, and I am thankful for her only in the sense that she taught my grandma exactly who not to be. I had Grandma Pryde as she was because of the horrible woman her mother was. Georgia was negative, selfish, greedy, demeaning, and abusive. It makes sense that at various points in her life, Grandma Pryde made conscious decisions to ensure she never resembled her mom in any arena, sometimes to her own detriment. She didn't degrade or blatantly acknowledge her mother's shortcomings as a human or a parent; instead, she emphasized that she just wanted to do different, to be better, to save us from the emotional scars thrashed upon her. As a result, she overcorrected and had some downfalls herself: toxic positivity,[1] ignoring her own needs for the betterment of others, hiding vulnerability until pushed to the brink, and people-pleasing at her own expense. These traits were born from the need to separate herself from what she saw growing up. The strength and admiration in that cannot be understated, as her intentions were courageous and selfless. Yet at the same time, it harmed her because her needs were on the back burner, simmering but ignored until something (or someone) boiled over. This approach had major implications for her identity as well. Her self-image was formed and connected to the welfare of others through her career as a nurse and the caregiver role she took in relationships. She programmed herself to ensure security and comfort for others while neglecting the same for herself.

She almost always had issues with her bones. She needed surgery in both feet as a teenager to treat bone spurs, and she had a slew of broken bones in her early adulthood, even delivering Tammy with a cast on her leg. Arthritis wasn't on her radar in early adulthood, but by her fifties, it was pretty clear something was developing. It began to affect her about the same time she was gladly tasked with the role of taking care of her eventual main reasons for living—Dalton and me. Both she and my parents lived in two-story homes with two sets of seven stairs in the center of the house. The most needed rooms were staggered on both levels. She had two grandkids full of energy who terrorized the whole space, meaning she, too, covered much ground each and every day. Osteoarthritis (the degeneration of joint cartilage and the resulting bone-on-bone friction causing stiffness and joint pain) first started in her right knee. There was no verbal indication of a problem brewing, but we first observed her slowing her pace around the stairs. She needed to be sure each foot fell flat on every stair. Steps were sometimes combined with the occasional squinting or quiet sighs after sharp jabs of pain. But she'd make the trip as many times as needed to ensure Dalton and I wanted for nothing. From the time we were born, her identity instantly altered into that of a doting grandma; there was nothing she wouldn't do for us. No pain was going to stop her from helping to ensure the smooth functioning of our family, and it didn't.

She was the motor that kept our machine running. When I was born, she rearranged her entire work schedule to accommodate taking care of me, a task she split with Grandma Becca. She showed up every single morning with surprises for us: not expensive or elaborate, just a small token to get us moving for the day. She would gently wake us up and carry or lead us to the living room, where she had breakfast waiting on the table. While we ate, she'd make our beds, pick out our clothes, and help us get ready for school. She tended to the household needs to help take the load off my parents. Dishes, laundry, errands, you name it. After school, she almost always treated us to a snack while she delicately listened to us retell every part of our day. Once home, it was all about homework and sports.

She never missed anything. Not a single performance, first or last day of school, athletic event, or doctor's appointment throughout my entire childhood and adolescence. Please take a second to put that into perspective. This was my grandparent, not my parent (and I did not have absent parents). We were truly her life, and it brought her immense joy and love to show up. Being a grandma was not just an internal identity but an external one as well. Everyone referred to her as Grandma Pryde. She volunteered in my classroom every year of elementary school, making deep and lasting connections with most of the teachers and students. For comedic relief, I will briefly mention my extreme emotional dysregulation that resulted from this. Long story short, I felt like she was *my* grandma, and I had no interest in allowing other kids to call her that (I even initially struggled with Dalton doing so). I was territorial and blunt when others referred to her that way. So, as much as she connected with her identity as Grandma Pryde, I reinforced it, demonstrating just how important it actually was.

Once the chronic knee pain affected her ability to care for us and her patients in the way she wanted to, she reluctantly decided to have a total knee replacement. I was in elementary school. There was a notable shift in our family's routine in the couple of months she needed for the healing process. The recovery was a disaster from the beginning. She never regained a full range of motion and was hindered by a combination of pain and declining function. She worked with a physical therapist and was a compliant patient (for being a nurse), but she never made the expected progress. Most appointments were full of agony, shrieks, and tears by the end. Concerned by what we'd heard, Dalton and I would ask, "Grandma, did that hurt today?"

As she wiped tears from her face, she'd reply, "Oh, it was a little stubborn to get moving, but then I got it moving good ... should we go get some french fries?" A positive spin and deflection in classic Grandma Pryde fashion. Her biggest concern was avoidance of any pain that Dalton and I might feel on her behalf (this concern never died down, by the way). Unfortunately, the surgery just didn't take, and the fear of another failed attempt and frustrating recovery was too much for her to handle. She made the conscious decision, more of a declaration, really, that she would never again allow a surgeon to cut her open. Given that she was the medical expert in the family, no one pushed back on her hopelessness regarding the potential for future surgeries. Now, I wish I could ask her if she had really considered or understood what that would mean for her over time as osteoarthritis waged a savage attack on the rest of her body.

As the snaps, crackles, and pops of her knees continued, her hands were the next area that drew our attention—about the same time I entered middle school. She developed nodules on her fingers, and when her hands were outstretched, her fingers naturally pointed in different directions. Swelling and tenderness became common with decreased grip strength. She would point out the funny shapes they made and rub them, often dousing them with ointments or creams that never really helped. There was no direct admittance of pain; she just noted it as an objective observation. She rallied per usual but became a bit slower with things, her decline following a trajectory similar to her knees. She didn't initially give up any of her hobbies, the most prominent being crocheting, and she made the most incredible baby blankets, hats, and booties for newborns. This started out as a fun pastime for her—making blankets for Dalton and me. Over time, she began to package the items for each new baby we would welcome into our family, friends' kin, and the babies in the NICU. Not only were these pieces beautiful and functional, but the love she put into them and the fact that they were a gift made by her were a big deal to the people who received them. The majority of lucky recipients still have their blankets and know exactly where they are to this day.

Looking back, I see that some of her slow-down coincided with the identity transitions she was forced to take as a result of Dalton and I growing up, especially once I started driving. We shapeshifted at the same time: me growing more independent, becoming bigger, while her duties shrank, making her feel smaller. Although she loved watching us grow, these milestones also brought disappointment with our growing autonomy; her role as grandma was the one in which she found the most pride and fulfillment throughout her life.[2] The less we needed her, the less she needed to move, and the more she would succumb to her pain (internally, that is). I never asked her (regretfully), but I can see how the slow, cumulative loss of her identity, of being Grandma Pryde the volunteer, the chauffeur, the basketball grandma, the cook, the teacher, the tidy-upper, and the savior created a sense of emptiness she always knew was coming but didn't know how to fill the holes it would create. It was grief, something much more painful than the irritation in her disgruntled joints. As my middle school years continued, she used more grit and tenacity to fight the progressive loss of mobility. The woman was insatiable, so dedicated to living up to the type of grandma she wanted to be. Her pain and resulting weakness robbed her of time and forced her to make accommodations, but those things still seemed to be an afterthought because of her commitment to supporting others. She knew what she should be doing to preserve her body but chose to put it off. She learned to mentally ready herself to cope with the chronic pain inherent in osteoarthritis,[3] honing a double-edged knack of avoiding the pain and convincing herself it wasn't that bad.

As I entered high school, the tides turned. The stairs in our homes became her nemesis, an opponent she was no longer a match for. This was intensified because, as her knees continued their tyranny against her desire to move, she began to overcompensate by using her other joints, unavoidably causing new problems. Havoc wrecked her lower back and both hips, making walking even on solid ground an exhausting endeavor. Our family became concerned about a possible fall and knew that things had to change. Emotionally, it was difficult for us to watch her try to walk, as anyone who has watched a loved one struggle with physical degeneration can attest to; it is a helpless and crushing thing to witness.[4] Conversations were initiated on the coattails of dread. She didn't want to admit the toll it was taking on her; she was scared. We didn't want to throw the loss of mobility in her face any more than her own body already was, but it needed to be addressed. My mom led the pack in coming up with a new game plan. First, we had to move her out of her house because the stairs were too dangerous. Grandpa Bill refused to leave their home, so we ended up getting her her own house that we could customize to create the least restrictive environment. She had always made things so easy for us, so now it was our turn to pay her back.

She was the poster child for toxic positivity during this transition. The move was hard on everyone, given the symbolism inherent in why it was happening. Nonetheless, once she was moved into the new home, she fell in love. This was one of the happiest periods of her entire life—I know because she used to say it all the time. She had wide areas to move around in, things were strategically placed for her to use with the least pain and effort possible, and she got full say-so in how every last item was arranged. Despite her failing body, she only spoke to the beauty in her life. I wish I were exaggerating that or misremembering fits of rage and anger about her ailments. I say "I wish" because I know there were many hardships she buried that prevented her from receiving the emotional and psychological support she was so good at giving to us. She deserved this support, and I wish she would have named these challenges, but she didn't. Instead, she raved about the organizational skills my mom executed to be sure her clothes and medications were easily put together for her. She was obsessed with the little devices and handiwork my dad would do around the house to make maneuvering around it easier, and of course, she loved any attempt Dalton and I made to come visit so she could showcase how she was adjusting to another small shift in her no-longer-abled body.

She still worked full time for an internal medicine clinic where she had also gotten me a job when I was sixteen. It served as a rare opportunity for the two of us to get to know each other in ways most family members never get to do. I got to see her flex her skills in perhaps her second-strongest identity: nurse. I heard stories of patients over the years, but to see the way people gravitated toward her was indescribable. I, of course, knew how special she was, so it wasn't surprising per se, but it was emotional to observe the ways she had touched others' lives. These snapshots of her at work helped me make sense of why her identity as a nurse was so important to her and aided my understanding of how painful it was for her to slowly lose it. It was a huge component of her self-worth, and it made sense; she was so damn good at it.[5] The patients, other nurses, and doctors all surrounded her for connection, advice, and support. Patients would rejoice when they saw her, requesting huge hugs and shedding tears of appreciation. "Oh Tasha, your grandma has been with our family through everything! We wouldn't have made it through without her!" They couldn't praise her enough. I also came to know just how comforting her bedside manner was. With bad news, staff would alert her, and she would take the extra time to make patients feel seen and heard and secure in a path forward. I remember a physician approaching her at her station once and whispering within earshot, "Pryde, this patient is having a really tough time. She asked if you'd come in and talk with us to help her figure out what to do next." Without another word, she was up and moving. When I was around, she would validate and meet her patients' needs first and then shift her focus to showing me off. "Here's my basketball star!" and "Tasha got straight A's again this semester!"

Her patients doted over me, always sure to remind me, "You don't know how lucky you are to have a grandma like Pryde, honey!" as if I really needed that. You have proud grandmas who will talk about their grandkids, and then you have Grandma Pryde. She took bragging to a whole new level, but because she cared so much for others, it felt as though her patients really cared about what they were hearing because we were an extension of her. She was a staple, relied on by generations of families, a steady force to support them through life.

As the beauty and pain dichotomy persisted, the joy she experienced in her home was matched by the continued deterioration of her body. We painfully watched as she transitioned from using walls and handrails as stabilizers to using a walker full time. She skipped the cane phase altogether because just switching sides to compensate for the feebleness wouldn't have helped; both legs needed time-outs. This would have been a decent time for a total hip/knee replacement to occur, but by then, her stubbornness wasn't the only barrier preventing this course of action. By her sixties, she had suffered four deep vein thromboses (blood clots) and a pulmonary embolism (blood clot in the lung) while being on blood thinners (I know, right!?). Investigation revealed that she had a genetic blood condition that made surgery riskier for her. Obviously, that sealed the no-surgery deal. She cared too much about life and wasn't willing to risk a complication or possible death that could result in her missing out on our lives. She vocalized her dislike of the walker initially but then began to speak to the ways in which it enabled a better quality of life for her. She even decorated it and used it as an accessory, trying to both normalize its use and shield us from showing concern or feeling pity. She tried to do little tricks with it, sitting on it and rolling around or using it to create obstacles to make other people laugh. Her lightheartedness was courageous—astounding, really.

The truth is, it broke her heart to have to succumb to the aging process in this way. She focused on what little she could control, not taking a day off work. She showed up on time and exceeded her responsibilities. The strength she demonstrated was inspirational to everyone around her, but inside, she was cracking, literally. We took her to arthritis specialists and received similar grim prognoses. She had the unanimous worst case of osteoarthritis they had ever seen, and nothing more than what we were already doing could be done, with the exception of introducing pain management. She absolutely hated this idea, but if pain medication could help restore a bit of functioning, she was willing to try it. And so, her journey with narcotics began.

Around this same time, the internal medicine clinic we worked for was a popular and thriving office, but eventually, the doctors admitted they weren't the most business savvy and needed to shut their doors. This meant that both Grandma Pryde and I would be out of work. Although somewhat stressful for me, it presented a much bigger stressor for her: a battle with her identity, not just that of a nurse but also of independence and the ability to provide for herself—something she had done since she was a teenager. She questioned whether another facility would hire her.[6] At the clinic, she had transitioned to a nurse emeritus, if you will, making phone calls and helping ease patients' pain, but by this point, she struggled to even use a blood pressure cuff properly. She wasn't ready to hang up her nursing hat, and to be honest, she needed the income to support herself. Again, in some ways, I wish I were lying, but there wasn't a single glimmer of negativity during this time. She admitted fear and was uncertain a viable solution would present itself, but she remained faithful, somehow sugarcoating it. She was diligent about checking the paper for jobs and getting a sense of what the community needed. Within a matter of a few weeks, a decades-long nursing friend of hers offered her a full-time position, this time at a home health facility. Grateful, she accepted, but on one condition. If I wasn't able to find another option, I would need to come along too. We were a package deal. She was my protector, and I was her legs. Because of who she was, this was an easy decision for our soon-to-be boss, even though she knew next to nothing about my actual work ethic. And thankfully, there we were again, working side by side.

She was forced to mourn more of her identity with this transition because traditional nursing was simply out of the question, and this new gig no longer had patients physically coming into the space. She rarely grieved this openly, but she did start to talk more about feeling burdensome.[7] She beat herself up for small mistakes and yearned for more direct patient contact and the fast-paced shifts she was used to. She brilliantly responded to her distress by accepting it and working to find purpose and meaning in the opportunities she still had. Her time at the home health agency was both inspiring and heartbreaking. Her body broke down much more concretely, and I am forever grateful to my now-best friend, Colleen, who would meet her outside at the beginning of each day and walk her out to her car each night to be sure no falls happened when I couldn't be there. It was devastating to watch her struggle getting in and out of the car and trying to organize her walker properly to get ready for the day. She took it all in stride, which served to build admiration and positive morale in our coworkers, who loved her like their own. Conflicting emotions pulled us all in varied directions. She was humble yet proud of the way she persevered through any level of pain. Simultaneously, immobility fostered misplaced guilt and shame, showcasing the many shadow losses that result from aging.

We went on this way for the better portion of a couple of years until the day after Christmas in 2010. Both she and I received the same out-of-the-blue call from our boss that we had been let go due to financial and staffing reasons. I was embarrassed and a bit panicked, given that the flexibility of the job made it easy for me to tackle it alongside my college studies. But for Grandma Pryde, this was a true betrayal and the last nail in the coffin of her nursing career. To be blindsided by her friend and approached without compassion and acknowledgment of what this would mean for her created emotional strife that she sadly held onto until she died. Although she had grieved aspects of her career as things were stripped away, her reasons for living and the social connections she found so much purpose in took a huge hit.[8] She knew that she would not be able to get another job given her physical state and couldn't put herself through the shame of trying. It was an unjust way to end one of the most rewarding and successful nursing careers of all time. To make matters worse, she feared what this financial blow would mean to the living arrangements she and Grandpa Bill had become accustomed to. She didn't display a "woe is me" reaction, but she was lonely. I wish I had had more fortitude to ask her to express herself more; grief was everywhere, and all she wanted to highlight was how lucky she was to have gotten to work with me for so many years.

Her forewarned fear was not irrational. We moved her and Grandpa Bill back together and into a new house shortly after we were let go. Finances were a primary reason, of course, but her physical deterioration was making us more anxious because of the increased time she was now spending alone. We could no longer risk the potential damage a fall would invite in her pursuit of independence. Plus, we were perturbed about the lack of social stimulation we knew she would not adapt well to. We also wanted her to be around Grandpa Bill to help us gauge what he was up to when no one was looking. His hoarding behaviors had skyrocketed since having his own space, and it was hazardous. Simply put, they needed each other again, even if it wasn't necessarily their first choice. We found a gorgeous home built specifically for elderly, handicapped people, and it was just a couple blocks away from my parents. This was more convenient for my mom, who, at this point, was visiting at least once a day to help make things safe and comfortable. New seeds of grief were planted as the two switched roles, another uncomfortable shapeshift of responsibility. My mom became a nearly full-time caregiver and supremely ensured the best quality of life possible. Just as my Grandma Pryde would have done anything for us, my mom began to model her commitment to do the same for Grandma Pryde, her identity also shifting from daughter to caregiver.[9] For my mom, "overwhelming" was an understatement, as she was sandwiched between taking care of her emerging adult children, my dad, my slew of other relatives who relied on her, and Grandma Pryde. It was arduous for her to know who she was supposed to be on any given day, and now she felt the sharp loss of no longer having her own mother as that steady force to fall back on. Meanwhile, Grandma Pryde's biggest task became sifting through the grief of losing another part of her self-worth, feeling guilty about the unwanted transition, and reorienting herself back to life with Grandpa Bill under the same roof.

As Grandma Pryde's identity was narrowing, mine was expanding.

This time coincided with my choice to pursue my doctorate degree. It was the biggest decision I had ever made for myself, and I heavily relied on her perspective every step of the way. I was completely torn once I was offered spots in programs around the country because it made real the idea of leaving behind everything I had ever known. I will never forget sitting on the couch next to her, sobbing silently yet uncontrollably. I was fixated on the anticipatory belief that I couldn't move away because of the prospect that something could happen to her and I wouldn't be there. My unusually high experience with death and the resulting recognition that you can lose someone you love at any minute played tricks on me in the sense that I felt culpable and selfish for considering the conflicting idea that you can live your life for yourself and still be loyal to your most trusted confidants, even if distance is between you. She knew she had to stay strong and unbiased for me because my parents were not able to offer the same encouraging support.

"I don't think I can do it, Grandma. I don't want to be away from you. It scares me that I can't get home fast enough if something happens. I don't think I should go. I know Mom and Dad don't want me to," I managed to say through choppy pauses to catch my breath.

"Sugar plum, I will be right here waiting for you to come home each and every day. This is good for you; you will go and do your job and then come home ... we will all be right here. Nothing is going to happen to me, and we will talk every day. You make me so proud."

After hours of broken-record conversations and her relentless patience and apt ear for listening, I sent the email from her living room to accept my admittance to Purdue University, while sitting on the floor in front of her rocking chair so she could see my fingers as I typed away and pressed send. Her mangled hand rested on my shoulder; our connection visible in every way. We sealed the deal together, marking one of the most onerous yet liberating moves I will ever make. It crushed her to see me move away for those three years, but not once did she make me feel guilty or question whether it was the right move for me. Instead, she ordered herself a Purdue blanket the very same day and came up with all these ideas of ways we could stay more connected while

I was at school. She promised me she would be there with me every single day, and she was.

She kept every promise she made. We spoke even more when I lived in Indiana. We started so many routines that strengthened our relationship and would become permanent fixtures in my day-to-day life until she died. On her end, one of the most important adjustments was working on being more honest about how she was actually doing, a transformation of its own. I was insistent about this because I couldn't just drive over and see it for myself anymore. Slowly but surely, she disclosed more about her pain and how it was impacting her but was careful never to turn it into a complaint. I needed to feel like I was there with her, which made it easier for us both to practice expressing vulnerability and admitting that things were really hard. Sometimes she acknowledged a fear of the future but quickly followed it with blind faith that she would be okay. She would vent about things that annoyed her or that she didn't understand. She talked through unfair feelings of worthlessness. She still yearned to be helpful and felt like no one relied on her for anything anymore, often reverting back to old stories with patients. This was the only time I was able to shine in the support department because I contended that she was the biggest reason I was able to make it through each day. Because she was. If she could live in her declining physical condition and waning quality of life without cessation, I could get through the bullshit that is graduate school, a broken heart, or whatever else. I loved the moments when I was able to remind her that the attention she provided me was a huge reason why I was a successful and productive human being. I was profoundly and unconditionally seen, loved, and supported each second of the day, and I knew it. What a privilege. I tried to give her random things to do for me to pass the time. Sometimes it was ordering me something online or asking her to do some research on a random topic I had heard about. Sometimes I'd even send her a few different shoe options I was considering and ask her to rank them. It was important to me to guarantee she felt like she was still helping and that she still mattered. Because she was, and she did, more than either of us realized.

The once-slow deterioration in her movement took a steep decline as if her body had officially tapped out without telling her. Her joints were all bone-on-bone except for one shoulder, and the incessant grinding wouldn't allow her to move anymore. The pain was unbearable, and we had to make yet another calamitous recommendation: a transition from a walker to a motorized wheelchair. Grief thickened, as we knew that limiting her potential for movement would only break down her body further, but her fall risk and pain were not worth allowing her to suffer in that way anymore. Plus, there really aren't any other transitions once you're in a wheelchair full time. She coped by internalizing her grief and diminishing pain, and we let her. The potential end of her life hung over us like dark clouds, eerily calm but undoubtedly carrying the worst storm we would ever face.

The only true movement she could execute was the excruciating struggle to lift herself from her bed or chair just enough to shimmy into the wheelchair and maneuver around. With her typical attitude, she remained overjoyed as she shared all the cool ways the wheelchair could move and what she had learned to do with it. She exclaimed how much easier it made things for her and would take pictures of little decorations she embellished it with and send them to us. She'd also try to make light of the "beauty marks" she'd add to the walls and furniture by accidentally running into things while turning her wheelchair into a racecar to get to the bathroom in time.

Despite her attempts at lightheartedness, she was terrified of falling and making her situation worse, so the prospect of leaving the house became out of the question. She had officially transitioned to homebound status.[10] Her social life, once so vibrant, became intermittent text or phone conversations with friends from a different time. She spent the day reading and watching old black-and-white movies on the AMC channel. She began to nap more, dozing unnaturally, waking up to kinks in her neck and guilt for dreaming the day away. If this sounds sad and isolating, then I've done my job. It was heart-wrenching to see her life whittled down to this routine. To hear someone say they miss going to the grocery store deepens a whole new level of understanding about the boredom and entrapment her body had created for her. Yet, her optimism never let her get too down, and she was always finding ways to look forward to things and rejoice in even the tiniest changes in her day. She lived for phone calls and visits from us. A simple text message from me lit up her world and made the pain she endured worth it. I know because she used to tell me that every day. I don't have words to explain what it's like to matter to someone that much. She was ever so present, engaged, and in tune with her guests when they were over. It didn't matter who it was. She made everyone feel like the most valuable person in the world. Her doctors, therapist, hairdresser, and even pedicurist all began coming straight to her, which I think speaks volumes about the respect, love, and dedication these individuals had for her. Their visits were typically used to talk less about her and more about Dalton and me. I know it was a challenge for any of them to redirect her back to actually addressing her own health and well-being, but they tried their best.

A huge portion of her bragging centered on the fact that I had finally crossed the finish line to Dr. Trujillo. Yet again, as her world was constricting, mine was swelling exponentially. There was joy from this accomplishment, and my career was shaping up nicely, but I was having a bit of my own identity crisis. I had been an ambitious, over-achieving, higher education aficionado for the better part of ten years, and suddenly I was "just working." As strange as it seems, I was lost. My identity veered off-track, as it so quickly molded from athlete in my teens to student that carried me through my twenties. I didn't really know what I liked to do for fun or with my free time because I had never had such an unstructured time in my life. I felt useless, which sounds stupid (yes, no self-compassion to be had here) given that I was working as a full-time psychologist, literally helping people. But it's true. I felt worthless, mediocre, and lacking the ever-present ambition I had lived my life by. I needed a way to channel my drive and find a purpose for me to feel worthy again, so I defaulted back to my old familiar friend: fitness. I set all sorts of goals, pushing myself well beyond my limits with suboptimal self-care to fuel recovery. I became fixated on training, trying to turn myself into a high-powered engine. The less food, the better; the more exercise, the better: whatever it would take to make me elite again. Malnourishment, injury, and frequent aggravation of my respiratory system were the primary results. But there she was, saving me from me. We continued our daily conversations.

"Sugar plum, you need to slow down. It's okay to have a rest. Don't work too hard, you already do so much. You don't want to get sick, you are too busy and too special, and Grandma loves you." This is a text I remember by heart.

She reminded me that self-worth is more than achievements (and who would know better than her by this point?). She was gentle, tentative, and cautious. She proposed I take honest looks at myself so I didn't get trapped in my perfectionism. She talked me through other opportunities I needed to lean into and reminded me that the discomfort I was feeling was temporary. I just needed to figure out how to reshape my identity without harming myself along the way. She was my rock, forever asserting her undeniable belief in my capabilities. Even though she was solely focused on meeting my needs, I wonder if these talks served the same purpose for her. I hope they reminded her that she was still needed. She needed to help save me from myself. And she did. Every day.

The final surrender to her failing body was made about six months before the end of her life, spurred by an unfortunate fall. She had gotten the arm of her robe stuck in her wheelchair, and as she tried to pull it out, she fell and broke her right humerus. As luck would have it, there were no options to heal the break except for a weak sling because of her surgery risk and where the break took place. On top of the arthritis continuing to destroy her body, the break made all of us feel powerless and angry. We swapped out a normal bed for a hospital bed to help make the transition in and out less pain-provoking and horrifying for her. We initially thought that she might not recover from this break and were terrified it might do her in, but just as sure as the sun rose and fell each day, she chose to push through it. Stubborn willfulness. As her distress intensified, doctors recommended higher doses of pain medication. No one really knew what to do with her, so pain control became the name of the game. Doses and types of medication were changed; we even introduced her to THC gummies. Devastatingly, we never found a concoction that brought her the much-deserved relief. She carried such guilt about taking pain medications and cannabis. Although she didn't misuse them, she knew that she was physically dependent on them over time, and that fact never sat well with her. Especially since they didn't eliminate her excruciating agony. Her body suffered other physical side effects from the medication, eating away at her teeth and skin, further eroding her sense of self and increasing her embarrassment for yet another thing her body took from her. She had moments of confusion and would sometimes say off-handed things that didn't really make sense. Logically, she knew she had no control over these effects, yet she couldn't help but allow them to deliver another heavy blow to her self-esteem. It was hard for her to have confidence when she came face-to-face with the withering state of her body. And still, she persisted. She woke each morning with gratitude for the opportunities to be a part of our lives. She used to say that being our grandma fueled her ability to fight through the pain. The unfairness in her story makes me irate. The pauses I've had to take while composing this chapter are tenfold compared to the other stories I've told. I sometimes question how much we let her down as her family and caregivers. Could we have done more? Sought out more specialists, demanded that they do more than dole out narcotics, and attempted more interventions outside of Western medicine?

I am absolutely disgusted with myself to write these next words, but they are true, and they are an important part of this story. As the obliteration of her body evolved over the last couple of years of her life, it became harder for me to look at her and to listen to her wince in pain each time she tried to raise her arm to her mouth to drink water or lift her leg a couple of inches to reposition it in her chair. Even the simplest moves would bring tears to her eyes, and then I would fight like hell to be sure they didn't come to mine. There wasn't a moment her body wasn't attacking her, and there was nothing any of us could do to stop it. I was wrecked and couldn't accept or face what this eventual decline would mean for her life or mine. She needed to stay alive for the rest of my life as far as I was concerned, and I selfishly teetered between the avoidance of watching her deteriorate and a ridiculous belief that she would simply have to live in this pain forever. Which I know she would have gladly done to stay by my side. I always counted on the fact that she didn't have any other severe medical ailments; besides the arthritis, she was truly healthier than I was.

But I was self-centered more than I'd like to admit. When we were together, sometimes I wouldn't be able to look at her for long, or I would be snappy and curt because I couldn't emotionally regulate the pain I experienced internally or externally. I was even mean at times, especially in her brief moments of cognitive fog. I knew it wasn't her, but it scared me. She remained so upbeat when she noticed my change in demeanor and would somehow turn the interaction into trying to make me feel better for what I was witnessing. She would lie about having a better pain day (a repeated flaw, for sure) or try to change the subject to bring a smile to my face. There she was, in literally debilitating physical and mental anguish, trying to protect me from my own emotional stunting and inability to be strong for her. It no doubt worsened her feelings of being a burden, but she was never a burden. I just avoided the acceptance and the uncertainty of life like the plague, which, in turn, made it harder for both of us. I would give anything to take back those exchanges and make it more about her. To lean into her suffering and be with her in it, even though we both knew there was nothing I could do. I wish I would have had the courage to keep looking. To put my fucking phone down and look at her when she spoke to me. She deserved more from me. I'm not asking for pity, sympathy, or positivity; it is just what happened. I hope that my vulnerability now is, by some means, honoring her, and maybe somehow, she will finally know the ways in which she completed our lives.

Without being able to interview her, I tried my best to consider what may have been pivotal moments for her in each story of this book. During my mom's hemorrhage, consider what it was like to get a call from your twenty-one-year-old son-in-law, frantically telling you that your daughter was bleeding out, about to die in their bathroom, while their two-week-old daughter fussed by their bedside. Imagine rushing down to another department in your workplace, prepping a group of professionals (your friends) for the arrival of your daughter, who had no pulse and a fatal blood pressure at just twenty years old. Envision watching your unresponsive, lifeless child covered in blood being carried off a stretcher and whisked into emergency surgery due to a mistake made by a doctor you know personally and called a friend—trusted even. Contemplate what it would be like to call your other children and tell them that they needed to rush home because their sister might die and that one of them would need to be prepared to give blood that could be the only thing to potentially save her life.

During my flight for life, I don't remember anything about the ambulance ride to the airport, and as the lone person who could fill in those details, her insight will forever be missed. As I recounted this tale, I was reminded just how immense her presence was in my life. She is the only witness who no doubt stood strong and steady through the entire escapade. We always had a particularly strong bond, perhaps because we shared the same name or because I was her first and only granddaughter. Regardless of the reasons, there is no other person on the planet I would have rather had with me on that chopper. I wonder if part of why I survived was because of the heroic manner in which she supported me. It turns out she was fearful of flying, particularly in small planes, and had to fight pangs of nausea the entire way. But she did it, probably without ever emitting an ounce of detectable discomfort. What I wouldn't give to thank her for that right now. Her bravery always showed through. In time, she described it to me as "uncomfortable" but dismissed any other recognition of what was clearly much more than just an uncomfortable ride.

These things are unfathomable. Yet I am told that she handled them calmly. Confidently. With ease, even. But we can't know what was happening for her internally. I can't ask her to walk me through some of the worst nights of her life. Life is infinitely different now without her. That realization brings paralyzing grief; however, it isn't just my own grief that hovers over these stories. It's all of ours—hers included. My mom's most tearful retellings of any story came when explaining the big and small parts her mom had to play in her life and remembering she is no longer with us in a physical sense. With each ping of reality, I could see the grief slowly take over my mom's facial muscles as she replayed each memory. The shakiness of her mouth, the veins that became more constricted around her eyes, and the urge to jump out of her own body were more apparent, all pointing out the despair sensed by reliving what it felt like to have her mother present for every major moment of her life.

A reminder that grief and loss are multilayered, messy, intense, and permanent. Yet if processed, there is unlimited potential growth from the roots of such despair,[11] an idea I know Grandma Pryde would get behind.

You may have noticed a few differences in how she showed up as a grandma and as a mother, and I feel empowered to comment more on this as I have tried to paint accurate pictures of each of us, even the ones I idolize the most. She made many mistakes as a parent with each of her children (not uncommon for any parent). Again, I feel hollow knowing I can't have more conversations with her about the recollections of her decisions. Try to put yourself in the shoes of a parent in the 1980s who has a child come out to you, knowing full well your husband will not be a safe and supportive confidant for him. Consider what it must have been like to hear your daughter retell trauma that both threatened and stole her innocence and safety. She did not always make the adaptive choice; my guess is that she just wanted the pain to go away. In contrast, some of her choices and needs induced hurt she never intended. There are striking dissimilarities between how she treated her children and grandchildren, and I wish I understood more about what developed over the years to allow for such a transformation. She never missed a single event of ours but missed several of her own kids' events. She knew all of our friends' names but very few of her own kids' friends. Times were different, and her identities and responsibilities were different, but the facts remain. It also reminds me how often I hear about 180-degree changes made once parents add "grand" to their title. What gives?

On a broader level, the cyclical grief that rotates in and out of our lives with the various roles we land, play, lose, and reshape is constant. Grief doesn't go away, and there are always new events lurking in the shadows, waiting to ignite a new fire born of loss. Our identities intersect with those of others and complicate our relationships and our understanding of ourselves, each other, and the world. Our identities can tear us apart when we lose them and make us feel whole when we refine them or embark on something completely new altogether. We reinvent so many aspects of the self throughout our lives. As they say, change is the only constant, but I'd argue that perhaps some things really do stay the same, even if they visually appear distinct from time to time. We have to accept that life is both pain and beauty, and you can't look at one while turning your back on the other. I tried to do this with her pain, and she suffered more because of it. We have to admit that uncertainty is everywhere, and learning to be comfortable with it is the key to unlocking our potential to fully live.[12] I hope that you, reading this, will be able to face your own vulnerabilities and fears more triumphantly. To be more like Grandma Pryde. To capitalize on opportunities you may take for granted and to bask in the goodness of the people you have since you never know when you will have them for the last time. Because when you lose them, and when you lose aspects of yourself, you have to accept completely that you will never be the same again.

12

EXISTENTIAL GLITCHES OF REALITY

Almost a month to the day before Grandma Pryde's death, she had been admitted to the hospital with a urinary tract infection (UTI). This was not her first bout with UTIs, as she was notoriously bad at drinking water and her diet had become more restrictive and unbalanced in her older years, partially because of ease and partially because of preference. These infections seemed to be her kryptonite. She usually didn't have notable symptoms, so the infections got severe before being treated, often requiring hospitalization. This illness was especially unsettling because we were in the middle of the COVID-19 pandemic. The world was completely shut down, and medical facilities were overwhelmed and strict with rules to avoid spreading the virus. Consequently, we couldn't be at the hospital with her. Although being a patient is not typically defined as a good time by many, because of who she was and the legacy she carried there, she got special attention, which was a huge consolation for us. She was treated like royalty because she was. Once they believed the infection had resolved, she was given the green light to discharge. She was released on oxygen, the only remarkable change. Hindsight bias has pointed out a few subtle changes we didn't really pay mind to but which could have been telling had we been more observant. For example, she slept more, although we chalked that up to the mundane and mostly uneventful existence she now led. She had more brief moments of confusion, which we intentionally avoided admitting because of our own discomfort. We weren't looking for signs of danger because we believed the infection had cleared itself. We saw what we wanted to see.

My mom received an alarming phone call from Grandpa Bill early Saturday morning, December 12, 2020. He was calm as he explained, "Lynn, it's me. Your mom is really cold, and we can't seem to warm her up. I have lots of blankets on her, but it isn't helping. And Lynn, she's throwing up and I'm not sure why ... I think you better come over."

My mom rushed over, bursting through the front door and into Grandma Pryde's room, where she lay in bed. She was barely conscious, which was strange in and of itself, to the point that my mom wasn't sure that her presence was even recognized. Knowing this was out of her wheelhouse, she called for an ambulance. As she waited for the paramedics to arrive, she got into bed with her mom and held her.

"Mom, I called an ambulance. We have to take you back to the hospital. Everything's going to be fine. I can't go with you because of this fucking pandemic, but I'll be there as soon as I can, okay?" She cringed as she swallowed the reality that her mom was too out of it to respond.

The paramedics, who looked like futuristic shapes of fabric around cutouts of human bodies, moved fast and were responsive to my mom's orders. She insisted they understand the extent of Grandma Pryde's arthritis so they didn't cause accidental pain while attempting to transfer her. My mom and Grandpa Bill watched the ambulance, lights on but no sirens, until it was out of sight. We didn't know it yet, but COVID was now our sworn enemy. The hospital had rules that no visitors were allowed, so she had to brave it alone. This caused warranted stress for everyone because no one knew her body as we did, and she was not conscious enough to assert her needs. We knew where she could be touched and the step-by-step routine to ensure as much safety and as little struggle as possible. No one knew better than my mom, in fact, yet that didn't seem to matter. There were no exceptions this time, not even for Grandma Pryde.

My mom had no idea what to do with herself, but she needed to stay busy. She started by making harrowing phone calls to alert us one by one. Most of those phone calls were brief and packed with emotion. Her call found me house hunting. My boyfriend at the time, Ramon, and I had become serious, and I had recently taken a job in Denver. We decided to take the big step of moving to a new city and in together. I was sitting in the passenger seat of his truck as I navigated us between the homes I had put into a detailed spreadsheet. I heard my phone ring, and I answered and heard sniffling and heavy breathing. She was crying.

"What's wrong, Mom?"

"Tasha, I just had to call an ambulance to come get your grandma again. They're taking her to the hospital."

Although I was alarmed and frustrated, Grandma Pryde had had a decent number of hospital visits over the last year, so I wasn't particularly concerned. "Do I need to be worried? I can come home now if I need to."

"No, it's probably the same shit as last time. She's just throwing up and a little more out of it right now. And with COVID, you can't see her anyway. Just stay there and look at your houses. Let me know when you get home. Please be safe. I love you."

"Okay, let me know, then. Love you, bye." Although I heard the tears and felt her fear, I honestly didn't ask if she was okay, a regretful oversight on my part. I let Ramon know what was going on, trying my best not to seem rattled. He asked if I wanted to cancel the rest of the tours and head home, and I said no. We needed to figure out a place to live. I said she would be okay. Even though I tried to play it off, my energy spoke otherwise and cast an odd shadow over us for the rest of the evening. I wasn't present, and Ramon had no idea how to maneuver dealing with me in this light, so he checked in occasionally but stayed at arm's length.

Back in Laramie, my mom remained anxious, expelling energy by cleaning everything in preparation for Grandma Pryde's unquestioned return. She wanted things to be fresh and ready to welcome her back home. She and Grandpa Bill conversed a bit, hypothesizing about what may be wrong this time. Neither of them had death anywhere in the vicinity of their conscious awareness. Meanwhile, the world just kept spinning, none of us aware of how derailed it would soon become.

Not even a full day after admitting her, the hospital staff contacted my mom and indicated that Grandma Pryde's status was rapidly worsening. She had a severe UTI that had induced sepsis with severe hypotension. They described her as critical but didn't explicitly introduce the idea of death. Apparently, the infection from several weeks prior had doggedly stuck around. Because she never had the telltale signs of a UTI, she didn't know there was a fast-approaching storm in her body. Their assessment revealed that her immune system had kicked into overdrive to try to counteract the infection still living inside of her. Because there was no timely treatment, her organs—kidneys, most specifically—had become overwhelmed and were shutting down. They reported that she was too critical to be treated locally and would need to be transported to a larger facility with better equipment. My mom gave immediate permission and was told they would deliver her to a trauma hospital in Loveland, Colorado, via ambulance. It is strange that this is the facility they transported her to because I happened to live in Loveland, and this hospital was literally right across the street from my condo. I could see it right outside my front windows and walk to it in a matter of minutes.

My mom, as Grandma Pryde's power of attorney, stayed in close contact with the staff at both hospitals throughout the transfer process. One change between the hospitals was that in Loveland, one visitor was permitted every twenty-four hours per patient. Given this knowledge, my mom and her siblings worked out how the three of them would tackle the shifts over the next several days, again insinuating that death hadn't found a place in their conscious psyche. Tom had the first one, so as soon as he was notified, he and Tammy made the drive from Denver to Loveland. As they walked inside the automatic glass doors, they searched the directory and made their way to the ICU. A man addressed them and reported that only one person could proceed. A bit flabbergasted but trying to remain polite, Tammy took a deep breath and stated she would wait in the car. You could tell the man was in a cognitive battle between his values and the superimposed rules of the hospital. Quickly, he acknowledged it was too cold for her to sit in the car and instead walked her to a chair in the hallway near the elevator. He told her to stay there and that she couldn't tell anyone he had allowed her to do so. Grateful for his kindness, she settled in and parted ways with Tom as she watched the doors of the elevator slowly close with him inside.

Tom stepped onto the nearly deserted floor and took a long look around before making a move. A nurse intercepted him and, after figuring out where he belonged, walked him to a window, where he was instructed to stay put until they finished settling Grandma Pryde into her room. The nurse reported, "Your mom seems to be in a lot of pain and was really disoriented. We're having a hard time getting things set up. She became a little aggressive, and we couldn't understand what she was trying to say. It will just be a little longer."

Furious but holding that back, Tom educated the nurse on her condition. "She is usually in a lot of pain. She has severe osteoarthritis and has lost most of her mobility and function in her legs, hips, and shoulders. She's recovering from a broken shoulder as we speak. You have to be gentle with her and cannot jerk or move her too quickly, especially her right arm."

The nurse gasped as things clicked for her, her eyes opening much wider, the only part of her face visible because of the mask she was wearing. Her newfound understanding was frustrating in that, had our family been present from the beginning, staff would have had the necessary information to keep her comfortable and eliminate their preventable confusion. Thanks, COVID.

After ten minutes, he received word that he could enter the room. Grandma Pryde was somewhat awake and coherent, so he took a seat next to her and started to joke with her.

"Mom! This is not the type of excitement we need to get you to come see Tasha in Loveland!" Although she didn't respond as she normally would, she released a notable sigh of relief at knowing how close she was to me, finally. She frequently expressed sorrow about not being able to travel to see my new home. They made a bit of small talk as the medical personnel continued to regulate her body. She dozed on and off while he held her hand and tried to bring positivity to the room, just as she would have done if she had more energy. Around 8 p.m., he was notified that visiting hours were over, even though he had only been there for about a twelfth of his allotted twenty-four. He obeyed, nonetheless. He kissed her and gave a simple, "I love you, Mom," completely unaware that this would be the last time he ever spoke to her. When he got off the elevator, he greeted Tammy, who hadn't made a single move from the lone seat she was given permission to occupy, and they made their way to the car. He called my mom and gave them both a play-by-play, reinforcing two key points that instilled false hope. One: Grandma Pryde was mostly coherent and in good spirits, and two: a procedure on her kidneys could do the trick and set her on the path toward healing. Audible solace echoed in the silence between them.

At about 1:30 a.m., Tom received a call from a nurse. It was an update with no update. Although appreciative of the call, it created an unsettled feeling that rendered him unable to achieve quality sleep for the remainder of the early morning. With a conflicted need to move and a desire to stay put, he started to get ready. A few hours later, he received another call, this nurse's voice more pressured.

"Hi Tom. Your mom has gotten sicker throughout the night, and we are at a point where we need your permission to intubate her."

He tried to slow down the conversation. "Wait, she was fine just a couple of hours ago. I need to talk to my sisters about this. I don't understand, but I need to talk to my sisters. I am not the POA; my sister Lynn is. I just need to make sure we are all on the same page. Can I call you back?"

He received pushback and was met with a rushed demand to give authorization. "We need permission to intubate now."

He pleaded his case. "I just need a little time. We will all be in Loveland in about an hour to reconvene. I just need a few minutes to make a three-way call with my sisters. Please, I will call right back." The nurse was disapproving but conceded and so he quickly organized a conference call. After he spilled the nurse's update, my mom was the first to break the silence, her high-pitched voice breaking in perfect rhythm with her heart. Her panic sent chilling waves through the phone as she helped them all grasp the seriousness of the situation. She knew intubation in any form was critical and introduced death out loud for the first time.

"She's going to die, you guys."

Tom kept repeating, "No, Lynn, she was fine just a few hours ago.

She was just fine!" The reality was now intolerable, avoidance blowing over them as easily as sagebrush across a desolate Wyoming prairie. The decision to intubate was a no-brainer. With shaky hands and a heart now skipping beats, my mom called back and gave verbal authorization. Now, in their effort to get to Loveland, our family wasn't just racing the typical traffic and weather problems of a Rocky Mountain winter; instead, they were competing against the hands of time and the mystical powers that decide when our physical forms no longer have a home.

December 13, 2020, was the worst day of my life. It was a Sunday morning, cold with snow but sunny. Sunday was Tammy's shift. Tom helped her prepare with questions and propositions once she had access to medical providers. They agreed hospice made the most sense. It would provide a more lenient and less sterile environment so that we could all be with Grandma Pryde while she recuperated. Tom pulled up curbside and watched helplessly from the driver's seat as Tammy exited and passed through the automatic doors and out of sight. After a stranger took her temperature and ensured she was masked and deemed safe to be there, she found her way to the ICU. She shook off chills from the apocalyptic vibes the silence was giving off. She walked around until she found the right room and was begrudgingly greeted by an irritable nurse sitting at the bedside. Tammy inched closer toward her mom, choking back intense bouts of fear that threatened to turn her legs around and run from the room at a dead sprint.

Grandma Pryde was lying motionless in the bed, her mouth unnaturally forced apart to accommodate the intubation tube now regulating her once natural and easy breaths. Tammy was shocked by the number of tubes and wires sticking out of nearly every visible surface of her body as she lay propped up at about a forty-five-degree angle. Under the fluorescent lights, the bed was the purist white color she had ever seen, a stark contrast to the gray tint her mom's skin displayed. Tammy's eyes were drawn to dry, bloody patches up and down her mom's arms where hospital staff had either been unsuccessful or removed and replaced medical instruments. Then, she noticed the deep gashes in her neck where thin hoses had been placed and replaced for reasons she didn't know. The horror must have been painfully obvious in Tammy's eyes, especially since the nurse couldn't see anything else. The nurse interrupted Tammy's inner dialogue.

"Your mom tried to rip out some of the equipment. We have cleaned things up as best as we can for right now."

Tammy couldn't respond and instead focused on the disconcerting sounds from each machine to which the various tubes were attached. There was no rhythm she could pick up to soothe her. Instead, it was chaotic and choppy, much like her thoughts. She needed some hint of positivity, so she stared hard enough until she decided that Grandma Pryde was actually having a pretty good hair day. She was finally able to catch her breath and used it to ask, "What happened?"

"Your mom's blood pressure was dangerously low, and her pain was uncontrollable, the combination of which led to intubation as the best choice."

"Okay, well, can she hear me?"

"Yes, why don't you move closer and grab her hand."

Tammy complied quickly, squeezing her hand and finding the calmest voice she could muster. "Mom, what happened? What the hell happened!?" The nurse emitted a burst of surprise and pointed out that there was clearly some life left in her because her heart rate had bounced up considerably at the sound of Tammy's voice.

Chattier now, after that encouraging glimmer of hope, the nurse asked Tammy, "Does your mom try to take her clothes off a lot? We had a hard time getting her to keep them on this morning."

Tammy chuckled and remarked, "Oh no, my mom is very modest. She is always fully clothed. Were you trying to move her right arm?"

"Probably," the nurse admitted.

Even though Tammy asked, she knew the answer; it was obvious from the dark red wounds, evidence of failed sticks.

"Well, that's what happened then. You can't move her arm right now because she's recovering from a broken humerus on top of arthritis." Again, the nurse gasped as she realized that straightening her arm would have been agonizing. Intense sadness and anger collided within Tammy as she recognized the harsh truth due to the COVID crisis.[1] They put her mom through unintentional but avoidable pain because she wasn't able to speak for herself and we weren't there. Of course she tried to rip those things from her arms! She was begging them to ease her pain in the only way she could. The nurse's eyes softened ever so slightly before she shut their exchange down to prepare Tammy for the doctor's arrival. A few brief minutes of silence carried another painful realization: the only person Tammy would or could have consulted with about what was going on was the person motionless in the bed. She had never felt more lost or alone.

The doctor arrived, this time a female. She was about Tammy's height, so they were at least able to look each other right in the eyes since nothing else was visible. Her scrubs didn't match, and Tammy had a negative reaction to it, knowing that in nearly five decades of nursing, Grandma Pryde never once left the house with scrubs that didn't match. She was zapped back to reality once the woman started talking. The doctor explained that toxins were quickly gaining momentum in their pursuit of Grandma Pryde's organs, and the only hope they had was to perform dialysis. The doctor wanted to know if they could proceed with the procedure. And then, she laid out the catch.

"Tammy, I want to be clear. This will either work and jumpstart an exceedingly long recovery that she still may not survive, or it will fail and the toxins will flood through her faster, leading to a quick death."

Trying to make sense of it all, Tammy responded, "I need to talk to my family. What can you do to keep her comfortable, and can we all come up to see her? What about home health, or hospice, or letting us take her home if the procedure doesn't work?"

The doctor shattered all hope. "Tammy, unfortunately, she is in grave condition. None of those are options at this point, and because of COVID, we can't allow more visitors."[2]

Tammy pleaded, "But my family is *literally* right across the street, and none of us have COVID. My mom doesn't even have COVID!"

The doctor redirected attention to the dialysis procedure and stood firm. "I understand how hard this is, but I need to know if you want to proceed with the procedure or not. No one else can come in at this time." Feeling intense defeat and anger, the only thing Tammy could muster was that they needed to do everything in their power to save her, that she was not ready to die, and that we weren't ready to lose her.

Meanwhile, in Laramie, even though they knew COVID rules were in place, my parents and Dalton urgently hopped in the truck and raced down to Loveland, trying to beat the final game clock we didn't realize had started. They chose not to bring Grandpa Bill because no one

was expecting that day to be Grandma Pryde's last. He stayed behind and agreed to stay near the phone for calls. It was snowing, of course, with low visibility and poor road conditions, but they had no choice. The ride wasn't silent as it had been during other rushed medical trips across state lines. Instead, there were nearly constant conference calls between my mom and her siblings. One of those calls carried more weight than the others in that Tammy had to rally her siblings to make a decision about whether to try dialysis. She sugar-coated nothing as she relayed the dire state their mom was in, reinforcing the idea of death as stated by someone with the knowledge and training to force unwanted objectivity. Not trying the procedure would lead to death and potentially more suffering. Even though she was intubated, we knew that Grandma Pryde didn't want to die (she said this often) and that we couldn't live without her (we didn't say this enough). There was unanimous agreement to initiate the last attempt we had at saving our everything. As my dad listened from the driver's seat, he realized that, once again, he was behind the wheel, reliving all the times in the past they had been in a snowstorm, speeding into Colorado. He tried to wrap his head around the words he heard but wasn't able to register. His mother-in-law was going to die and with her, a part of all of us.

My dad looked around the truck to gauge how everyone was. Dalton was in the backseat silently crying, his sunglasses on, head against the cold glass, but not wincing, even a little. He was being pulverized inside but couldn't let it show. He wanted to create a united front of strength between him and our dad for our mom. Our mom was gasping for air as she cried, trying to come to terms with the fact that she had just agreed to put her mother's life in the hands of physicians who did not know who she was, what her struggles were, or that the sickly body they were working on held the soul of the most important woman on the planet for all of us. They couldn't see our faces or hear our voices, and even if we were there, they would only have been able to see the fear and desolation in our darkened eyes. The masks covered everything else. My dad knew no words to help console the hearts he felt breaking in the truck, his own included. He had relied on Grandma Pryde in some form every day since he was fourteen. He pushed the gas pedal a bit harder and focused on getting to me as quickly as possible. I was the missing quarter of the family. He couldn't stop our hearts from breaking, but he could at least get us together: the family that was Grandma Pryde's proudest purpose for living.

My mom took a few minutes after she hung up to compose herself and used her shaky fingers to dial my number. I heard the phone ring as Ramon and I were pulling into my condo's parking lot. He abruptly stopped the truck in the alleyway where the garages met the sidewalk. I answered, heard the sniffles, and asked what was going on. My mom whispered, "Tasha, your grandma is not going to make it." I felt a surge of adrenaline wash over me from my toes up, threatening to propel me from the truck like a rocket, yet at the same time, I felt a sinking feeling, like I had been glued to the seat of the truck. I was unable to move, yet energy erratically tried to escape through every nerve in my body. I stayed composed but terse.

"What are you talking about?"

"Tasha, they are going to try dialysis on her kidneys, but it probably isn't going to work, and when it fails, she's gonna die. Even if it does work, she still may not make it, Baby." I could hear her gasp for a breath. "Tasha, I am so sorry."

I tried to be strong for her as I took in these words, and that apparently came across as logistical. "When will you be at my house?" That was it. No acknowledgment of our world slipping away, just the organization of it all. Ouch.

I finished the call without an ounce of breakage in my tone, but I was absolutely destroyed. I started shaking uncontrollably and torpedoed my phone onto the dashboard and heard it crash into the windshield as I threw my head into my hands and started bawling. I knew Ramon was right next to me (meaning I would normally try to be calm), but I needed to release the energy pent up inside of me. I simply couldn't stop it. His energy was the exact opposite of mine; he sat behind the wheel, frozen. He had no idea what to do. He had never seen me like that, and both the visual and audible displays were terrifying and heart-rending to process. He didn't need me to tell him what I had heard based on my reaction, but I still mustered, "She's going to die," followed by another loud yowl, the jarring sound of my anguish.

He felt like all the air had been sucked from the truck as he quietly asked, "Tasha, I am so sorry. What can I do?" When I heard the question, I picked up my head and forced myself to stop crying, judging myself as being unreasonable and dramatic. I just needed to go inside and wait for my family. I asked him to go home. I thought the vibe would be distressing and didn't want to subject him to such intensity, as I figured it would be uncomfortable for him. The truth is, I knew it would be uncomfortable for *me* to keep displaying such raw emotion, and I was making unfair assumptions, trying to protect him from my own projections. Life is uncomfortable, and he just wanted to be there for me. Even so, I sent him away as soon as I saw Uncle Tom round the corner and park in front of my condo. Ramon's eyes confirmed he didn't want to go, but he didn't fight me and slowly drove away.

Back at the hospital, after my mom relayed the family's decisions, Aunt Tammy was briskly relocated to another part of the hospital so they could initiate the procedure. She sat in the abandoned waiting room, staring out the humongous glass windows with a view of the mountains, nearly cracking the screen of her phone due to the force with which she held it. She could see my house from her chair but had never felt further from civilization in her life. Her mind tortured her, grasping at every straw that it could, trying to make sense of how we had gotten to this moment and why she was all alone, with no one to hug or talk to in the flesh. She tried to get a grip on her reality but couldn't shake the iciness from the haunting sensory deprivation, the environment matching the hollowness she felt mounting in her chest. She tried to reorient herself by checking the time, anxiously awaiting the notification of my family's arrival at the house she could see but might as well have been worlds away from.

When my family arrived, Uncle Tom and I were already inside. The TV was on, NFL games, the world totally unaware that ours was blowing up by the second. I muted it, only keeping it on so that it provided a picture for us to stare at. The walls' stillness was suffocating. As they walked in, tension mounted. It was as if we each needed to carry around our own pair of scissors to cut through the grief that rushed in with the opening of the door. Like a jungle never before touched by human hands, our emotions flooded the room, bouncing to and from all angles, making it difficult to carve out any personal space at all. The strategizing we were doing in our heads contrasted starkly with the paralyzed personification we all seemed to be stuck in. Dalton was completely mute, my mom couldn't stop crying, my dad was pacing, Tom was caretaking, and I was trying to take control of anything and everything—the controllable and uncontrollable.

One of the first decisions we had to make was when and how to bring Grandpa Bill down. We considered having one of us drive back to Laramie to pick him up. We debated about asking a few family members who might brave the wintry conditions, when something clicked for me. I needed to call not only my best friend but also one of Grandma Pryde's best friends, Colleen. Colleen held a very special space in my grandma's heart. They were friends before we were. Colleen needed to be the one to bring Grandpa Bill to us. It is the only way Grandma Pryde would have wanted it, and I wonder if she had a hand in making sure my best friend would be there with me. When I brought it up, there was no hesitation from anyone, and so it was decided. I ran to the closet in my bedroom and called her, trying not to sound like I was crying. She hated to drive and was even more fearful of it during the winter, but I knew she'd do anything for Grandma Pryde and me, and in that moment, I needed her more than I ever had before. She could sense that through the phone. We didn't yet know if any exceptions could be made to get Grandpa Bill into her hospital room, but we had to give it our best shot, and that couldn't happen if he was still in Wyoming. Barely letting me finish, Colleen agreed to bring Grandpa Bill to be beside his wife of sixty-three years on her last day of life.

Next, I called Grandpa Bill and let him know the plan. I tried so hard to remain calm and steady so that I didn't induce any panic—in myself more than in him, probably.

"Hi, Princess. What's going on?"

"Hi, Grandpa. Things don't look good. We need to get you here, just in case ... we, we don't think she's going to ... make it. I don't know if you can go into her room, but we are going to have Colleen come pick you up and bring you to Loveland so that you can hopefully see—go be with her, okay? Please get ready. She's coming now." I couldn't use the word die. I stuttered as if me speaking the word out loud would send the angels of death directly to her room before we were ready. But we would never be ready.

"Oh, Princess. Oh. Are you okay?"

"Yeah, I have to go. I will have Colleen call you," was all I could express.

Colleen called him and echoed similar sentiments. I didn't hear the exchange, but I can guarantee she was warmer than I was and more accommodating to his needs. Once the calls ended, Grandpa Bill tried to process what he had heard. He gathered his coat and hat and put his shoes on, sitting on the couch opposite his wife's chair, staring at its emptiness. He repeated to himself over and over again that if he was being called down to be by her side, it meant that her body was failing. That she was *dying*. He now heard the seriousness of the words I had verbalized a few minutes before. He read between the lines. He felt a growing tenseness squeeze his heart, holding it hostage by terror as he envisioned what would happen to our family without Grandma Pryde.

Sometimes life is strange, unexplainable, and mysterious, even. The best way for me to describe what happened next is spiritual, mental fuckery. I can only conclude that Grandma Pryde had some sort of oversight in the chain of events, but I can't say how. I just feel it in my bones, and it helps me make sense of it and ease the uncertainty that consumes my mind. The doctor entered the waiting room and startled Aunt Tammy, the only person there. Her voice was calm, but her eyes were frightened. She explained, "Tammy, I am so sorry. The procedure did not work, and we are trying to make her comfortable." In shock, Tammy gathered the remaining courage she had left and asked one last time, "Is there *any* chance you can make an exception to let my dad be with her? I will leave if it can only be one person. They've been married for sixty-three years, seriously. He is on his way."

After a desperate pause, the doctor agreed. "One person can come. Where is your dad? He needs to hurry; she likely doesn't have much time left now."

Tammy's heart plummeted to her feet. She stayed focused on her win, the fact that her finagling had led to a small change of heart, but only if he could make it in time. Tammy stood motionless, irate, and relieved as the mismatched scrubs scurried off around a corner. She couldn't process her feelings, so instead, she dialed my mom's number as she followed distantly behind the doctor and reentered the hospital room. She put us on speaker phone as she gathered with the nurses and urgently requested an update on Grandpa Bill's ETA.

Then, she delivered a bittersweet update. "Guys, they said one person can come. Dad can come. We need to get him here now!"

It is unimaginable to have to choose just one soul to be granted the chance to be present when our family had six people who all desperately wanted the chance to be there. Yet, the unimaginable was our reality. Although no one fought it, there was silent hesitation, vicious jealousy, and reluctant moral give-in to the fact that the other person had to be my Grandpa Bill, even though we each wanted it to be ourselves. He had only just arrived and begun to take off his ball cap and jacket, but instead, we spoke to the time crunch, trying to race and beat death. "Take him, Tom. Get him there now!" my mom yelled with closed fists and a shallow breath.

As Grandpa Bill and Uncle Tom drove away from my house, Ramon returned. I had been staying in contact with him via text and had evaluated the situation enough to feel decent about asking him back over. As he walked in, he immediately noticed the quiet, a rarity for our family. He sat down on the couch opposite my dad, not wanting to be in the way. He was not new to our family but new to experiencing grief with our family, so he didn't want to say the wrong thing, as if there were actually a right thing to say.

When Tammy ended the call with us from Grandma Pryde's room, she took a huge deep breath and met the eyes of the irritable nurse. Her eyes seemed kinder than before, or perhaps Tammy just convinced herself of that because she wanted to believe that when someone's mother was dying, anyone would look at the bereaved with kind eyes. The nurse's demeanor had shifted. Now, she seemed better able to empathize with the fact that this woman she knew nothing about would soon lose her life while her family watched helplessly on FaceTime. Two other nurses had been suiting up in their hazmat attire in the hallway, and they entered. Tammy watched them take their places as if this scene were being rehearsed for a movie. Then, out of what felt like thin air, another woman appeared, identifying herself as the chaplain.

The woman got straight to business. "Are there any passages or prayers your mom would find comfort in?" Internally, Tammy screamed at every kind pair of eyes to go away, that there were no prayers, no words her mom needed in this moment, just healing. But instead, she briefly explained Grandma Pryde's religious history and said the only prayer she could think of was The Lord's Prayer. Hand in hand with four pairs of eyes belonging to faces she knew she'd never be able to identify, Tammy stood and repeated the words in unison with a group of strangers. "Our Father, who art in heaven, hallowed be thy name ..." Tammy leaned in close and gave her mom a blessing, murmuring, "Mom, if it's time to let go, that's okay. You can let go. Mom, Dad's on his way."

Aunt Tammy phoned us again and fought back tears as she explained the situation and got FaceTime set up with the help of the nurses. As she spoke, she watched the staff detach a few of the machines and expose wounds left behind she knew would never heal. They cleared out a few of the items to make more space to surround her. With FaceTime now set up, Tammy handed the phone to a stranger to hold and beseeched the crabby-turned-kind nurse to keep her mom alive long enough for her dad to arrive. She then let her tears begin to fall.

Uncle Tom parked right in front of the hospital entrance and hopped out quickly, helping his dad's aching body fight the cold and wind. After a brief exchange with the attendant, within seconds, two nurses greeted them. Tom had secretly hoped that they would feel his heart breaking. That maybe they would spot pieces of his heart in the air and they'd have to dodge them and allow him entry, too, but instead, they forced meaningless pleasantries and turned their focus to Grandpa Bill. They each took one side of him, locked arms, and led him toward the elevator. The urgency was so obvious; they basically lifted and ran with him. Tom stood there dumbfounded, his whole body curling in on itself. He felt stuck, a crippling effect of anticipatory grief, making him begin to appear as small as he felt. Exasperated and confused, he swallowed the fact that his only choice was to turn around and drive away, back to us.

When Grandpa Bill walked into the room, the first thing he noticed was an open chair he assumed had his name on it. He sat down and made brief eye contact with Tammy, greeting her desperate, crying eyes without solutions to offer. He surveyed the room and settled in to study the chaos surrounding Grandma Pryde's body. He felt that the cords and tubes looked more like the wires people pile up and throw behind computer desks than they did tools used to save lives. He noticed a nurse who appeared to be the puppeteer of the many strings keeping his wife alive. He traced each solid line from the starting place on her body to identify the machine it was attached to. There were tubes in her arms and hands, her chest, her neck, and her mouth. He had no idea what most of them were for and suddenly realized that the only person he would have felt comfortable asking was the only person who could no longer answer. He tried to assess if there was any stream of consciousness left in her and concluded that he didn't think so. Even so, he grabbed her hand, so cold and lifeless, and leaned in close. He simply said, "Oh my, Pryde, I love you." He kissed her on the forehead. There was no response, no indication that she was aware he was now by her side. Defeated, he tried again, thinking maybe his voice could be the cure to will her back to consciousness. He wondered if she was in pain as he silently accepted that she could no longer speak, even if she wanted to.

Back at my condo, we were watching the worst movie ever broadcast on the small screen. My mom settled on the bed in my guest room and held the phone the whole time, extending her arms out in front of her so we could see the life drain from Grandma Pryde's desecrated body. My dad sat in the living room nervously until I went out and yelled at him.

"Dad, get your ass in here and sit by mom."

It is no secret that he doesn't handle emotionally loaded situations well. He needed direction from me and was glad to take orders (and I'm pretty good at giving them, clearly). Dalton stuck close by my mom but said nothing. I had flashbacks to when I was in the same role against Grandma Becca's leg when her mom died. It reminded me how similar Dalton and I are, always trying to hide our emotions and stand as tall as possible in the quicksand of human suffering. Acting as if we can both conquer it somehow, especially around my mom. I bounced aimlessly between rooms, checking on everyone and trying to expel the nervous energy that wouldn't let me stay in one place. The phone was handed between several people whose faces and hands we never got to see. We could hear Aunt Tammy and Grandpa Bill talking, but there were no visuals to match their words. Instead, the camera stayed fixed on Grandma Pryde from about her chest up. She looked nearly translucent, with no color to her face at all. The white of the pillow her head was on seemed to match her pallid appearance. The intubation tube was taped to her face for safekeeping. There weren't any other cords visible that we could see, making our visual experience vastly different than the real-life one.

We could hear the nurses in the background, sometimes addressing us and guiding us on what we could/should be doing. They encouraged us to talk to her as much as possible, facilitating the flow of conversation so that each one of us took our turn appropriately. Someone asked if she could hear us and if she was in pain. Our questions were fool-hearted attempts to help us better understand her situation and to get others to speak for her in a way we damn well knew they couldn't. They reassured us that she could hear us and to keep communicating because it made a difference. But honestly, what kind of difference? And, how the fuck would they know, and why did we even ask? We confessed our love as best as we could. Uncle Tom tried to paint a picture of our scene for her because had her eyes been open, she would have been viewing us through a screen too. He described the room we were in and the placement of each of us, reiterating that we were all together and we were all with her.

It was one of the most cruel and grueling experiences I will ever live through. She made no movements. She gave us no indication of whether she could hear us. We didn't know if she was in pain, if she was scared, or if she had already left our world for the next. Hearing the pleading of my mom and brother made my stomach feel as if it had been sliced by a thousand knives all at once. I didn't recognize my own voice as I spoke, imploring her to please remember how much I loved her and wanted to be there with her and that it was okay for her to let go. But I think I was lying. It wasn't.

Back in the hospital room, a nurse suddenly halted Grandpa Bill's internal dialogue with a question that sounded like it was in a foreign language. She addressed both him and Tammy, trying to look both of them in the eye simultaneously, and gently asked, "Are you ready for me to turn off the machine?"

They made eye contact with each other, speechless. Grandpa Bill acted first, bowing his head and slowly, almost imperceptibly nodding up and down, unable to conjure up any words but not wanting that decision to stem from Tammy. Grateful, Tammy affirmatively nodded but did not give verbal confirmation either. She was miraculously able to swallow her shattered heart that had bubbled up into her throat and reported the final seconds to us, giving us a detailed play-by-play. The nurse didn't hesitate at their authorization but moved cautiously and respectfully, indicating the lifesaving measures were quitting the one job they were given. An eternity of silence passed as we all watched her. Two in person, getting to hold her hands and provide human contact and comfort, as it should be in someone's final moments. And six of us via a fucking screen, less than two minutes away, not able to see her hands, to feel her skin, or to offer trust in our physical presence. After a few moments, the nurse indicated that her heart had officially stopped.

Just like that, it was over. My dad, Uncle Tom, and Colleen were huddled with us around a smartphone, all awkwardly trying to hold one another up as each of us was falling into a numb abyss.

We sat in silence as the nurse said, "She's gone."

We stayed, staring at her lifeless body on a fucking screen, all gobsmacked. The crying commenced with those sharp but honest words, the daggers of reality cutting the emotional embankment that stored what would be nonstop streams of tears. Behind the scenes, a nurse must have tried to close the open window curtains. We faintly heard Aunt Tammy say, "Please stop. Leave that open and let the sun set as it should, with my mom, one last time. She loved sunsets."

It was Aunt Tammy's turn to tell us what we already knew, and she did so, repeating the same words a few times, "Grandma is gone, you guys. She isn't in pain anymore. She looks really peaceful, guys. I love you." She choked back tears with each word.

No one wanted to end the call, but there was no reason to remain on the line.

Aunt Tammy leaned in close and hugged her mom as tightly as she could. She realized there were no jolts of pain anymore and pointed it out to the nurse first and then to her dad, letting them know they could now touch her arm without inducing any more harm. All Tammy wanted in that moment was to feel a hug back. She needed her mom now more than ever and couldn't wrap her head around the fact that she was gone. Grandpa Bill wanted to comfort his daughter but had no idea how to do so. He figured nothing would come close to what his wife could have done for their daughter if their roles had been reversed. He thought of the things Grandma Pryde might have said and repeated a few of them, not sure how they landed. Eventually, the once-crabby nurse gently initiated the process of escorting them out to the car. She led Tammy, with a second nurse grabbing hold of Grandpa Bill.

That was our moment; that's how we said goodbye. Running from myself, I moved from my guest room into the living room, where Ramon and Dan (Colleen's boyfriend) were standing, and I announced that she was gone. Hugs ensued, and we all collectively sat in heartbreak for ourselves and for Grandma Pryde. I ran into the closet and made a couple of other phone calls. First to Grandma Becca, and second to Corina. I knew they would handle the rest.

Uncle Tom left to make the longest two-minute drive of his life to pick up his dad and sister. He saw the mean nurse first and was surprised when she embraced each of them with a huge hug and said the most overused phrase of all time: "I'm so sorry for your loss." Her tune had changed, and she was now expressing what felt like sincere condolences. Perhaps death doesn't just harden us but may soften us some too.

She addressed all three of them, hitting home: "Her pain is over, but I know yours is just beginning."

Tom couldn't stand the fact that his mom would now be lying in an unfamiliar hospital, all alone. "I'd like to get her body back to Laramie as soon as possible. I don't want her alone here for very long, please."

The nurse seemed to understand the emotional reasoning. "Tom, I'll take personal responsibility for overseeing this process. It will be prompt and smooth." With that, they all parted ways. It was eerie to think that these two nurses witnessed one of the biggest tragedies of our lives, but we would never even know what they looked like. Exposed eyes would be the only visual memories of the humans who couldn't save her life.

When they walked back into my condo, a procession of hugs were exchanged, with squeezing being the nonverbal permission to ease tears from our eyes. There were a lot of "I'm sorrys" in between admissions of disbelief. The thickness of the tension before had now been replaced with gripping condensation of fear and despair. We were all drowning at different speeds and into different depths, clinging to one another for upward pulls, just trying to stabilize. We all had similar questions, completely lost and unsure of how to proceed with the day. How do you keep living? Why do you keep going? Eventually, we decided that everyone needed to return to their own dwellings, where just a few hours ago, everything in the world was different. Part of me wanted to stay by myself in Loveland, but I knew that wasn't the right idea. I didn't know when they would transport her body back to Laramie, and I felt disgusted with the idea that she would be staying in Loveland by herself (something I didn't learn I had in common with Uncle Tom until his interview). I never spoke this into existence but instead fought with myself about it internally. I decided she would have wanted me to be with my mom to help ease her aching heart, and so I messily packed a bag and followed my parents back to my hometown, realizing for the first time in my life that my favorite person in the world wouldn't be available when I arrived.

I felt like I held it together pretty well the whole day. It could have been shock, or, as we have established, maybe it was my uncanny ability to shut off some switch in my brain that's connected to appropriate and natural human emotion in times of such suffering. I remember nothing about the drive home or the evening, but my memory became crystal clear about 10 p.m. that night, just about the time I laid down to sleep, hoping this was all a horrible nightmare I needed to awaken from. As I got into bed, I instinctually went to text Grandma Pryde because that's what I did. *Every. Single. Night.* My entire life, I had either texted, called, or been with the woman I had just lost. When I realized she wouldn't be responding, I lost my fucking mind. The tears began to swell, and I felt a heavy warmth wash over me. My head started to pound as all the air in my lungs escaped me. I stood up, dizzy, with blackness overcoming my eyes, and as I started to cry louder, I ran to my parents' room. They were both already in bed, not sleeping but nonetheless alarmed by the unraveling of their typically stoic and calm daughter. I crawled into bed. They both tried so hard to soothe me, but I was helplessly inconsolable. I couldn't catch my breath and was trying to talk but couldn't put my thoughts together. As the decibels became louder, I remember thinking I literally was going to die, and if I'm being completely honest, I wanted to. My parents were immobilized with fear. I had never displayed such primal anguish, and they were concerned that I might never stop. I knew I needed Grandma Becca to make it through the night. I yelled in disbelief, "I only have one grandma left. I need her here with me. I need my Grandma Becca. Please." I know it was one of the most primitive and bitter displays of despair that any of us had ever seen. I scared my parents, and I scared myself. They reacted as any loving parents would. My dad shot out of bed like a firecracker and sprinted out of the house, calling Grandma Becca to tell her we needed her. My mom just held me and let me cry, working hard to give me space.

"I know, baby, I know ... I know ..."

When Grandma Becca arrived, she knew what to do. She burst into the bedroom unapologetically, moved us over, and found her spot in the bed. "Ayy linda mi jita, I know, Grandma's here." She held me through the night, not repositioning herself once so as not to disturb me. She rocked me as the four of us became acclimated to my screeching pain that would carry us through the night.

The meetings we held to organize the arrangements could not have gone smoother. Dalton and I were flexible. We did our best to stay quiet unless directly addressed. I am in pure awe of and possess a great deal of gratitude for the unity Grandpa Bill and his three children displayed. There was no arguing; it was nearly perfect harmony. We were all able to tap into the positivity and selflessness Grandma Pryde had and seemed to be on the same page with how to honor her. I spoke only two times during the whole meeting. First, the casket selection. As we walked into the room to look at the options, my eye immediately caught a violet, nearly periwinkle chrome casket with yellow flowers embroidered on it. Grandma Pryde's favorite color was yellow, although she sort of forgot that once I came along. My favorite color is purple, and because I love it *so* much, she seemed to switch her tune and started to identify more as a purple lover. But we all knew yellow was actually her favorite color. As soon as I saw it, I thought to myself how strange it was that out of all the caskets from all the magazines from all the companies this funeral home could have had, the absolute perfect one was staring right at me. This one was it. Price didn't matter; nothing mattered. I'd buy it myself if I needed to. It was decided on in seconds.

My second declaration is admittedly a bit less flattering. Honestly, I was the most difficult person to deal with during the planning. Because of COVID, we weren't able to do some of the usual ritualistic practices that accompany our family's traditions of honoring our dead.[3] One of the changes was limiting who was invited to the funeral, and the other was not having a meal together post-burial to properly execute the order of mourning I was familiar with. I understood the constraints, but this upset me so much. To me, we weren't able to honor her in the "right" way (or so I thought), and I fought it. I wanted as many people as possible. I wanted to celebrate her in the most extravagant way imaginable (even though that wasn't really her at all). And I wanted a damn dinner. Again, I comprehended the limitations but also tried to validate my anger with the situation we were in and had been in since this whole COVID bullshit started. My family did their best to listen to me and acknowledged that they, too, saw the unfairness in it, but they reminded me that we couldn't be careless in the time of a global pandemic.

The only other part of the planning that left me feeling exasperated, alone, and turned off to all of humanity was figuring out who was going to speak at the services. I was tasked with writing the obituary and delivering the eulogy. The priest explained that we would have two readings during the services as well. I picked out the pieces and then informed the family I didn't want to read them. I already had such a big role and was overwhelmed. My request was met with crickets. No one in my immediate family felt they could do it, and I was annoyed but tried to be understanding. Not everyone can get up and speak during such times of sorrow, and I wanted to be more open to not demonizing any one way of coping (I didn't get the A+, but passed). So, I turned to others in my extended family and was told no by several people. They were kind and insisted they would do nearly anything else to help, but not that. I felt a complete sense of loneliness, one that I had never experienced before. People often reach out in times of distress, expressing things like, "Let me know if you need anything at all." I was doing that (rare in and of itself), and no one showed up. I was angry because I wasn't asking for me; this was to honor Grandma Pryde and all the things she did for everyone else. I was livid that no one could stretch themselves enough to do the same for her. I decided that I would do both readings and the eulogy and likely hold grudges for the rest of my life, and I left it at that (the jury is still sort of out on that last piece).

Some traditions still held steady in the few days following her death. Our home was a revolving door of food and well-intentioned offerings of comfort. I oscillated between wanting everyone to go away and knowing that I needed to be around people, too. I cried at the drop of a hat, something no one, including myself, was used to. I know that my goddaughter Reegan, just eight at the time, became scared at seeing her Nina (how we refer to Godmother) in such pain and not understanding how to react to me. Despite her obvious unease, she sat with me and pushed her body into mine, and I let myself cry. Not the howling cries from before, but silent tears, pulling her close and trying to be honest and real with her, but also strong. I needed to protect her, just like Grandma Pryde always tried to do with me. But I also needed to teach her about the inherent pain in life without the splash of optimism. You can't have one without the other. The symbolism in her leaning into me suddenly clicked. I had pressed into Grandma Becca, Dalton drew closer to my mom, and now Reegan angled herself to be my anchor in the face of death. I guess that is what humans do; we must align with another's pain and help them see it through. Reegan had no idea what a powerful role she now played in my life, nor did she realize how much Grandma Pryde loved her.

We held the viewing at the funeral home instead of the church, a first for our family, but necessary given COVID. It was an open casket. She was placed at the front of the room, diagonal to the French doors you had to cross to enter the area. Dalton and I had no part in picking out her clothes, but as I approached her, I recognized exactly what she was wearing and felt it was perfect. I remembered her alive, well, and happy in the shirt she had on. Most importantly, even though we couldn't see it because only the top half of the casket was open, she was wearing her favorite Denver Broncos slippers. That fact provides an unexplainable dose of succor for all of us. She looked somewhat different than in life, partially because she had makeup on. It wasn't overdone, just unusual because she never wore any. The thing I noticed most is that she was lying completely flat, without any indication of pain on her face. She lived with intense, unmendable arthritic pain for many decades, but now, she could actually lie flat, completely void of torment. My joy for her to be out of pain, and the sorrow for me to have somehow absorbed what I assume was equal amounts of emotional suffering, strangled me. I stood over her casket, rubbing her hand and trying to tell myself to remember the feeling. To describe it, to capture every detail as best I could. I spoke to her internally, saying, *I love you* repeatedly, hoping it would bring her back to life. Sometimes I glanced around the room to see who had arrived or was interrupted by hearing the quintessential taglines offered to the bereaved while giving people hugs they may or may not even want. I noticed people catching up, laughing even, and felt the strangeness of the whole thing. When it's your turn, you think you'll never laugh again, and you never want to. When it isn't, you can compartmentalize someone else's grief while also talking about the weather or how your lower back has been feeling. Some people steered clear of the casket altogether, some paid respects quickly and quietly, and some reached out to touch her.

Uncle Tom stood out in that he stayed by the casket, just staring at her, silent unless interrupted by someone. I didn't know what to do to help him and was trying to play mind-reader instead of simply asking, "How are you, *really*?" even though the answer to that question is usually forged in these situations anyway. The fact is, there's no way to know what anyone's internal dialogue is without asking, yet I know this experience captured the human response to death in both transformative and confusing ways. I often question what should be expressed in these moments and what shouldn't.[4] How much of the grief process and experience is for us as individuals, and how much should be brought out into the collective? How much do you honor each individual's needed way of coping, even when it makes no sense to you? Or if it makes perfect sense to you, how do you cope with the envy because you cannot bring yourself to emulate the same? Perhaps answerless questions but ones I can't help but ask.

The funeral was held the following day and was a traditional Catholic service. The front of the church had plants and flowers everywhere, perhaps more than normal because of COVID. Bouquets of flowers replaced bodies in the pews. The church was not nearly as packed as I remember it being for Aunt Do or Grandma Claire or the handful of others we had lost up to that point. I know it isn't a competition. It was still a decent showing, but nothing like it would have been pre-pandemic. It infuriated me, and I tried to remember that the number of people at a funeral does not equate to the legacy of the person being honored, but my god, it stung. In my opinion, she was still robbed, and to this day, I can't seem to figure out how to reconcile my logical understanding of the restrictions and the emotional tsunami of damage these facts leave me with.

My first goal was to knock her reading out of the park. When I got up to read the eulogy, I realized that the people listening would learn more about her past after her death than they ever did when she was alive. She didn't speak ill of the people in her life that caused her harm, and she didn't let on to the significant traumas she had faced in life. I spoke to some of the challenging dynamics of her past and how she chose to cope with them by learning to be the opposite of everything she observed. There was surprise alongside the tear-soaked faces below me, and the intended reactions were right on cue, so I concluded that I did my job. To learn she became who she was against the odds showcased her heroism. I didn't question whether she would have been proud of me, as that would have conflicted with the relationship I had with her. Even if I had tanked the speech, she would have been overjoyed, her eyes closed to my shortcomings. She would have beamed with pride. My confidence in her undying support offered great comfort and is something I will always carry close.

My second goal was to make a valiant effort to be as in tune with Dalton during the reading as possible. I have been talking *for* him literally his entire life, and I knew there were certain parts of the tribute he wanted me to share with the world that he was not capable of doing himself. In those moments, I forced myself to make eye contact and get his approval that I did the right thing to honor the bond between him and Grandma Pryde. I could tell by the slight eye twitches and the turning of his head inward that I had done their relationship justice. We didn't hold eye contact for long, but it was enough for us both to simultaneously start crying as we grasped the reality of our world being turned upside down, never to be repositioned in exactly the same way. As a sidebar, my cousin Brittany eventually let me know that she would be willing to do one of the readings. Out of all my memories of those few days in my life, Brittany showed up all the way and helped me carry out the acts to best honor Grandma Pryde. She was nervous and shaky as she did it, but she absolutely nailed it, and I will forever remember it (thank you, B).

The burial was frigid. Despite COVID, people huddled together to conserve warmth. There was actually a huge turnout at the cemetery despite the cold, which induced a warm solace for me. We arrived to see the casket glowing as the sun hit it perfectly. On top were seven identical crucifixes in a straight line, waiting to be handed out to each of us by the priest after a short blessing. Within seconds of splashing holy water over the crosses, visible icicles formed, a physical representation of the delicate isolation our hearts now felt. As the final honoring of her passage from this life to the next came to an end, I remember hearing loud crying as I buried my head into my hands and against the shoulder of whoever was standing next to me. As the pitch became more muffled in the back of my ears, I realized it was me. I had never wanted to be "that person" at a funeral, but I couldn't help it, and for once, I couldn't think about who was witnessing the sorrow that had swallowed me whole. Walking away from her casket was one of the hardest things I have ever done. I worried about how cold she would be and pictured myself sneaking back to the cemetery later to place blankets over her, criticizing myself for such a foolish thought. My brain was trying to catch up with the loss my heart was desperately bearing. Just like the viewing, Uncle Tom was the last to go. He sat with a fixed stare at the hole in the ground, now home to the broken body his mom finally got to leave behind. Following the burial, we had a small, informal, and non-broadcasted dinner at my parents' house. Sort of a "come-at-your-own-risk" invitation. It went well, and no one got COVID.

Before I synthesize the ways in which my family has been impacted by Grandma Pryde's death, I want to mention how this section of the book came together more in-depth. I began with one-on-one interviews, similar to the rest of the book's composition. Then, I wrote the first part of this chapter, got everyone together to read it, and asked for feedback. Next, I asked more hard questions. I wanted to have a discussion with all of us in the same space at the same time to dig into how we had each changed since her death. To name what's been admirable or perhaps hard to keep looking at. These were beautiful conversations that evoked conflict and resolution. I hope my compilation of our thoughts helps not only my loved ones but also you and yours. I challenge you to think about how loss has changed you and the ones close to you. What's working, and what isn't?

The cumulative losses of the pandemic created unknowns for our family that we will spend the remainder of our lives sorting through. It kicks off piercing pain to wonder if Grandma Pryde was scared, lonely, or wishing we were by her side. Why couldn't there be exceptions? She didn't die from COVID. She was negative, in fact. All of us were negative and gladly would have taken as many tests as needed to prove that. The hospital itself was desolate, devoid of everyone but the necessary. *We* were necessary. I can't help but stir up more wonderings about the selection or exclusion of who gets to be there when someone dies. Perhaps Aunt Tammy was there so that she could actualize the strength of the bond she had with her mom that she too often questioned. Perhaps my mom wasn't there because Grandma Pryde knew that it would help her start to detach before she left this world. Perhaps Grandpa Bill needed to be there because, despite their lackluster love for one another over the years, he was still responsible for giving her the people who made her life worth living. That could all be a big pile of nonsense, or maybe not. I have no encouraging explanation for why I wasn't there. No ideas of comfort, just confusion and anger. Maybe it will change someday, maybe it won't. My dreams have attempted to work this out in my subconscious, to no avail. I often think about dreams and how death affects the world of our subconscious. She has visited some of us (myself multiple times), and others not at all. Some dreams have been peaceful and healing; others have been fraught with terror and tension that extend into the entire next day. I question dreams' purpose, how they come to be, and what they are trying to tell me. Answerless thoughts tend to reverberate in the boundaries of my brain, especially at 4 a.m., my mind's conditioned favorite time to consider the unknown.

One thing I know is that we are not special. We are not unique in that thousands of other families also had to say goodbye to loved ones in this way because of the pandemic. Virtually, with masks on, from parking lots and homes near and far away, all alone. But Grandma Pryde *was* special. She was unique. She wasn't perfect, but she deserved to have her family by her side on her deathbed. And her closeness to us, only being allowed to be shared through the pixelated virtual world of FaceTime in her dying moments, is an absolute tragedy. Immoral. Inhumane. In many ways, it makes it even worse that we were just across the street. Physical proximity was close, but the rules made us feel oceans apart. She was robbed and cheated yet again. This parallel sparks many intrusive thoughts about my understanding of how taken advantage and overlooked she was by her own family growing up. Intense disappointment has mounted over time, marking territory I'm not sure I'll ever get back. COVID plagued us with infinite questions that have no answers. Had we been more physically present, would it have made a difference? Were the doctors really on top of their game, or had COVID fatigued their sharpness and decision-making abilities? Would being more forceful have impacted the outcome at all? The rumination can and does drive us all crazy at times, and it's hard to disconnect and simply accept what is. Maybe we do it because, by trying to make sense of it, we can somehow conclude a stronger sense of control. If you can somehow make yourself responsible for things your logical brain knows you can't own but do anyway, I guess it makes it easier to digest. An unsafe home for invented blame. I sure spend a lot of time there.

I've tried to lay out the gains born of tragedy throughout these stories to honor Grandma Pryde's positivity (the healthy aspects of it), so I must share a comforting triumph from her death. We have remained united as a family. I don't believe our foundational bonds have changed, even though our internal aptitudes for coping with life have. Our togetherness is a welcome relief and is in stark contrast to some of the ways grief has etched change into my dad's side of the family. I am assured by how close we still are, always reaching out to support, trying to emulate little pieces of Grandma Pryde that we can provide for each other. At the same time, there is also a lot of tip-toeing around one another (frequently me), uncertain of whether we can bring her up in conversation. We have an awareness of competing needs but seem too fearful to actually ask or simply take a risk and name the cumulative losses we carry now. This has improved with time, but now there is focused ultra care, which I admit is a great disservice to our own grief and to her honor. The only way to cope with grief is to go through it, and thwarting the process prevents us from the only thing we can really "do," which is to simply "be" with it in all its messiness.

It's beautiful to see our collective bonds flourish, yet individually, we all seem a bit more detached from the world around us. We're each reinventing aspects of our identity that no longer fit. There is newfound surprise at how reliant we were on Grandma Pryde's positivity, always comforted by her energy, even if we knew it was just a little too much at times. We were securely connected to her, and her loss has created forced uncertainty about what other attachments are worth holding onto. Similarly, we contemplate what physical afflictions we may inherit from her brutal battle with osteoarthritis (a debate that has led me to have four surgeries in the past six months—thank you, running and genetics). Comments are often subtly infused into conversations that we simply can't imagine her journey ourselves and don't think we could possess the same strength and bravery that she did. Then, we cringe at our own selfish desire to reduce our own suffering.

It is displacing to realize that in profound loss, so much changes, yet so much stays the same. My grandparents' house still looks like it is patiently waiting for Grandma Pryde's return. Her items are mostly untouched; her presence is still everywhere. The lone exception is that the items she was most embarrassed by and served to be the biggest symbols of her ailing body have disappeared to preserve her dignity. None of us sit in her chair, even if there aren't enough seats anywhere else in the living room. The tools my dad crafted to ease her needs stay in the same places, waiting once again to be helpful to their owner. In some ways, this brings comfort that her presence is still close enough to touch and envision. Yet in other ways, it makes the hole in my chest feel deeper, blacker, and more desolate. A total brain tease.[5] There is no right or wrong, and I honestly can't even settle on what would make me feel better. But that is not my call; it is up to my grandpa, uncle, aunt, and mom.

Our needs born from loss can be so varied. Some may want to keep things just as they were; some may want to clear any and all reminders in order to simply survive. Because that's what we all seem to do right now. It doesn't seem like we *live* anymore; we just stumble and *survive.* Integrating her loss is still in its infancy for us all, and I am not convinced that the ways in which our hearts have been frayed will allow for repair. Of course, they won't be fixed, but perhaps repaired enough to weather the ongoing tension that exists in this life. We have all created new rituals, some known, some secret, to either feel more connected to her or to handle the obvious disconnection. Perhaps not even fully sure why we are doing what we are doing, just trying to seek comfort in moments of distress and find the strength to keep pushing forward.[6] Hanging on by a thread has a whole new meaning to me now.

My mom lost her identity as Grandma Pryde's caretaker and is riddled with manufactured guilt about not doing or being enough for her. She has no idea how to fill the time that used to be dedicated to keeping her mom alive and comfortable. She also struggles to manage the overflowing emotion with the daily reminders of her mom's absence, causing her to take several unwanted pauses and restroom breaks to regain composure. Her anxiety has worsened and with it, her tolerance for coping with distress. She is sadder, more irritable, and more terrified. She went from taking care of Dalton and me to taking care of her mom. Now, she has no one to take care of in such a primary way. Further, she expresses immense culpability for somehow not supporting Dalton and me enough with our grief. Her conflicting roles of grieving daughter and strong mother often make her feel like she's let us down (but I assure you, she hasn't in this department).

Dalton is more withdrawn in general than he already was (which is hard to imagine, but he has miraculously achieved it). He is more in tune with our mom now and tries to make her life easier and protect her, often by "doing," just like our dad.[7] He ensures she has the latest gadgets and top-notch experiences, and he has taken over many of the chores she doesn't care for. He tries hard to make her space feel cozy. He came up with the concept of custom-made shadowboxes for each of us to display in our homes. Each box is a different theme of Grandma Pryde's life, complete with memorabilia to honor an aspect of her identity. It is a tangible way to highlight important parts of her and our connection to her. For example, my mom's is filled with sentimental holiday items, the love for the holidays being something the two of them shared. Aunt Tammy's sports a collection of vintage nursing gear and the major accolades from her career. Each box is a bit different, with the exception of the crucifixes from her burial and a single golden-encrusted glass rose engraved with her name, date of birth, and date of death, which were from our dad. If you're wondering, my box is the only box not completed yet because I still haven't been able to identify the theme to make it ... you guessed it ... perfect.

Aunt Tammy has struggled with down moods and coming to terms with her manufactured guilt about being the only child with her mom when she died. Hindsight bias eats at her in that she didn't realize how close she was with her mother until she no longer had her. Uncle Tom is more easily defeated now. He struggles to feel as connected to people as he once did and feels an eternal sense of loss and emptiness he can't escape. Grandpa Bill *seems* the most the same, something I find angering more than anything. I have been both hurt and irate that he doesn't seem to have the public display of grief you might expect from a bereaved husband. Then, I have to chastise myself for unfairly putting expectations or my own needs/desires onto someone else's grieving process.

While interviewing him, I asked, "What has her death actually been like for you? It's hard to tell; you always seem like you're fine."

I was pleased to hear, "Well, Princess, there is always so much more than what the surface tells us. No one really knows what I am going through or how I grieve, you included."

He wears a mask, and we may never get to see what's behind it. And to that I told him, "Touché, Gramps, you are right about that."

I was put in my place, and it reminded me not to make assumptions or judgments. So much of this process is invisible. The lone verbal change he emits is that he's had the courage to tell us his wishes when it is his turn to die. No machines, no cords, no unnecessary holes in his body that wouldn't save him anyway. Grandpa, I get it, and we will honor you.

And then there's me. There was complete agreement from every person interviewed that I have changed the most since Grandma Pryde's death. And no, unfortunately, there isn't much of a positive Grandma Pryde spin on their observations. I can't put into words what it is like to know that you are truly someone's entire world, unconditionally. That no matter what happened in life, you were never alone. To be someone's everything, not just with words but with emotions and actions, consistently, for thirty straight years, is a rare and unmatched experience for many. That privilege is not lost on me. And now she only lives in my memories, my dreams, and my middle name. Consequently, I have turned away more from my family. I don't show up like I used to. I avoid events I used to crave and no longer carry a zest for the future. My nightly check-ins are only with myself and are often filled with self-criticism and an extreme difficulty in relaxing. I remain an emotional mystery, but less so in that I will at least say I am miserable now, even though I don't elaborate. Although this book is quite the counterpoint to that assertion, wouldn't you agree?

I avoid talking about Grandma Pryde as much as I can, which is a horrible way to honor her, something my true love once pointed out to me, but delving in too much makes me feel unable to breathe, in all forms of the word. An obvious example of this comes out in my writing style. I cussed more in these two chapters than I did in the whole book, showcasing plenty of feelings either untouched or fiercely positioned. I already knew it when she was alive, but as much as Dalton and I were her world, she was also ours. Watching her decline gave both of us time to come to terms with her mortality but not to prepare for it. It was as if she were intentionally taking away small pieces of herself gradually so that we could adapt to the changes, never being too settled before another ache or pain would take more of her away from us. Dropping hints that death was eventual, even for Grandma Pryde. She was still teaching and nurturing us, even with these painful transitions. Dalton and I never spoke to each other about this during the process, but we were sorting through the internal dread of it all simultaneously. While I was painstakingly visualizing her being absent at future moments we would have as a family, Dalton was taking snapshots of her in the present, trying to remember her before the arthritis would capture something else. A picture of her on her walker or in her wheelchair, a picture of nothing but their hands intertwined when she was hospitalized. One thing I wish she could have more fully understood: we both truly believe that she would have been on the podium, the best of the best in the world, for every Olympic cycle—then, now, and forever. And, because of her life and because of her death, we will never be the same again.

EPILOGUE

AFTER LIFE

You are likely wondering how this book has impacted my family since it came to be. In the immediate sense, the answer is *profoundly*. I forced them to look at themselves and each other and communicate about past, present, and future circumstances that are equally heartwarming and heartbreaking. Insight has been built, some connections have been strengthened, and some connections have been made more distant or confusing. For most of them, my interviews were the first time they were willing to speak openly about many of the hardest moments of their lives. They were led to confront their memories, their behaviors, and their emotions and speak to the lasting impacts these events had not only on themselves but also on those they love the most. Although it reignited pain, there is much benefit observed in allowing them to sit with and process their true feelings about these memories. Seeing this unfold was palpable in the room and created clean air they could inhale to foster some semblance of adjustment, as opposed to remaining suffocated by the failed attempts to flee the discomfort.

In the months since they've heard the final product, there have been random echoes of deeper reflection and some improved communication, addressing some of the things they'd buried for years.

There have also been more of the same cyclical patterns still burning holes through our foundation. It initiated an acknowledgment of things they had seen but chose to never put words to or wondered about but never felt strong enough to ask about. There is greater understanding and empathy for each other's previously misunderstood or unheard perspectives, even if they strongly differ from one another. The lesson here is that speaking about it has allowed the ups and downs of life to be given the rightful time and space they deserve to foster connection and the ability to grow and adapt more appropriately to the inevitable suffering we simply cannot run from. Being more aware of what the future may hold and taking care to be more intentional with living in the present have also become clear. As for our future, the answer is uncertain, as we all will have to continue to practice what was started by the openings of old but ever-present wounds. In doing so, we will grapple with deep despair but also meaningful love and connection, the very combination that allows us to live.

So ... look at yourself now. Your family, your friends, your history, and your future. Talk about what's hard. Lean into what's uncomfortable. Wrestle with what's uncertain. Celebrate what is hard-fought and deserving. Mourn what has been lost. Appreciate what's meaningful and makes life worth living for you. Feel angry about what is unfair, unjust, and unfixed. Analyze your values and act accordingly while using more empathy to respect the values of those with whom you may not see eye to eye. Embrace that we can feel multiple polarizations at one time and, although confusing as all hell, it is life, and it is blindingly beautiful.

A final point about me, the thread that strings together the many lives you just learned about through the narratives of my family's history. I agree with my family's conclusion that I have changed the most since Grandma Pryde's death. Even though I tried to come up with a rebuttal (I enjoy being right ... and perfect), I wasn't able to compose much to counter their points (rare and bothersome). In my defense (do I need to defend myself?), the rain has continued to pour and hasn't let up much since her death. Two weeks afterward, I had some of the biggest changes of my life occur. I moved from Loveland to Denver on New Year's Day, in with Ramon, and started a new job three days after. This was my first professional job outside of academia and presented me with a huge opportunity to change the trajectory of my career and my life. And I didn't have her by my side to process any of it. Nonetheless, I recognized the potential to move forward[1] with my life in ways that would continue to honor her and all that she gave me. The job was huge in terms of my academic journey finally coming to an end and being the early career professional I had talked with her about for years. She was thrilled for me to start. I was in a serious relationship with a man I thought I might spend the rest of my life with. A man she met and expressed approval of. I was finally in the city I had been wanting to live in for the preceding fifteen years of my life. A city she was comfortable with because I had family to watch over me. In all the grief, there was hope for happy moments again, although I knew my life would never be the same. As life would have it, somehow, you just keep going. Supposedly.

But one month into my new life, everything changed. Three months into my new life, I began to transform. Four months into my new life, I had a completely different trajectory and was enthralled with the premise. My relationship, my house, and my plans for the future no longer fit. Yet I felt complete in a way I never had before and never have since, and *that* is the reason you now hold this book in your hands. The culprit: I met ... *her*. And then I lost her, and along with that I lost myself, what could have been, and my perception of what I should be. And I will never be the same again.

ACKNOWLEDGMENTS

It has been challenging to know exactly how to categorize this book along the way because it is more than a personal memoir. It crosses clear-cut genres and boundaries because it isn't just my story. It is a multigenerational and collective memoir, mentioning many of the people whom I love deeply, some who challenge me greatly, and some I live my life for. I'd like to start by thanking my parents. Their courage and vulnerability are admirable. They allowed me to address incredibly challenging aspects of their personhood and their parenting and were gracious enough to give their permission to share it with the world. I hope I have honored them in ways they can be proud of and that they both know how grateful I am for all that they have given me (and for putting up with me on my rather challenging days—which have been quite frequent in recent years). To Dalton, I know you, in particular, have been nervous and quiet (per usual) about the composition of this work. Thank you for letting me tell some of our stories, and more than anything, I hope I depicted your relationship with Grandma Pryde in a way that can bring you a little comfort in the dark moments.

To Grandma Pryde, I think about you every day. I miss you with fierce yearning and always will. I know you would be proud of this, yet it still kills me that I can't see it for myself. Anyone who has the chance to learn about you is lucky, and those of us who knew you are indebted beyond words.

I am in debt to you, Uncle Tom and Aunt Tammy, who allowed me to read every draft of this out loud and have been such steadfast supporters every step of the way. Your encouragement and consistent presence in my life mean the world to me. You are genuinely happy and supportive of me and our family with every success and have been steady forces in the roller coaster of my life the last few years.

To all of my extended family and friends who I interviewed, I hope that I have done your memories and recollections justice. I know that I don't always get it right, and so I will continue to be open to changing my mind. I am deeply moved by your brave demonstrations to show me a side of yourself that is raw and unapologetic and to allow your light to be seen by strangers. Your stories matter. You matter.

To Dr. Heather Servaty-Seib, Dr. Riley Nickols, Cole Imperi, Chris Diaz, Brody Tate, and Lorrie Lynch, thank you all for being my first (and expert) readers and giving me critical feedback to keep moving forward with this. Many of your comments were simply trying to convince me not to ditch this project and run for the hills, to remain confident in the usefulness these stories could bring to others. I thank you all for the push to persist.

To William Dalton, I could not have asked for a more beautiful cover. You are a brilliant artist and a cherished cousin. This project is all the more special because of my ability to professionally collaborate with you.

To my editor, Bobby Haas ... you gave me exactly what I was looking for. Hard realizations, self-awareness, all the right kinds of doubt and fear, and consistent belief in my vision to help this become a reality. To Angelina and Desi, I cannot thank you enough for your help in managing so many aspects of getting my business off the ground and helping me with all the things that give me the utmost anxiety. To Polly, thank you for your quirky personality and sharp prowess in the book publishing world. I have learned so much and am grateful I took this chance with you.

And to *her*—I am not sure I ever would have had it in me to bring these words to life without being shattered. There may yet be much unwritten in our story, and I welcome a day when it can be penned.

FREE DISCUSSION GUIDE

Thank you for reading *And She Was Never The Same Again.* I hope you found my story to be inspirational and helpful.

Please leave a review on Amazon.com. Reviews are extremely helpful to authors.

Get a Free Discussion Guide

Click this link or scan the QR code to receive a free discussion guide to deepen learning and exploration of the issues covered in this book.

ABOUT THE AUTHOR

Dr. Trujillo is a licensed counseling and sport psychologist who obtained her doctorate degree in Counseling Psychology from Purdue University in 2019, where she participated in a grief and loss research team throughout her tenure. She works primarily with current and former athletes and performers, specializing in issues pertaining to grief/loss, eating disorders, trauma, anxiety/depressive disorders, perfectionism, and performance psychology. She conducts individual therapy, team/coaching interventions, consultation, and education in groups, presentations, and workshops. She is also recruited to help build/refine protocols for teams/organizations looking to address mental health support and to write content on various mental health and sport psychology topics. She remains a fierce competitor, soaks up all things sport, and is an avid lover of the written word. She currently lives in Denver, Colorado and is in private practice.

To learn more about Dr. Trujillo and how you can work with her, you can visit www.npttherapy.com or follow her on Facebook, Instagram, and LinkedIn.

To learn more about the book and ways to keep the lessons going, you can visit https://andshewasneverthesameagain.com/.

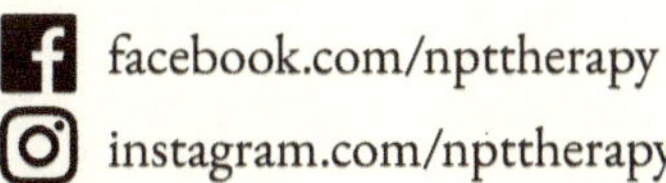

facebook.com/npttherapy

instagram.com/npttherapy

linkedin.com/in/natasha-p-trujillo-phd

RESOURCES FOR FURTHER LEARNING

FOREWORD

1. Servaty-Seib, H. L. (2014). Using a gain/loss framework to measure impact: The Perceived Impact of Life Event Scale. *Journal of Loss and Trauma, 19*(4), 331–354. https://doi.org/10.1080/15325024.2013.781468.
2. Servaty-Seib, H. L. (2020). *Benefits of Making Death Talkable*. TEDx Talk. Purdue University.

1. THE NEAR-END OF THE BEGINNING

1. Pérez, O. F. R. and Morales, A. (2020). Machismo. In *The Wiley Encyclopedia of Personality and Individual Differences* (Eds. B. J. Carducci, C. S. Nave, J. S. Mio and R. E. Riggio).
2. Conrad, M. (2022). *What is Anticipatory Grief and How Does it Work?* Forbes Health. Retrieved July 13, 2023, from https://www.forbes.com/health/mind/what-is-anticipatory-grief/
3. Sweeting, S., & Gilhooly, M. (1990). Anticipatory grief: A review. *Social Sciences and Medicine, 30*(10), 1073-1080. DOI: 10.1016/0277-9536(90)90293-2.
4. TEDx. (2020, April 13). *Benefits of making death talkable | Heather Servaty-Seib* [Video]. YouTube. https://www.youtube.com/watch?v=T_pfV5SyRN4
5. Cramer, P. (2006). *Protecting the self: defense mechanisms in action*. Guilford Press. Retrieved July 17, 2023.
6. Webster, B. (2015). *Distinguishing Primary and Secondary Loss*. Grief Journey UK. Retrieved July 13, 2023, from https://griefjourney.co.uk/startjourney/for-the-grieving-person/articles-for-the-grieving-person/distinguishing-primary-and-secondary-loss/
7. Ozcan, O., Hoelterhoff, M., & Wylie, E. (2021). Faith and spirituality as psychological coping mechanism among female aid workers: A qualitative study. *Journal of International Humanitarian Action*, 6(15).
8. Neimeyer, R. A., Burke, L. A., Mackay, M. M., & van Dyke Stringer, J. G. (2010). Grief therapy and the reconstruction of meaning: From principles to practice. *Journal of Contemporary Psychotherapy, 40*, 73–83. https://doi.org/10.1007/s10879-009-9135-3
9. McNally, R. J. (2005). Debunking myths about trauma and memory. *The Canadian Journal of Psychiatry, 50*(13), 817–822.

2. BEASTLY BEAUTY

1. Gaddis, L. (2017). *Moving On Is Very Different From Moving Forward*. Still

Standing Magazine. Retrieved July 22, 2023, from https://stillstandingmag.com/2017/07/05/moving-different-moving-forward/

2. Doka, K. J., & Martin, T. (2010). *Grieving beyond gender: Understanding the ways men and women mourn.* Routledge.
3. Overton, B. L., & Cottone, R. R. (2016). Anticipatory grief: a family systems approach. *The Family Journal, 24*(4), 430–432.
4. Raffaelli, M., & Ontai, L. L. (2004). Gender socialization in latino/a families: Results from two retrospective studies. *Sex Roles, 50*, 287–299.
5. Roots of Empathy Symposium. (2019). *The neuroscience of touch | Jean Clinton and Tiffany Field* [Video]. YouTube. https://www.youtube.com/watch?v=L58MrCQtKRo
6. TED-Ed. (2013, March 7). *The difference between classical and operate conditioning | Peggy Andover* [Video]. YouTube. https://www.youtube.com/watch?v=H6LEcM0E0io
7. Rauvola, R. S., Vega, D. M., & Lavigne, K. N. (2019). Compassion fatigue, secondary traumatic stress, and vicarious traumatization: A qualitative review and research agenda. *Occupational Health Science, 3*, 297–336.
8. White, T. (2021). *How Intent and Impact Differ and Why It Matters.* Healthline. Retrieved July 22, 2023, from https://www.healthline.com/health/intent-vs-impact#the-difference
9. DBT Tools. (n.d.). Emotional Regulation Skills. Retrieved July 22, 2023, from https://dbt.tools/emotional_regulation/index.php
10. Piaget, J., & Inhelder, B. (1969). *The psychology of the child.* Basic Books.
11. O'Connor, M-F. (2023). *The grieving brain: The surprising science of how we learn from love and loss.* HarperCollins Publishers.
12. Chodron, P. (2003). *Comfortable with uncertainty: 108 teachings on cultivating fearlessness and compassion.* Shambala Publications, Inc.
13. Neimeyer, R. A., & American Psychological Association. (2001). *Meaning reconstruction and the experience of loss (1st ed.).* American Psychological Association.
14. Servaty-Seib, H. L. (2014). Using a gain/loss framework to measure impact: The perceived impact of life event scale. *Journal of Loss and Trauma, 19*(4), 331–354.
15. Joseph, S. (2011). *What doesn't kill us: The new psychology of posttraumatic growth.* Basic Books.

3. THE GROWTH IN ULTIMATE SUFFERING

1. Newcomb, M. E., & Mustanski, B. (2010). Internalized homophobia and internalizing mental health problems: A meta-analytic review. *Clinical Psychology Review, 30*(8), 19–1029.
2. National Alliance on Mental Illness. (n.d.). Trauma and Internalized Shame. Retrieved July 23, 2023, from https://www.nami.org/Your-Journey/Identity-and-Cultural-Dimensions/LGBTQ/Trauma-and-Internalized-Shame
3. TEDx. (2020, July 14). *From shame to pride – and everything in between | Kris Barz Mendonca* [Video]. YouTube. https://www.youtube.com/watch?v=c28KESnrzEo
4. Slepian, M. L., Kirby, J. N., & Kalokerinos, E. K. (2020). Shame, guilt and secrets on the mind. *Emotion, 20*(2), 323–328.

5. Sutton, J. (2020). *Socratic questions in psychology: Examples and techniques*. Meaning and values: Positive Psychology. Retrieved July 23, 2023, from https://positivepsychology.com/socratic-questioning/
6. Kubler-Ross, E. (1969). *On death and dying: What the dying have to teach doctors, nurses, clergy and their own families*. Simon & Shuster, Inc.
7. Robinson, L., Segal, J., & Smith, M. (2023). *Coping With a Life-Threatening Illness or Serious Health Event*. HelpGuide. Retrieved July 23, 2023, from https://www.helpguide.org/articles/grief/coping-with-a-life-threatening-illness.htm
8. O'Hara, B. (2021, November). *Whose Death is it Anyway? How We Die Matters* [Video]. TEDx Talks. https://www.ted.com/talks/whose_death_is_it_any way_how_we_die_matters
9. Juth, V., Smyth, J. M., Carey, M. P., & Lepore, S. J. (2015). Social constraints are associated with negative psychological and physical adjustment in bereavement. *Applied Psychology, Health and Well Being*, *7*(2), 129–148.
10. Josue, M. (Director). (2015). *Matt Shepard is a Friend of Mine* [Film].
11. Brown, B. (2010, June). *The Power of Vulnerability* [Video]. TEDx Talks. https://www.ted.com/talks/brene_brown_the_power_of_vulnerability?language=en

4. SKID MARKS AND BANISHED TEARS

1. Neimeyer, R. A., Baldwin, S. A., & Gilles, J. (2006). Continuing bonds and reconstructing meaning: Mitigating complications in bereavement. *Death Studies*, *30*(8), 715–738.
2. Gruhn, M. A., & Compas, B. E. (2020). Effects of maltreatment on coping and emotion regulation in childhood and adolescence: A meta-analytic review. *Child Abuse & Neglect, 103*, 104446.
3. Wolfelt, A. D. (2023). *Acknowledging the illusion of control*. Center for Loss and Life Transition. Retrieved July 25, 2023, from https://www.centerforloss.com/2023/04/acknowleding-the-illusion-of-control/
4. Melnick, J., & Roos, S. (2007). The myth of closure. *Gestalt Review*, *11*(2), 90–107.
5. Straus, M. A., Kinard, E. M., & Williams, L. M. (2001). The multidimensional neglectful behavior scale. *Family Research Laboratory*, 1–23.
6. Gruhn, M. A., & Compas, B. E. (2020). Effects of maltreatment on coping and emotion regulation in childhood and adolescence: A meta-analytic review. *Child Abuse & Neglect, 103*, 104446.
7. Lopez, C., Vazquez, M., & McCormick, A. S. (2022). Familismo, respeto, and bien educado: Traditional/cultural models and values in latinos. In *Family Literacy Practices in Asian and Latinx Families: Educational and Cultural Considerations* (pp. 87–102). Springer International Publishing.
8. Isobel, S., McCloughen, A., Goodyear, M., & Foster, K. (2021). Intergenerational Trauma and Its Relationship to Mental Health Care: A Qualitative Inquiry. *Community Mental Health Journal*, 57(4), 631–643.
9. Cacciatore, J. (2017). *Bearing the unbearable*. Wisdom Publications.
10. Brown, B. (2021). *Atlas of the heart*. Random House Publishers.
11. TEDx. (2017, May 5). *When someone you love dies, there is no such thing as moving on*

| *Kelley Lynn* [Video]. YouTube. https://www.youtube.com/watch?v=kYWlCGbbDGI
12. Harvey, J. H. (2001). The psychology of loss as a lens to a positive psychology. *American Behavioral Scientist*, *44*(5), 838–853.

5. LOSING THE ILLUSION: SHATTERED PERFECTION

1. Flett, G. L., & Hewitt, P. L. (2022). Core themes and definitions. In *Perfectionism in childhood and adolescence: A developmental approach* (pp. 11–24). American Psychological Association.
2. Fairlamb, S. (2022). We need to talk about self-esteem: The effect of contingent self-worth on student achievement and well-being. *Scholarship of Teaching and Learning in Psychology*, *8*(1), 45–57. https://doi.org/10.1037/stl0000205
3. Mills, K. (2022, July). Perfectionism: When good is never good enough (No. 198) [Audio podcast episode]. In *Speaking of Psychology.* American Psychological Association. https://www.apa.org/news/podcasts/speaking-of-psychology/perfectionism
4. Adams, V., Howell, J., & Egan, S. J. (2023). Self-compassion as a moderator between clinical perfectionism and psychological distress. *Australian Psychologist*, *58*(1), 31–40.
5. Hewitt, P. L., Flett, G. L., & Mikail, S. F. (2017). Perfectionism: A relational approach to conceptualization, assessment, and treatment. Guildford Press.
6. Gilbert, P., Durrant, R., & McEwan, K. (2006). Investigating relationships between perfectionism, forms and functions of self-criticism, and sensitivity to put-down. *Personality and Individual Differences*, *41*(7), 1299–1308.
7. Klonsky, E. D. (2007). The functions of deliberate self-injury: A review of the evidence. *Clinical Psychology Review*, *27*(2), 226–239. doi: 10.1016/j.cpr.2006.08.002
8. Nock, M. K. (Ed.). (2009). *Understanding nonsuicidal self-injury: Origins, assessment, and treatment.* American Psychological Association.
9. Taylor, P. J., Jomar, K., Dhingra, K., Forrester, R., Shahmalak, U., & Dickson, J. M. (2018). A meta-analysis of the prevalence of different functions of non-suicidal self-injury. *Journal of Affective Disorders*, *227*, 759–769.
10. Cornwall, G. (2022). When 'Perfect' Is a Pitfall. *School Library Journal*, *68*(8), 30–33.
11. Basco, M. R. (2000). *Never Good Enough: How to Use Perfectionism to Your Advantage Without Letting It Ruin Your Life.* Touchstone.
12. Brown, B. (2010). *The Gifts of Imperfection.* Hazelden Information & Educational Services.

6. THE MATRIARCHAL ANCHOR

1. Organista, P. B., Organista, K. C., & Kurasaki, K. (2003). The relationship between acculturation and ethnic minority health. In K. M. Chun, P. Balls Organista, & G. Marín (Eds.), *Acculturation: Advances in theory, measurement, and applied research* (pp. 139–161). American Psychological Association.

2. Ospino, H. (2015). Hispanic ministry in Catholic parishes: A summary report of findings from the national study of Catholic parishes with Hispanic ministry. Our Sunday Visitor Press.
3. Simmons McConnell, V. (1999). The San Luis Valley: Land of the six-armed cross, second edition. University Press of Colorado.
4. Segal, E. A., Gerdes, K. E., Mullins, J., Wagaman, M. A., & Androff, D. (2011). Social empathy attitudes: Do Latino students have more? *Journal of Human Behavior in the Social Environment*, *21*(4), 438–454.
5. Counihan, C. M. (2009). A tortilla is like life: Food and culture in the San Luis Valley of Colorado. University of Texas Press.
6. Lehto, R. H., & Stein, K. F. (2009). Death anxiety: An analysis of an evolving concept. *Research & Theory for Nursing Practice*, *23*(1), 23–41.
7. Zimmermann, C. (2004). Denial of impending death: A discourse analysis of the palliative care literature. *Social Science & Medicine*, *59*(8), 1769–1780.
8. Umberson, D. (2003). *Death of a parent: Transition to a new adult identity.* Cambridge University Press.
9. Kelly, M. L. (2020, December 14). Psychologist on why funerals are fundamental to processing grief: Christy Denckla [Radio broadcast]. *All Things Considered.* https://www.npr.org/sections/coronavirus-live-updates/2020/12/14/946402101/psychologist-on-why-funerals-are-fundamental-to-processing-grief
10. WPSU. (2023). *Secondary Losses.* Speaking Grief. Retrieved July 30, 2023, from https://speakinggrief.org/get-better-at-grief/understanding-grief/secondary-losses
11. Harvey, J. H., & Miller, E. D. (1998). Toward a psychology of loss. *Psychological Science (0956–7976)*, *9*(6), 429.
12. Olberding, A. (2017). *Is the death of an elder worse than the death of a young person?* Aeon. Retrieved July 30, 2023, from https://aeon.co/ideas/the-death-of-our-elders-not-the-young-is-the-worse-loss
13. Martinez, N. (2022, April 6). Language, culture, and assimilation. Julissa Arse, Omar Valerio-Jimenez, & Ernesto Casteneda [Radio broadcast]. *The Source: Texas Public Radio.* https://www.tpr.org/podcast/the-source/2022-04-06/language-culture-and-assimilation
14. Calhoun, L., Tedeschi, R., Cann, A., & Hanks, E. (2010). Positive outcomes following bereavement: Paths to posttraumatic growth. *Psycholgica Belgica, 50*, 125–143.
15. TEDx. (2022, May 29). *Why talking about dying matters | Robert McDermid* [Video]. YouTube. https://www.youtube.com/watch?v=cK4gAN44EmM

7. TRAUMA SHADOWS

1. Baumeister, R. F., & Robson, D. A. (2021). Belongingness and the modern schoolchild: On loneliness, socioemotional health, self-esteem, evolutionary mismatch, online sociality, and the numbness of rejection. *Australian Journal of Psychology*, *73*(1), 103–111.
2. Sandstrom, M. J., & Zakriski, A. L. (2004). Understanding the experience of peer rejection. In *Children's peer relations: From development to intervention* (pp. 101–118). American Psychological Association.

3. Brown, B. (2012, March). *Listening to shame* [Video]. Ted Conferences. https://www.ted.com/talks/brene_brown_listening_to_shame?language=en
4. Azmitia, M., Syed, M., & Radmacher, K. (2013). Finding your niche: identity and emotional support in emerging adults' adjustment to the transition to college. *Journal of Research on Adolescence, 23*(4), 744–761.
5. Van der Kolk, B. A. (2014). *The body keeps the score: brain, mind, and body in the healing of trauma*. Viking.
6. Smith-Morris, C., Morales-Campos, D., Alvarez, E. A. C., & Turner, M. (2013). An anthropology of "familismo": on narratives and description of mexican/immigrants. *Hispanic Journal of Behavioral Sciences, 35*(1), 35–60.
7. Trickett, P. K., Noll, J. G., & Putnam, F. W. (2011). The impact of sexual abuse on female development: lessons from a multigenerational, longitudinal research study. *Development and Psychopathology, 23*(2), 453–76.
8. Crenshaw, K. W. (2017). *On intersectionality: essential writings*. Faculty Books. 255. https://scholarship.law.columbia.edu/books/255
9. Kornbluth, J. (2021). *Othering and belonging* [Video]. Citizen Brain. https://www.youtube.com/watch?v=8E2DRW0Zfi8
10. Diana, C. (2023). Pregnancy loss: consequences for mental health, *3*.
11. Williams, H. M., Topping, A., Coomarasamy, A., & Jones, L. L. (2020). Men and miscarriage: a systematic review and thematic synthesis. *Qualitative Health Research, 30*(1), 133–145.
12. Weitzel, E. C., Glaesmer, H., Hinz, A., Zeynalova, S., Henger, S., Engel, C., Löffler, M., Reyes, N., Wirkner, K., & Witte, A. V. (2022). What builds resilience? Sociodemographic and social correlates in the population-based LIFE-adult-study. *International Journal of Environmental Research and Public Health, 19*, 9601.
13. Maier, S. F., & Seligman, M. E. (2016). Learned helplessness at fifty: Insights from neuroscience. *Psychological Review, 123*(4), 349–367.
14. TEDx. (2020, March 5). *Shadowloss: Shedding light on our hidden grief | Cole Imperi* [Video]. YouTube. https://www.youtube.com/watch?v=SqeKwOz3DMQ
15. Trujillo, N. P. (2018). Non-suicidal self-injury in first-year college students: The testing of a nonlinear integrated model. *Open Access Dissertations*. 2085. https://docs.lib.purdue.edu/open_access_dissertations/2085
16. Harden, K. P. (2014). A sex-positive framework for research on adolescent sexuality. *Perspectives on Psychological Science, 9*(5), 455–469.
17. Bhatt, A. (2021, October 20). Trauma and addiction: Ashish Bhatt [Radio broadcast]. *Straight Talk with the Doc.* https://www.addictioncenter.com/community/episode-32-trauma-addiction/
18. Holland, J. M., Currier, J. M., Coleman, R. A., & Neimeyer, R. A. (2010). The integration of stressful life experiences scale (ISLES): Development and initial validation of a new measure. *International Journal of Stress Management, 17*, 325–352.
19. Dalbert, C. (2009). Belief in a just world. *Handbook of individual differences in social behavior*, 288–297. Guildford Press.

8. IDENTITY'S SCOREBOARD

1. Trujillo, N. P. (2015). Non-suicidal self-injury: What physical and sport educators should know. *Strategies: A Journal for Physical and Sports Educators, 28*(5), 34–38.
2. Reid, R. (2011). Losing to win: A clinical perspective on the experience of loss among elite athletes. *Coping and emotion in sport: Second edition.* Taylor & Frances.
3. Houltberg, Wang, Qi, & Nelson. (2018). Self-narrative profiles of elite athletes and comparisons on psychological well-being. *Research Quarterly for Exercise and Sport, 89*(3), 354–360.
4. Ronkainen, N. J., Kavoura, A., & Ryba, T. V. (2016). Narrative and discursive perspectives on athletic identity: past, present, and future. *Psychology of Sport & Exercise, 27*, 128–137.
5. Edison, B. R., Christino, M. A., & Rizzone, K. H. (2021). Athletic identity in youth athletes: A systematic review of the literature. *International Journal of Environmental Research and Public Health, 18*, 7331.
6. Hagerty, S., & Felizzi, M. (2023). The impact of authoritarian coaching styles on athletes' anxious states. *Sport Social Work Journal, 3*(1), 67–76.
7. Lizmore, M. R., Dunn, J. G. H., & Causgrove Dunn, J. (2017). Perfectionistic strivings, perfectionistic concerns, and reactions to poor personal performances among intercollegiate athletes. *Psychology of Sport & Exercise, 33*, 75–84.
8. Ohlsson Walker, S., & Stern, R. (2023). *You said it: Boundaries, anyone? Gaslighting and athlete safety.* Better. Retrieved August 8, 2023, from https://better.net/life/you-said-it/you-said-it-boundaries-anyone-gaslighting-and-athlete-safety/
9. Dhanaraj, C., & Kohlrieser, G. (2020). *The hidden perils of unresolved grief.* McKinsey Quarterly. Retrieved August 8, 2023, from https://www.mckinsey.com/capabilities/people-and-organizational-performance/our-insights/the-hidden-perils-of-unresolved-grief
10. Miller, E. D., & Harvey, J. H. (2001). The interface of positive psychology with a psychology of loss: a brave new world? *American Journal of Psychotherapy, 55*(3), 313–322.
11. Magness, S. (2022). *Do Hard Things: Why We Get Resilience Wrong and the Surprising Science of Real Toughness* (Unabridged). HarperCollins.
12. Menke, D. J., & Germany, M. L. (2019). Reconstructing athletic identity: College athlete and sport retirement. *Journal of Loss and Trauma, 24*(1), 17–30.
13. Orlick, T. (2016). *In pursuit of excellence* (Fifth Edition). Human Kinetics.

9. THE GAMBLE OF DENIAL

1. Lee, Y., & McCormick, B. P. (2002). Sense making process in defining health for people with chronic illness and disabilities. *Therapeutic Recreation Journal, 36*(3), 235–246.
2. Handron, D. S. (1993). Denial and serious chronic illness: A personal perspective. *Perspectives in Psychiatric Care, 29*(1), 29–33.
3. Henriques, G. (2020). Groupthink and the Evolution of Reason Giving. In D. M. Allen, & J. W. Howell (Eds.), *Groupthink in Science.* Springer.

4. Burke, P. J., & Stets, J. E. (2022). *Identity theory: revised and expanded* (2nd ed.). Oxford University Press, Incorporated. Retrieved August 9, 2023, from https://public.ebookcentral.proquest.com/choice/PublicFullRecord.aspx?p=7132626
5. Park, C. L., Lechner, S. C., Antoni, M. H., & Stanton, A. L. (2009). *Medical illness and positive life change: Can crisis lead to personal transformation? (Decade of Behavior)* (1st ed.). American Psychological Association.
6. Arantzamendi, M., García-Rueda, N., Carvajal, A., & Robinson, C. A. (2020). People with advanced cancer: The process of living well with awareness of dying. *Qualitative Health Research, 30*(8), 1143–1155.
7. Lloyd, L., Calnan, M., Cameron, A., Seymour, J., & Smith, R. (2014). Identity in the fourth age: perseverance, adaptation and maintaining dignity. *Ageing & Society, 34*(1), 1–19.
8. Knox, M. (2017, December). *Talk about death while you're still healthy* [Video]. TED Conferences. https://www.ted.com/talks/michelle_knox_talk_about_your_death_while_you_re_still_healthy
9. Rotstein, G. (2018). Near death, seeing dead people may be neither rare nor eerie. *AP News*. Retrieved August 11, 2023, from https://apnews.com/article/5a33106183af4d22a51172e35e9104d5
10. TEDx. (2015, December 2). *I see dead people: Dreams and visions of the dying | Christopher Kerr* [Video]. YouTube. https://www.youtube.com/watch?v=rbnBe-vXGQM
11. Lekes, N., Martin, B. C., Levine, S. L., Koestner, R., & Hart, J. A. (2022). A death and dying class benefits life and living: Evidence from a nonrandomized controlled study. *Journal of Humanistic Psychology*.
12. Wyatt, K. (2017, February 13). Managing family conflict at the end of life [Radio broadcast]. End of Life University. https://eolupodcast.com/2017/02/13/ep-77-managing-family-conflict-at-the-end-of-life/
13. Sanders, C. M. (1983). Effects of sudden vs. chronic illness death on bereavement outcome. *Journal of Death and Dying, 13*(3), 227–241.
14. Smeenk, F. W. J. M., Schrijver, L. A., van Bavel, H. C. J., & van de Laar, E. F. J. (2017). Talking about end-of-life care in a timely manner. *Breathe, 13*(4), e95–e102.
15. Stahl, S. T., & Schulz, R. (2019). Feeling relieved after the death of a family member with dementia: Associations with postbereavement adjustment. *American Journal of Geriatric Psychiatry, 27*(4), 408–416.
16. Secondary and cumulative losses. Coalition to Support Grieving Students. Retrieved August 11, 2023, from https://grievingstudents.org/module-section/secondary-cumulative-losses/

10. AN UNRAVELED STORYBOOK ENDING

1. Cauce, A. M., & Domenech-Rodriguez, M. (2002). Latino families: Myths and realities. *Latino children and families in the United States: Current research and future directions*, 3–25.
2. Schwarz, S., & Stahlberg, D. (2003). Strength of hindsight bias as a consequence of meta-cognitions. *Memory, 11*(4/5), 395.
3. Stoeber, J. (2012). Dyadic perfectionism in romantic relationships: Predicting

relationship satisfaction and longterm commitment. *Personality & Individual Differences, 53*(3), 300–305.
4. Clark, M. S., & Beck, L. A. (2011). Initiating and evaluating close relationships: A task central to emerging adults. In F. D. Fincham & M. Cui (Eds.), *Romantic relationships in emerging adulthood* (pp. 190–212).
5. Davis, C. G. (2008). Redefining goals and redefining self: A closer look at posttraumatic growth following loss. In M. S. Stroebe, R. O. Hansson, H. Schut, & W. Stroebe (Eds.), *Handbook of bereavement research and practice: Advances in theory and intervention* (pp. 309–325). American Psychological Association.
6. Rodriguez, L. M., Øverup, C. S., & Neighbors, C. (2013). Perceptions of partners' problematic alcohol use affect relationship outcomes beyond partner self-reported drinking: Alcohol use in committed romantic relationships. *Psychology of Addictive Behaviors, 27*(3), 627–638.
7. Beckmeyer, J. J., & Jamison, T. B. (2020). Is breaking up hard to do? Exploring emerging adults' perceived abilities to end romantic relationships. *Family Relations, 69*(5), 1028–1040.
8. Wilder, S. E. (2016). Predicting adjustment to divorce from social support and relational quality in multiple relationships. *Journal of Divorce & Remarriage, 57*(8), 553–572.
9. Jamison, T. B., & Lo, H. Y. (2021). Exploring parents' ongoing role in romantic development: Insights from young adults. *Journal of Social & Personal Relationships, 38*(1), 84–102.
10. Gui, T. (2023). Coping with parental pressure to get married: Perspectives from chinese "leftover women." *Journal of Family Issues, 44*(8), 2118–2137.
11. Chickering, A. W., & Reisser, L. (1993). *Education and Identity* (2nd ed.). The Jossey Bass Higher and Adult Education Series.

11. THE SHAPESHIFTS OF BECOMING

1. Goodman, W. (2022). *Toxic positivity: keeping it real in a world obsessed with being happy*. Tarcher Perigee, an imprint of Penguin Random House LLC.
2. Reitzes, D. C., & Mutran, E. J. (2004). Grandparent identity, intergenerational family identity, and well-being. *The Journals of Gerontology Series B: Psychological Sciences and Social Sciences, 59*(4), S213–S219.
3. Rice, D., McNair, P., Huysmans, E., Letzen, J., & Finan, P. (2019). Best evidence rehabilitation for chronic pain part 5: Osteoarthritis. *Journal of Clinical Medicine, 8*(11), Article 1769. https://doi.org/10.3390/jcm8111769
4. Yorgason, J. B., & Hill, M. S. (2019). Grandparents and health. *Grandparenting: Influences on the dynamics of family relationships*, 201–216.
5. Kristoffersen, M. (2021). Does professional identity play a critical role in the choice to remain in the nursing profession? *Nursing Open, 8*(4), 1928–1936.
6. Phillips Lassus, L. A., Lopez, S., & Roscigno, V. J. (2015). Aging workers and the experience of job loss. *Research in Social Stratification and Mobility, 41,* 81–91.
7. Van Orden, K. A., Bamonti, P. M., King, D. A., & Duberstein, P. R. (2012). Does perceived burdensomeness erode meaning in life among older adults? *Aging and Mental Health, 16*(7), 855–860.

8. Heaven, B., Brown, L. J. E., White, M., Errington, L., Mathers, J. C., & Moffatt, S. (2013). Supporting well-being in retirement through meaningful social roles: Systematic review of intervention studies. *Milbank Quarterly, 91*(2), 222–287.
9. Ziemba, R. A., & Lynch-Sauer, J. M. (2005). Preparedness for taking care of elderly parents: "first, you get ready to cry". *Journal of Women & Aging, 17*(1-2), 99–113.
10. Lee, J. H., Suh, Y., & Kim, Y. (2022). Multidimensional factors affecting homebound older adults: a systematic review. *Journal of Nursing Scholarship: An Official Publication of Sigma Theta Tau International Honor Society of Nursing, 54*(2), 169–175.
11. Bonanno, G. A. (2009). *The other side of sadness: What the new science of bereavement tells us about life after loss.* Basic Books.
12. TEDx. (2020, January 30). *Curveballs and blindspots: Navigating uncertainty | Bobbie LaPorte* [Video]. YouTube. https://www.youtube.com/watch?v=XMJifVonVAo

12. EXISTENTIAL GLITCHES OF REALITY

1. Hart, J., Summer, A., Yadav, K. N., Peace, S., Hong, D., Konu, M., & Clapp, J. T. (2021). Content and communication of inpatient family visitation policies during the COVID-19 pandemic: Sequential mixed methods study. *Journal of Medical Internet Research, 23*(9), e28897.
2. Downar, J., & Kekewich, M. (2021). Improving family access to dying patients during the COVID-19 pandemic. *The Lancet. Respiratory Medicine, 9*(4), 335–337.
3. Lynner, N. B. (2023). Death in a Pandemic: Funeral Practices and Industry Disruption. *UCLA Law Review, 70*(1), 154–205.
4. Calderwood, K. A., & Alberton, A. M. (2024). Consoling the bereaved: Exploring how sympathy cards influence what people say. *Omega: Journal of Death & Dying*, 1572–1590.
5. TEDx. (2018, October 17). *Lost in loss: A window into the grieving brain | Zoe Donaldson* [Video]. YouTube. https://www.youtube.com/watch?v=n4n1hKvT2CM
6. TED. (2019, April 25). *We don't move on from grief: We move forward with it | Nora McInerny* [Video]. YouTube. https://www.youtube.com/watch?v=khkJkR-ipfw
7. Doka, K. J., & Martin, T. L. (2010). *Grieving beyond gender: Understanding the ways men and women mourn* (Rev. ed.) Routledge/Taylor & Francis Group.

EPILOGUE

1. Harvey, J. H., & Miller, E. D. (1998). Toward a psychology of loss. *Psychological Science 9*(6), 429.

www.ingramcontent.com/pod-product-compliance
Lightning Source LLC
Chambersburg PA
CBHW020436130626
46549CB00001B/175

9798989544301